GW00645286

The Book of

St Dennis and Goss Moor

A Moorland History

By Kenneth H. Rickard

Halsgrove

First published in Great Britain in 2004

Copyright © 2004 Kenneth H. Rickard.

This book is dedicated to
Emily and Dominic.

All rights reserved. No part of this publication may be reproduced, stored in a retrieval system, or transmitted in any form or by any means without the prior permission of the copyright holder.

British Library Cataloguing-in-Publication Data
A CIP record for this title is available from the British Library

ISBN 1 84114 330 8

HALSGROVE

Halsgrove House
Lower Moor Way
Tiverton, Devon EX16 6SS
Tel: 01884 243242
Fax: 01884 243325
email: sales@halsgrove.com
website: www.halsgrove.com

Frontispiece photograph: *A group of local GWR lengthmen pose for the camera in the 1930s.* Left to right, back row: *Joe Brewer, Herbie Taylor, Len Grose, Reg Knight, Percy Davey;* centre: *Tom Kent, Fred Luke, Bill Barkwill;* front: *Art Greet, Fred Laing, Phil Greet.* KHR/Coll

Printed and bound by CPI Bath.

Whilst every care has been taken to ensure the accuracy of the information contained in this book, the publisher disclaims responsibility for any mistakes which may have been inadvertently included.

Foreword

For those whose livelihood or interests lie in mid Cornwall, Ken Rickard has provided the most scholarly and detailed record of its very heart. St Dennis and Goss Moor, their people, their work, institutions, customs and their stories have been studied and presented in this volume of rural history with manifestly a deep affection for the subject. As a native of the area it could not be otherwise – a fascinating revelation in which no stone is left unturned.

Sir Alan Dalton, CBE, DL

Left: *Parish boundary stones which mark the meeting point of the St Dennis, Roche and St Columb parishes on Goss Moor.* KHR

Right: *This scene captured in 1920 from the Carne Hill Chapel field shows the primitive swings of that time and the building in the background which was used as the Sunday school from 1868–92.* KHR/Coll

Left: *This recent photograph of St Dennis village shows its situation amongst the northern outcrop of the St Austell granite mass.* Imerys Minerals Ltd

The WVS at work in the 1940s.* Left to right: *?, Mrs Williams, Mrs Tucker, Mrs May, Mrs Hawke, Mrs Gilbert* (in the front), *Mrs Grose, Mrs Bray, Mrs Goudge, Mrs Hawke. KHR/Coll

Below: *The War Memorial Institute with some old-time posers and Miller's shop in the 1930s.* KHR/Coll

Below right: *The Goss Moor Tin Alluvial Ltd Company used this type of dredge in their tin-mining operations in 1911. This is an Alfa dredge working at Breney Common.* KHR/Coll

Below: *A fine village view prior to 1969; in the centre is the cottage which was later demolished to make way for the bungalow which subsequently became the Rectory.* KHR/Coll

Left: *Mr Sammy May using a cleaning axe to dress china stone at Rostowrack Quarry, c.1949.* Goonvean Ltd

Right: *Goonvean China Stone Quarry in 1958, with not a mechanical device in sight. This was one of the typical jobs involving manual labour which men had to accept in those days.* KHR/Coll

Contents

Left: *This scene in the blacksmith's workshop at Hendra clay works shows Mr Alfred Kent at the anvil accompanied by two unknown assistants in 1905. Alfred, who was a toolsmith by trade, had only recently returned from his previous employment in the diamond mines of South Africa.* KHR/Coll

A threshing scene at Carnegga in 1955. The Burrell steam engine called 'Ponto', registration number ERB 351, belonged to Mr Ambrose Matthews. Pictured, left to right, top: *Douglas Stoneman, Dick Pethick, Ern Westlake, Mrs Matthews;* bottom row includes: *Russell Dyer, Ed Endean, Jack Tippett, Stewart Varcoe, Bryne Kendall, Ephram Osborne, Alec Cawrse, Merlin Key, Russell Key, Robin Key, Donald Grigg. The engine driver (not in view) was Sid Matthews.* KHR/Coll

Left: *One of Mrs J. Penhaligan's many fashion shows which raised several hundred pounds for charity in the 1960s. Seen here are seven of the models.* Left to right: *Mrs L. Hawke, Mrs D. Trevenna, Mrs J. Rickard, Miss S. Penhaligan, Mrs P. Luke, Mrs J. Allen and Miss A. Lagor.*

Trerice Bridge. KHR

Acknowledgements

I would like to record my sincere thanks to the following people, without whose help this book would not have been possible.

These are the people who have loaned photographs, books, etc., and provided verbal and written information. To each one of them I am greatly indebted:

Revd Colin Allen, Frank Andrews, Kalim Anwer, Harry and Muriel Barrett, G. Bassett, Betty Bell, Peter Belton, Alan Best, Roy Best, Peggy Bilkey, John Blewett, Ivor Bowditch, John Brush, Richard Budge, Mrs Bullock, Tom Bullock, Jack Burnett, Ralph Burnett, Basil Coad, Michael Cole, Pauline Cole, Garfield and Betty Craddock, Ron Craddock, Norman Crews, Rex Curtis, Maurice Dart, Alan Davey, Martin Davey, Hugh Davies, Billy Davis, Callum Deveney, Charlie Dunstan, Bill Edyvean, Dennis Ellery, Jennifer Fouracres, Peter Gray, Stuart Gregor, Saxby Hatton, Ken Hannaford, Dennis Harris, Rex Harvey, Audrey Hemmings, Sheila Hill, Lawrence Holmes, Stuart Hutchings, Corinne Jenkin, Ivor Johns, Glynis Keast, Jonathan and Joan Kent, Ronald Kent, Adrian Kessell, Clarence Key, Alan Martin, Colin May, Stan May, Thelma May, Peggy McCaughan, Hilda Metherell, Peggy Metherell, Jack Michael, Colin Morcom, Barry Nance, Victoria Northcott, Dorothy Olford, Merle and Billy Oliver, Hilary Osborne, Beatrice Ould, Derek Penhaligan, Douglas and Josie Penhaligan, John Preston, Graham Reed, Richard Riley, Alan Rowe, Revd Tim Russ, Jackie Salmon, Brian Skews, Shirley Smith, Nicky Stephens, Douglas Stoneman, Dudley Taylor, Peter Taylor, Dorothy Trudgeon, David Turner, John Vaughan, Mavis White and Alan Wilson. Sadly, since the main text for this book was completed, Doris Bullock, Michael Fouracres, Jack Liddicoat, Hazel Nobes and Mabel Taylor have passed away. All contributed valuable information, which was greatly appreciated, and I feel privileged to have received their cooperation. (Those captions followed by the reference KHR are pictures from my own private collection. Those with the reference KHR/Coll refer to pictures loaned to me for inclusion in the book.)

Thanks also to the County Libraries at Bodmin, St Columb, St Austell, Truro and Redruth, plus the County Record Office at Truro.

This 1930s scene shows a St Dennis butcher serving a customer at Trerice from his horse-drawn cart. **KHR/Coll.**

Thanks must go to the staff at Halsgrove, and at ClayTAWC Ltd in St Dennis, Klick in St Austell, Staples in Truro, English Nature and Cornwall Wildlife Trust.

Special thanks to my wife, June, for her support and encouragement, and to Mrs Christine Best for carrying out the arduous task of deciphering my handwriting and amendments while processing the text. Also, thanks to Martin Davey and English Nature for their contributions.

To those whose names I have unwittingly omitted, I offer my apologies.

Kenneth Rickard, 2003

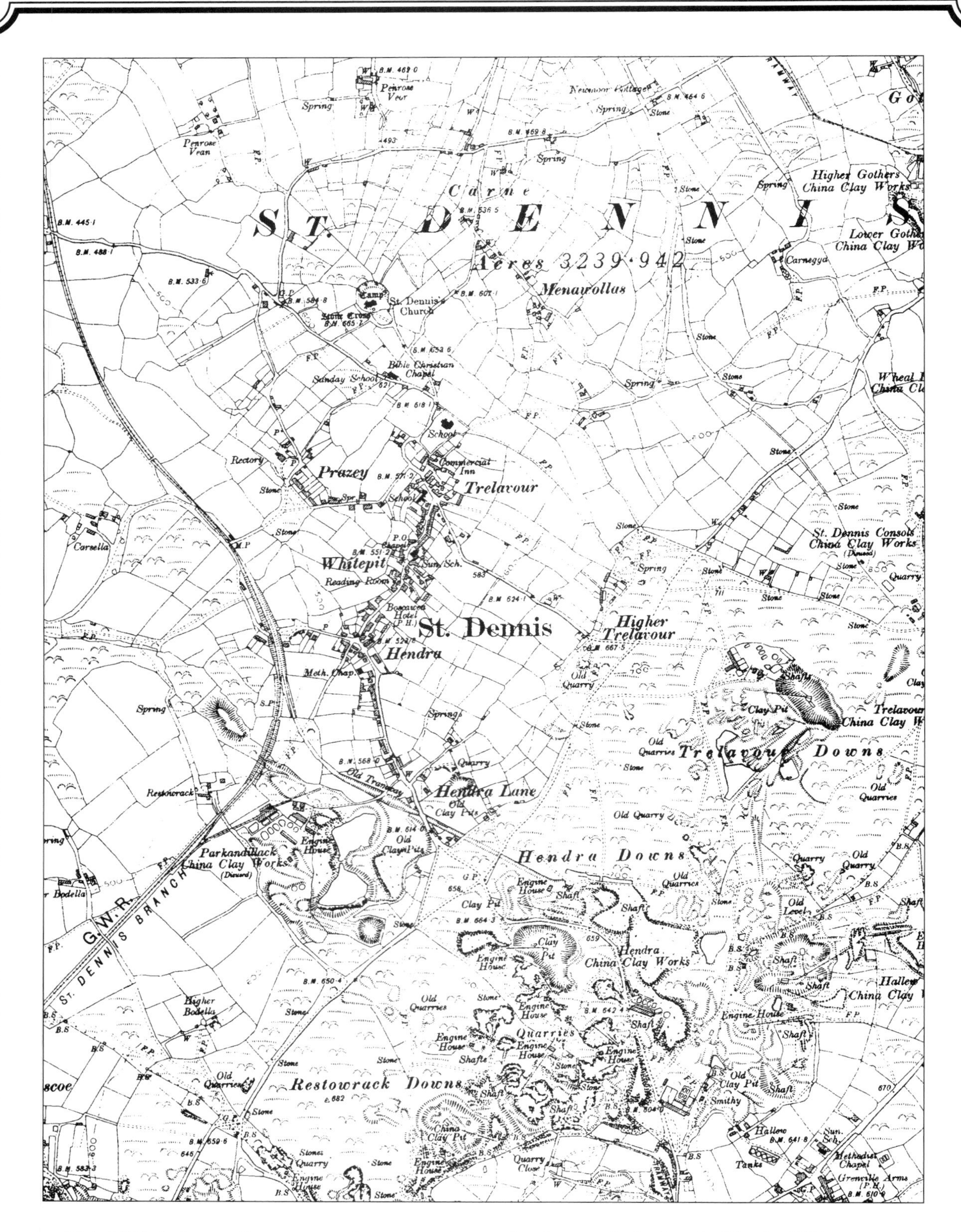

This 1908 Ordnance Survey map shows many interesting features including the Hendra Hill tramway connecting the china-clay works on Hendra Downs to the railway loading wharf at Hendra Prazey, the medieval field pattern around St Denys Parish Church and the complexity of china-clay works and stone quarries. Only the Parkandillick drying complex, the Rostowrack clay pit and the Prosper stone quarry remain in use today.

Chapter 1

Introduction to the Story of St Dennis

The Early Years

The complete history of St Dennis can never be written in full because the details of long periods of the past were never recorded. To compile a history one can only use the documentation and memories which are available at the time.

Emerson, the American philosopher, once said that 'History is a pageant – not a philosophy'. The pageant of St Dennis is grim and forbidding – one long struggle against nature, poverty and isolation. However, our forefathers were tough and laid the foundation of a community which is second to none in our wonderful county.

In the *Chronicles of British Kings*, written by Geoffrey of Gloucester in 1135, it is recorded that Dimelihoc was a secondary fortress (or dinas) of Gorlois, King of Cornwall. Gorlois and King Arthur, who had taken refuge in Cornwall, were continually in conflict, and Gorlois chose Dimelihoc as his fort; indeed, it was here that he eventually perished. Arthur abandoned the dinas and it later became the site of a church dedicated to St Dionysius, or Denis, or Denys.

The eastern slope of the dinas was a burial-ground. Some stones were later removed and used for hedge building. It is hoped that the remaining stones will not be disturbed again as there are very few old sites like this remaining today.

A public gathering in the field behind the War Memorial Institute for VE Day celebrations which involved the Special Constables, and representatives from the Red Cross, Home Guard, Boy Scouts and other organisations. A makeshift band provided the music. KHR/Coll

The Domesday Book compiled in 1086 records that Dimelihoc was a hill-fort surrounded by a moat and landed estate, governed by a baron and situated some 20 miles from Tintagel. The Dimelihoc manor occupied a position on the western slope of the hill and included 'Ennis' or 'Enys', the home farm. In the twenty-first century, Domellick, as it has become known, is the name of the farms which cover all the estate recorded in the Domesday Book.

The parish of St Dennis lies in the centre of the Cornish peninsula approximately ten miles from the English Channel and the Atlantic Ocean coastlines, positioned some 500ft above sea level on the B3279 road. It is surrounded by the parishes of Roche to the north-east, St Stephen-in-Brannel to the south-east and St Enoder and St Columb Major to the west. St Dennis is named after St Denys the Martyr, although as the Parish Church is located on top of a hill, the name may have originated from the Cornish word 'dinas', which means hill-fort.

During the reign of Henry VIII, St Denys was the

Above: *Girls' Training Corps, 1942/3.* Left to right, back row: *?, ?, ?, Barbara Currah, Edna Varcoe, ?, Phylis Snell;* centre: *?, ?, Mrs Sara, ?, ?, Betty Mundy, ?, Olive Grigg, ?, ?, Helen Herring, ?;* seated: *Mr Magor, ?, ?, ?, ?, ?, ?, ?, Revd Old.* KHR/Coll

Right: *This was the St Dennis Auxiliary Unit – people selected to act as resistance leaders in the event of the country becoming occupied by enemy forces in 1940.* Left to right: *P. Magor, H.S. Estlick, Johnny Bunt, S. Willcox, ?, ?, ?, C. Dunstan, E. Trethewey, T. Kessell.* KHR/Coll

Left: *Second World War Special Constables.* Left to right, back row: *Alwyn Bunt, Cyril Strongman, Percy Smith, Len Trudgian, Edwin Stoneman, George Allen, Harry Cory;* front: *Joe Thomas, Will Solomon, E. Pascoe, C. Gifford, Elias Allen, PC W.H. Taylor.* KHR/Coll

only parish in Cornwall to have 'Saint' as a prefix. The original parish consisted of the villages of Hendra, Whitepit, Trelaver (Trelavour), and Ennis-Caven (Enniscaven). A notable local feature, to the north, is the well-known Goss Moor which is bisected by the River Fal. This area has a history of its own, which will be explored in Part Two of this volume.

Industry

The countryside around St Dennis is dotted with a number of small villages and hamlets which were created by people who made their livelihoods in the tin-streaming and china-clay industries, as well as farming. All these industries have declined in recent years and people have had to diversify and travel to make a living.

The china-clay industry was born in the nineteenth century and by 1807 there were seven different clay works in the St Dennis and St Stephen parishes. However, although the number of clay works increased over the years, which created more employment, it did not affect the general standard of living as the work was hard and the wages were low. Conditions remained hard through the 1930s and during the Second World War when the clay industry slumped. The steady recovery in the demand for china clay in the 1950s heralded the exceptional market for this mineral in the following years.

St Dennis, along with other nearby villages, thrived in the 1960s, '70s and '80s, largely as a result of the boom in the china-clay industry which led to good times for local people and businesses, services, and social outlets. The policy of the clay-producing companies of restructuring, or 'downsizing' as industry calls it, which started in 1989, has resulted in less than 30 per cent of the 1980 employee total being employed today. Indeed, it is a widely held view that the modern industry, which was built on the backs of our forefathers, has little regard for the loyalty demonstrated by its employees and the wider communities.

The china-clay pits and waste tips lie around the eastern and southern edges of St Dennis, with the village designated as an island settlement; the industry is therefore unable to encroach upon its boundaries. In 2003, St Dennis had a population of approximately 2,500 people, and at the end of the twentieth century it was reputed to be the largest populated village in the county.

Religion

Methodism has a strong history in the village, and at one time there were three Methodist chapels in use. However, in 2004 this has been reduced to two. The church at St Dennis overlooks the village, Enniscaven, the Retew Valley and Goss Moor from its home on top of a hill. It is surrounded by small fields, with drystone hedges constructed centuries ago.

Listed Properties

The parish has 11 entries in the official records of Grade II listed buildings/monuments. These are: the church, a font, the Varcoe, Riddler, Truscott and Gill monuments, plus an unidentified monument all in the churchyard, as well as the Parkandillick Engine House, Trerice Bridge, a house east of the Old Rectory now known as 'Biddicks' House, and an old house with a galvanised-iron roof opposite the old chapel at Enniscaven.

Left: *Parkandillick Engine House.* KHR

This picture: *Biddicks House.* KHR

Below: *The house at Enniscaven.* KHR

Clockwise from top left: *The Gill monument of 1801; the Truscott monument, 1829; the Riddler monument, 1827; the Varcoe monument, 1826; the unidentified monument, 1835; the church; the early-twelfth-century font; the old Celtic cross.* KHR

The Second World War

During the war, along with the rest of the county, St Dennis played its part and overcame the problem which war brings to a rural community. The recently formed Red Cross unit came into its own, and a Home Guard unit, an auxiliary fire service, a squad of 12 Special Constables, an auxiliary unit and an air-raid warden were all formed from people not eligible for military or war effort service. A Girls' Training Corps was established and trained by Mr and Mrs P. Magor. In addition, villagers accommodated 60 evacuees along with their teachers in housing far below the standard that we take for granted in the twenty-first century. A Women's Voluntary Service (WVS) group was also formed to help with emergencies. All this was achieved without the presence of the breadwinners, who were often away on active service.

There was a British Army Ordnance depot in the clay dries at Gothers which brought heavy traffic to the roads. This was increased further during the build-up to D-Day; US troops and weaponry overran the whole area.

Auxiliary units were established at the beginning of the Second World War to carry out resistance work mainly in coastal areas, in the event of enemy occupation. These units were given three responsibilities (special duties, fighting patrols and signals) and were issued with arms, ammunition, explosives and 14 days' supply of rationed canned food. This food was hidden in secret locations, which in the case of St Dennis was near Hendra Pit.

Training and lectures were carried out at the church. In the event of enemy occupation, the St Dennis unit was instructed to prioritise the destruction of the Domellick Bridge. The unit consisted of: Claude Dunstan, Percy Magor, Eric Trethewey, Johnny Bunt, Ralph Burnett, Tommy Kessell, Harry Estlick, Arthur Gregor and Sidney Willcox. This information was classified as secret until 1995 when the 50 years' secrecy limit was reached.

A regrettable statistic from this war was that a dozen men from the village were killed in action.

Housing and Utilities

The standard of housing, apart from some grand houses and manors, was generally poor in the early-twentieth century when thatched roofs and garden toilets were commonplace.

Housing began to improve with the building of mains sewerage and the Robartes Road council-houses after the First World War had ended. Incidentally, Robartes Road was named after the Rt Hon. T.C.R. Agar-Robartes, the Liberal MP of this constituency who was killed during this conflict.

Mains water did not arrive until the early 1930s. Prior to this drinking-water was obtained from pumps positioned around the village. Research has failed to obtain from the respective bodies the actual dates when water, sewerage and telephones were installed in the parish. That said, we do know that electricity was available from 1931.

New council-houses were constructed on Hall Farm land, beginning in 1947, and soon they numbered over 100 new homes. They were all made using prefabricated units that were manufactured locally at the Gothers concrete works.

Warden-controlled bungalows designed to house elderly people were built in the 1970s. The 1980s also saw a boom in house building. Private developments have been built at Kellow Estate, Parc-an-Brae, Whitegate Meadows, Kents Close, Dunstan Close and Whitegate.

There was a time when most households had a garden or allotment where vegetables were grown, or a few fowls or an odd pig were reared. At the start of the twenty-first century, however, this has all changed as people have the resources to purchase all their requirements from general stores and supermarkets.

Leisure

From the early days of the twentieth century the village has been known for the talents of its inhabitants. Over time it has produced many fine marching and dance bands, plus choirs, singers, dance troupes, drama and pantomime groups, as well as various teams and individuals.

St Dennis has had its share of dance bands, especially in 1930–50, when names such as Blue Moon, White Aces, Rhythmic Six, Duchy, Lyric, Roselyn Boys, Paramount and Rhythm Stars were popular.

During the 1930s the village had its own string orchestra and at one time in the early-twentieth century Enniscaven had its own brass band and a fife-and-drum band. Since 1836 the village has had a Silver Band, although it has not always been known by that name. St Dennis' band was once very famous, competing with the likes of Sunlife and Grimethorpe Colliery Bands. However, it fell on difficult times but remained active and at the start of the twenty-first century continues to work towards achieving its previous high standards.

Since the 1930s local youngsters have participated in social groups such as the Cubs and Scouts, Brownies, Rangers and Girl Guides, the Crusaders and the youth club. Although some of these have existed intermittently, they have all played an important role in preparing the youngsters for adulthood.

'No-one wants to come here but once here no-one wants to leave'

The Institute, social clubs, and public houses have provided facilities for darts, billiards, snooker, pool and various card games. Many fine players have emerged over the years, some of whom have represented the county in their chosen fields. Football has long played its part in village life, with the St Dennis AFC, Newmoor Rovers and St Dennis United all providing outlets for those with a talent for soccer.

The church and chapels, apart from worship, have also provided social activities for the community, especially in the mid-twentieth century.

After the Second World War, a women's hockey team was formed which played in the bottom part of the football field. Mr Albert Williams was well known as the referee as he was probably the only person in the village that knew the rules! This sport only lasted a few years.

St Dennis has its own branch of the Old Cornwall Society which was formed in 1986. The instigator Mr Douglas Creba was elected as chairman. He was made a Bard of Kernow in 1994 and given the name of Den an Carrygy, which means 'Man of Rocks'. In 2003 the branch had several members and had Mrs Heather Stanley as secretary.

A Darby and Joan Club was formed in the 1960s to provide a social amenity for the elderly people by way of weekly get-togethers. This ran for many years before changing its name to the Good Companions, which continues in 2004 under the guidance of Mrs B. Hayward who regularly organises coach outings for its members.

After an absence of 15 years the village carnival was revived in 1970 and is held annually in July. Since its revival it has raised thousands of pounds for the Silver Band and the St Dennis AFC, and to a lesser extent some of the smaller village organisations. Since the 1970s the carnival has been organised and operated by a loyal band of supporters ably led and encouraged by Mr Rex Harvey.

The British Legion

A branch of the British Legion existed in the village before the Second World War, which was active and supportive to ex-servicemen and women after the conflict. Sadly the branch no longer exists, although the village still has a wreath- and poppy-sales co-ordinator. A Remembrance Day celebration has been held continuously since the early days of the branch. These days it consists of a parade to the church for a service by representatives of all village organisations, led by the Silver Band, then back to the Institute for a wreath-laying ceremony. During the 1960–80 period a large contingent of airmen from RAF St Mawgan attended. However, over the years, this representation has been reduced to two airmen. For many years Mr Stuart Gregor was the parade marshal.

Cancer Research

St Dennis has a very active Cancer Research (UK) committee which was formed in 1962 at a meeting held in the Church of England School chaired by the Devon and Cornwall organiser Mr Household. Many dedicated people have served as committee members and worked tirelessly to raise funds. Certain founder members are still serving, as is chairman Ralph Burnett who has retained that position since day one. The annual efforts of the St Austell Golf Club continue to result in a major contribution to the funds. To date this village committee has raised over £120,000 for Cancer Research.

A New Millennium

The dawn of the new millennium was celebrated in 2000 by a parade of village organisations, led by the village band, visiting the purpose-built Celtic cross at Carne and the sundial at Trelavour Prazey, with a service held at each conducted by the Revd Tim Russ. All parish children were given a special medal to commemorate the occasion.

Gone are the days when the household refuse was collected by horse and cart then dumped on a tip at Hendra Prazey. In modern times the village benefits from weekly council collections and recycling is encouraged with monthly collections, with alternative facilities provided in the Wellington Road car park.

As the twentieth century progressed, the shopping habits of the village inhabitants changed; people used to buy all their goods and groceries in the village, such was the selection of shops. Nowadays, however, people have to travel to St Austell or Truro for even the most basic things. Subsidised bus services run to various locations but more often than not the buses are virtually empty. The standard of living and quality of life afforded by most enables the motor car to be an accepted amenity for the majority of people in rural areas such as ours.

During the twentieth century and possibly before, village organisations, whatever their size, religion or otherwise, were created, supported and appreciated by very loyal and dedicated people. By doing so these individuals and groups played their part in creating the community of the village. The most important part of any organisation is its people and St Dennis is no exception. Although in today's changing times a strong sense of belonging still survives, other characteristics which made our close-knit community are gradually diminishing. No longer are nicknames such as Whiskers, Ticker, Saddler, Dempsy, Mac, Tug, Micky, Kitch, Dickie Smut, Dessie, Newquay, Dyke, Sparrow, Donkey, Dick Skit, Wilder, Bronco, Dinger, Tinker, Rip and many more being used.

I am sure that people's memories highlighted in this book will remind them of the part they have played and hopefully they will gain some satisfaction from reflecting on their contribution.

Chapter 2

A History of Commerce

This chapter serves as a brief index of remembered and known businesses and services which have served the community over the years.

Hendra Road (Lane)

Penwyn Garage, built 1949

Mr Frank Julian, 1949–59: motor repairs and haulage.
Mr Arthur Kent, 1959–74: motor repairs and haulage.
Smith and Treffry, 1974–77: motor repairs and haulage.
Mr Stanley Metherell, 1977–79: motor repairs, etc.
Mr Graham Brokenshire, 1979: motor repairs, sales, etc.

Shed near Penwyn

Richards and Mitchell, 1932: fruiters, etc.

Penwyn Garage, 2003. KHR

Penawyn

Mr Bert Stephens: milk and ice-cream sales.

St Dennis Band Club, built 1983

Coach Garage, built 1920, demolished 1989

Mr Harry Crowle, 1920–1834.
Western National Bus Company.
Mr Combellick: salvaged vehicles workshop.

Garage, built 1920

Harry Crowle, 1920–34: coach servicing.
Mr Dave Yelland 1934: motor repairs and fuel sales.
Mr Hodge: motor cycle spares sales.
Mr K. Geach: motor repairs.
Wisdom Signs: sign making.

'Harwena'

Dr C.M. Wilson, 1963–74: doctors' surgery.

Right: *A 1927 scene, taken from Hendra Corner, showing Mr John Kessell's shop and his horse-drawn delivery vehicle.* KHR/Coll

A Hendra Road scene in 1933 showing two of Harry Crowle's buses, one opposite his petrol pump. The policeman is PC 'Bobby' Taylor. KHR/Coll

No. 38
Mr M. Martin, 1986: UPVC installations.

'Broomhill'
Dr Manson's surgery.

Denzil House
Mr M. Coombe: cigarettes and ice-cream sales.

Shop, converted to dwelling 1973
Mr R.H. Yelland: butcher.
Mr E. Davies: butcher

Carpenter's workshop, now Jubilee Terrace
Mr Percy Magor: carpenter

Shop, converted to dwelling 1960
Mr John Kessell: grocery sales.
Messrs Tucker and Grigg: cycle sales and repairs.

Shop (Hendra Corner), converted to dwelling, c.1970s
Mr G. Richards: chip shop.
Mrs Trethewey: sweets, etc.

Hendra Manor Yard
Mr Claude Grose: mason and builder.
Mr Eric Grose: mason and builder.

Hendra Bakery
Mr Arnold Kessell: baker and coach operator.
The Bestwetherick Bros: bakers.
Mr and Mrs J. Philbrook: bakers.
Mr and Mrs Mountstephens: bakers.
Mr and Mrs J. Rowe, 1977: bakers.
Mrs P. Rowe & Sons: bakers.

Fore Street

Greenwich House, converted to dwelling 2000
Mr Tom Morcom: patent medicine sales and jeweller.
Mr Hugh Morcom: newsagent and jeweller.
Mr Arthur Kent, 1955–69: newsagent and general store.
Mr R. Juleff: newsagent and general store.
Mr D. Osborne: newsagent and general store.
Mr Peppiatt: newsagent and general store.
Mrs A. Gregory, 1999–2000: newsagent.

Public house, returned to domestic use 1894
The Wagoners.
The Miners Arms.

A 1920s view from Hendra Corner. KHR/Coll

Inset: *Hendra Bakery, 2003.* KHR

This picture: *A view from Hendra Corner showing the baker's shop, the Miners Arms and, on the right, Tom Morcom's shop.* KHR/Coll

The Boscawen Yard stable building before it was modernised, 1990. KHR/Coll

The Red Cross building in Boscawen Yard, which at the time of writing is up for sale. KHR

Left: ***The old smithy in Fore Street, 2003.*** KHR

Right: ***The St Dennis Pharmacy, 2003.*** KHR

Above: *Mr Percy Varcoe outside the smithy in 1926.* KHR/Coll

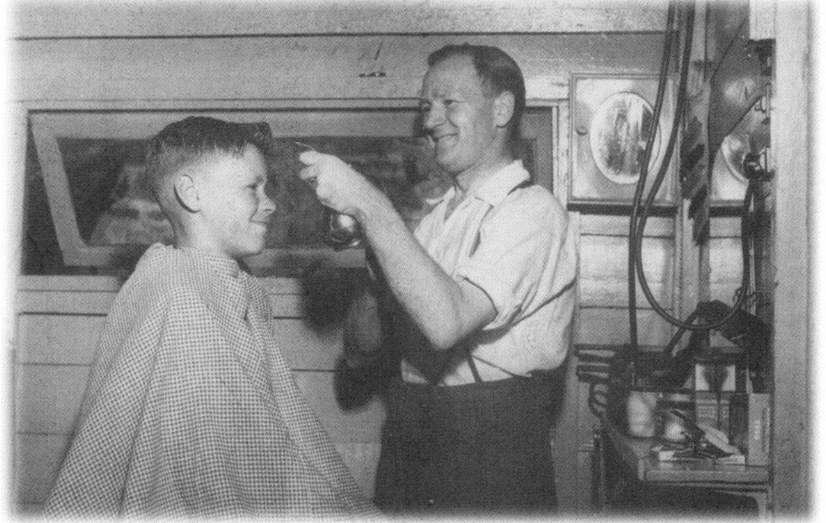

Right: *Mr Bill Taylor at work in his barber's shop putting the finishing touches to his son Dudley's hair in 1948.* KHR/Coll

Mr Elah Nance (left), *his son Richard* (centre) *and Mr Cyril Best, 1923. On the left is Elah's hardware shop and on the right is his carpenter's workshop and saw-pit, which served the village, the local clay works and his undertaking business. The site, known in those days as the 'Army Yard', was cleared in 1930 to make way for a new cinema. At that time Elah moved to new premises, previously occupied by Mr Tremain, a butcher, which became the home of the family business for many years.*

Coal yard, converted to car park 1970s
Mr William Pollard: coal merchant.
Mr 'Queenie' Best: coal merchant.

Doctors' surgery, purpose built 1970

Boscawen Yard Building, closed 2003
Garages and stables.
Messrs R. and S. Gregor: dairy storage.
Red Cross centre: modernised in 1991, first floor used for various functions.

Boscawen Hotel, built 1895 for Lord Falmouth

Chemist's shop, purpose built 1927
Mr S.H. Estlick, 1927–40: chemist.
Mr H.S. Estlick, 1940–65: chemist.
H.S. and G. Estlick, 1965–90: chemist.
Mrs S. Burgess, 1990–94: chemist.
Banns Pharmacy, 1994: chemist.

Shop, built 1970s
Mr T. Cornelius: TV and music sales.
Mrs B. Pascoe and Mr M. Honeywell, second-hand goods sales.
Mr D. Morcom: butcher and groceries.
Mr L. Pearce, 1994: butcher and groceries.

War Memorial Institute, built 1922

Cinema, closed 1930
Mr Elgar
Barclays Bank: built on old cinema site in 1960.

Shop, converted to dwelling 2003
Mr Tommy Varcoe: gents' outfitter.
Mr Cyril Miller: electrical and wool sales.
Mr Claude Bunt: shoe sales, etc.
'Peggy' Sue: ladies' fashions.
Lloyds Bank.
Dolphin – Mr E. Withers: swimming-pool engineer.
Mr E. Withers: second-hand goods sales.

Fore Street during the 1950s. KHR/Coll

Angove Villa (hut in garden), closed 1975

Mr Bill Taylor: hairdresser.

Blacksmith's shop, closed 1973

Mr Richard G. Varcoe: blacksmith.
Mr Percy Varcoe: blacksmith.

London House shop, converted back to dwelling 1994

Mrs Jessie Trudgeon, 1920s: groceries and sweets.
Mrs Olive Taylor: egg sales.
Village Home Guard HQ during Second World War.
Mr H. Bullen, 1955–61: fish and chip café.
Mr and Mrs Male: café.
Mr H. Treloar: ladies' fashions.
Mrs Frampton: ladies' fashions.
Mr E. Ward: grocery sales.

Shop next to blacksmith's before cinema was built

Mr Elah Nance: hardware sales, etc.

The Army Yard

Salvation Army hut: used by Reading & Recreation Society.
Mr E. Nance: carpenter's workshop and saw-pit.

The Plaza Cinema, built 1930, demolished 1964

Shop next to cinema, demolished 1964

Mr James, 1930s: tailor, Singer sewing-machine agent.
Miss M. Tucker: ladies' hairdresser.
Mr D. Richards: general goods.
Messrs C. and G. Bunt: shoe sales and repairs.

Shop, Central Café

Mr Arthur Trudgeon: barber's and chip shop.
Mr Francis Ellis: boot repairs and chip shop.
Mr Rex Harvey, 1974–79: fish and chips.
Mr Gerald Saunders, 1979–91: fish and chips.
Mr Gerald Kelly, 1992: fish and chips.
Mr Mel Hill, 1992: fish and chips.
Mr Tony Gummow, 1993–2000: fish and chips.
Mr Steve Gummow, 2000: fish and chips.

Corner Stores

Mr Jim Osborne: grocery store.
Mr Henwood: café.
Messrs Albert and Stanley Key: grocery store.
Mr Roy Bennetts: grocery store and café.
Mr R. Hayes: grocery store and café.
Mr Epsom: grocery and butcher's shop.
Mr Blackham: grocery and butcher's shop.
Mr and Mrs L. Chapman, 1986: general stores.

Whitepit

Mr C. Odgers: drapery sales.

Stores, closed in 2000

Mr Tremain: butcher.
Mr Elah Nance: hardware, carpets, undertaker.
Mr R. Nance: furniture, hardware, carpets, undertaker.
Messrs J. and B. Nance: furniture, hardware, carpets.
Mr J. Nance: furniture, hardware, carpets.

Left: *Outside Mr Trudgeon's barber's shop, 1922.* Left to right, back row: *Harry Cory, Jim Rundle, 'Whiskers' (Mr Trudgeon), Harry Best, Mervyn Trudgeon, Stan Rapson, Reg Colewell, Mr Trudgeon's father;* centre: *Fred Bennetto, ?, Fred Waters, Albert Goudge, Wesley Goudge;* front: *Alfie Richards, Bert Keast, ?, Cyril Best, ?, George Grose, ?, Henry Hill.* KHR/Coll

Below left: *Mrs Ellen Knight* (left) *with her daughter Florence, holding a young Derek Colewell, outside Mr Trudgeon's barber's shop and village water pump, 1928.* KHR/Coll

Below: *Central Café, formerly Trudgeon's barber's shop, 2003.* KHR

Left-hand column, from top: *Mr Jim Osborne and family outside their corner shop, 1934* (KHR/Coll); *Nance's furniture showroom after closure, 2003* (KHR); *Butcher William Kellow's house and shop in Fore Street, 1920s.* (KHR/Coll)

Right: *Outside Veall's Bakery in 1925* (left to right)*: Mrs Emily Veall, Miss Eva Marshall and Miss Rhoda Bullen. The children's names are unknown.* (C.H. Barrett)

Right-hand column from top: *Richard Nance's LWB lorry in the yard at Whitepit. This vehicle was essential to the timber and firewood trade, which was a considerable part of the family business during the 1950s* (KHR/Coll); *John Nance's vintage Albion – a 1929 LB41 Boxvan, with the registration number UH6939* (KHR/Coll); *Kays Fish and Chips, 2003.* (KHR)

Left: *'Saddler' Kellaway outside his Fore Street shop in 1930.* C.H. Barrett
Centre: *Mr Edgar Coombe outside his hairdresser's shop in Fore Street in 1935.* C.H. Barrett
Right: *Hazel Common, as a baby in the arms of her sister Florrie, outside No. 21 Fore Street in 1909, before the property was utilised by Lloyds Bank.* KHR/Coll

Myra Villa

Mr William Kellow: butcher's and farmer.

Café, known as 'Kays' in 2003

Mr Jimmy Rundle: chip shop.
Mr Monty Lobb: chip shop.
Mr Bert Stephens: chip shop.
Mr Ted Kessell: fish and chip shop.
Mr Henry Bullen: fish and chip shop.
Mrs Kay Martin: fish and chip shop.
Mr Dennis Kent: fish and chip shop.
Mrs Key and Mrs Bilkey: fish and chip shop.
Mr S. Gummow: fish and chip shop.

Post Office – 'Tremont' – from 1922

Rose Cottage – Old Post Office up to 1922

Shop – No. 35, converted to dwelling 1992

Mr T.M. Kellaway: saddler, engineer, equipment and taxi hire.
Mr Oscar Dunstan: hardware sales.
Mr Trevor Geach, 1976–92: cycle spares and video library.

Bakery, converted into flats 1986

Messrs E. & M. Veall: bakers.
Mr J. Tippett: baker.

Saloon (Hut)

Messrs E. & R. Coombe: hairdresser.
Miss S. Truscott: hairdresser.
Mrs K. Lobb: hairdresser.
Mrs J. Ford: hairdresser.
Mrs L. Craddock, 1976–86: hairdresser.
Mrs R. Sargeant, 1986: hairdresser.

Cobblers Workshop – No. 23, ceased trading 1970s

Mr A.E. Strongman: shoemaker.
Mr C. Strongman: shoemaker.

Barclays Bank – No. 23, part time

Lloyds Bank – No. 21, part time

Lloyds Bank at 21 Fore Street (opened on a part-time basis on Tuesdays) in the 1940s. KHR/Coll

Above: *Mr and Mrs J. Bell's Fore Street shop in 1960.* KHR/Coll

Left: *Mrs Arthur Gregor in the doorway of the family shop in Fore Street, c.1920.* KHR/Coll

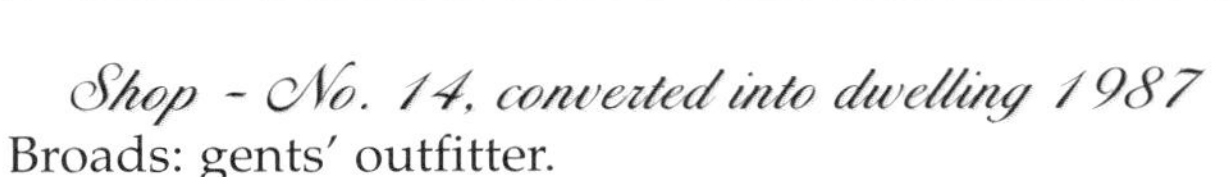

Shop – No. 14, converted into dwelling 1987

Broads: gents' outfitter.
Parish Office and travel agents.
Mr A.J. Gregor, 1928: outfitter and electrical sales.
Mr J.A. Gregor, 1987: outfitter and electrical sales.

Shop – No. 4, converted into dwelling 1991

Mr L.G. Hooper: general stores.
Mr G. Allen: general stores.
Mr and Mrs J. Bell, 1959–78: general stores.
Mr G. Allen: motor accessories.

Shop – No. 11, closed 1989 and combined with dwelling 1990s

Mr E. Harris: greengrocer.
Mr A.J. Strongman: greengrocer.
Mr P. Walker: greengrocer.

School House – shop (Hut)

Mrs Stribley: pork sales, etc.

Capenter's shop – No. 1

Mr G. Bullock: carpenter.

Trelavour

Shop – No. 6, combined with dwelling 1993

Mr E.D. Jenkin: hairdresser.
Mr F. Mugford: hairdresser.
Mrs E. Buckingham: hairdresser.
Mr W. Ellery: hairdresser.
Mrs H. Metherell: general stores.
Mr F. Metherell: hairdresser.
Mr L. Best, 1984–88: general stores.
Mrs M. Elliott, 1988–93: general stores.

Shop – No. 10, combined with dwelling 1982

The Maltsters public house.
The Globe public house.
Mr W. Yelland: butcher's shop.
Mr C. Pope: grocer and fruiter.
Mr S. Pope: grocer and fruiter.

Shop – No. 14, rebuilt as a residence 1997

Mr W. Yelland: blacksmith.
Mr 'Doc' Martin (Nanpean): cement store.
Mrs J. Rabey: cycle spares, oils, etc.

Left: *Mr G. Bullock's carpenter's shop in the 1920s which in 2003 is the residence known as 1 Fore Street.* KHR/Coll
Centre: *No. 1 Fore Street, 2003.* KHR
Right: *Butchers Richard and Elizabeth Yelland outside their premises at Trelavour in 1932.* KHR/Coll

Mr S.H. Estlick and his wife outside their chemist's shop in Trelavour in 1926. C.H. Barrett

Mr S. Hore: ladies' fashions.
Mrs J. Penhaligan, 1960–72: ladies' fashions.
Launderette.
Mrs S. Uddy: hairdresser.

Shop (Hut) - No. 1, demolished 1977

Mr H.S. Estlick, 1912–26: chemist.
Mr A. Strongman: greengrocer.
Mr E. Penhaligan: greengrocer.
Mr S. Penhaligan: greengrocer.
Mr and Mrs R. White: music sales.
Mr P. Trebilcock: hairdresser.

Shop - established 1850 - No. 16

Mr R. Hore: grocer.
Mr S. Hore: grocer.
Mr Jones: grocer.
Mr P. Trebilcock: 1958–95: hairdresser and grocer, etc.
Colin and Di, 1995: grocers and fuel, etc.

Above: *D. and J. Penhaligan's ladies' fashions shop at Trelavour (1960–72).* KHR/Coll

Shop, No. 2 the Square, combined with residence 1980s

Mr Currah: grocer.
Mr T.M. Kellaway: saddler.
Mr R.H. Yelland: grocer, decorator and chimney sweep.
Mr Midwinter: grocer.

Shop - No. 9A, converted into dwelling 1990s

Eliza Bunt: general stores.
Mr T. Huddy: plumbers' supplies.
T & GWU: office.
Messrs F. & G. Stoneman: chip shop.
St Dennis AFC: committee room, etc.
Mrs H. Metherell: children's clothes shop.
Miss A. Knight: hairdresser.
Mr T. Cornelius: TV sales, etc.
Mrs D. Best: wool sales.
Mrs R. Gill: fishmonger.
Pet food sales
Mr L. Spry: greengrocer, etc.

Hall Farm - Trelavour Manor, land sold for building development 2000

Mr E.S. Hext, 1889–1917
Mr W.G. Blewett, 1917–40
Mr M. Lewarne, 1940–43
Mr J.D. Thomas, 1943–68
C.E. and C.M. Dunstan, 1968

The Commercial Inn

Premises in Trelavour Square known as 'Ontario' in 2004

Mr Tom Bullock, 1870–1927: carpenter.

Shop - No. 10, converted to residence 1990s

Mr W.J. Yelland: butcher.
Mr P. Burnett: butcher.
Mr R. Burnett 1951–86: butcher.
Mr P. O'Brian 1986–92: butcher.
Miss M. Hancock: hairdresser.

Trelavour Farm

Mr J. Thomas: coal merchant.
Mr J. Matthews: vehicle repairs and sales.

Wellington Road (Well Lane)

No. 8, ceased trading 1988

Messrs S. and W. Honey: wholesale egg collectors.
Mr W.F. Oliver, 1955–88: dairyman.

Co-Operative Society Store, built 1915

St Dennis Branch, 1915–84: grocer, draper, provender.
Mr G. Allen: vehicle storage.
Mr A. Taylor: general stores.
Mr D. Rowe: second-hand goods sales.
Mrs A. Gregory, 2000: newsagent.
K. & G. Sheds 2000: carpenter's workshop.

Left: *Carnival celebrations in 1960, also showing Mr R.F. Yelland's corner shop in Trelavour Square.* KHR/Coll

Below: *Mr W. Blewett at Trelavour Manor (Hall Farm) in 1938.* KHR/Coll

Below left: *Wellington Road shops, 2003.* KHR

Left: *Staff of the St Dennis branch of the Co-op pose for a group photograph in 1935.* Left to right, back row: *Mr D. Lobb, Miss P. Kent, Miss P. Bunt, Mr B. Broad, Miss L. Collett, Mr Symmonds;* front: *Miss S. Pethick, Miss S. Wade, Miss N. Angilley, Mr Willcox, Miss R. Baglow, Miss J. Luke, Miss B. Bullen.* P. Bilkey

Above: *Mrs P. Burnett in the doorway of the family butcher's shop at Trelavour, 1930s. The old butcher's shop and the hut of many ventures that stood next door in Trelavour, have since been converted into homes.* KHR/Coll

Right: *An aerial view of Arthur Kent's coal yard, c.1960.* KHR/Coll

'Lamorna'
Mr C.H. Barrett, 1954–2003: photographer.

Coal Yard, closed 1989
Mr Bert Kent, 1900–46: coal merchant.
Mr Arthur Kent, 1946–74: coal merchant.
Mr Stanley Metherell: vehicle repairs, etc.
Smith and Treffry, 1975–89: coal merchants.

'Glendale'
Mr G. Bullen: carpenter and undertaker.
Mr M. Martin: UPVC store.

Stonemasons Yard
Mr A. Pedlar & Son: stonemasons.

Trelavour Prazey

Glyn Vale Dairy
Messrs S. & R. Gregor: dairymen.
Mr R.W. Lyndon: dairyman.

Whitegate

Garage, demolished 1994
Mr T. Kessell: car sales and motor repairs.
Messrs T. & A. Kessell: motor repairs and vehicle hire.

Rural Workshop Estate comprising six units
English Nature (two units).
Oasis Community Care.
Wisdom Screen Print.
Altiman.
Computer Forms Services.

Boscawen Park - St Dennis AFC and Social Club

Robartes Road

The Osborne Building, closed 1972
Mr Henwood: shop and café.
Mr E. Lobb: shop.
Mr Brown: chip shop.
Drs Wilson and Crabtree: surgery and dispensary, as well as a part-time dentist and optician's practice.
Drs Therwell and Winslade: surgery.

Garage
Messrs G. & D. Richards: motor repairs and fuel.
Demolished 1964 and rebuilt as a café, domestic premises and a filling station.
Mr R. Hayward, 1947–67.
Doctors' Surgery, 1976.

Old Fire Station
Mr Moffitt and Mr C. Miller started a motor-repair and electrical business here. Mr C. Rabey later replaced Mr Moffitt.
The fire service moved in in 1951.
Closed as the fire station in 2002.

'Dee-An-J'
Mr R. Odgers, 1981–99: carpenter and decorator.

No. 8 - Shed in back garden.
Mr P.T. Snell: butcher.

No. 5
Mrs Ellery: shop and agency.

Builders Yard
The Lobb Bros: builders.

Hut
Mr Marsh Kessell: shoemaker.

Hut
Tucker and Grigg: cycle repairs, 1930s.

Garage, purpose built 1959
Messrs T. & A. Kessell, 1959–97: filling station, shop.
Mr A. Grose, 1997–2001: filling station, shop.
Trident Civil Engineers.

Trelavour Road (Downs Lane)

Workshop (Hut)
Mr C. Coombe: shoemaker.
Mr C. Bunt: shoemaker.
Mr Brown: shoemaker.

Carpenter's shop
Mr G. Bullock: carpenter, wheelwright, undertaker.
Mr T. Bullock: carpenter, wheelwright, undertaker.
Mr S. Metherell, 1984: saw-servicing workshop.

Kingdom Hall, converted to domestic use
Mr J. Trudgian, 1889–1925: organ factory.
Gospel Hall.
Youth Club, 1940s.

Hut (on site of present filling-station forecourt), demolished 1949
Mr Tom Trudgian, 1930s: watchmaker.
Mr Tom Underwood: hairdresser.

Trelavour Road Garage, built 1963
Stanley Metherell: general repairs specialising in Land Rovers, a filling station.
Saw-sharpening service, 1984. Called Mid-Cornwall Saw Service in 2004.

Slaughterhouse
Mr R. Burnett, 1951–70: butcher.

Left: *A rare view of the Kessells' garage at Whitegate with one of their fleet of rental caravanettes, which formed part of their business in the 1970s.* KHR

Below: *Boscawen Park, home of St Dennis AFC.* KHR

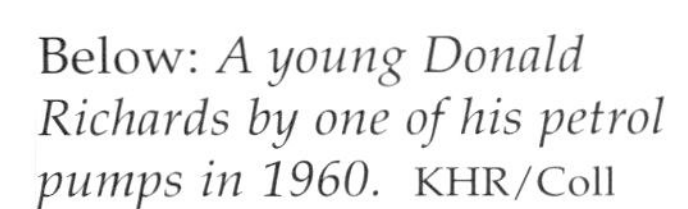

Below: *A young Donald Richards by one of his petrol pumps in 1960.* KHR/Coll

Right: *A 1963 scene showing the Army Yard cottages and Donald Richards outside his garage.* C.H. Barrett

The Pyramid site in 2003. **KHR**

The Old Filling Station – used as offices in 2003. KHR

Right: *Mr C. Coombe's shoemaker's hut at the bottom of Trelavour Road. Unfortunately the picture has been badly damaged.* KHR/Coll

Below: *One of Harold Gould's lorries.* G. Gould

Above: *Mr Eric Trethewey started his concrete-block business in the early 1950s near the Parkandillick clay pit where there was a supply of sand and water. This business, which employed five men in its heyday, closed in the early 1970s. The production site is shown here.* KHR/Coll

Above: *Mr John Trudgian outside his organ factory in Trelavour.* C.H. Barrett

Mr Tom Bullock's carpenter's shop, 2003. In 1984 it became part of the Metherells' saw-servicing business. **KHR**

Trelavour Road filling station and garage, 2003. **KHR**

'Highfield'
Mr R. Key: mason.

Copperstones
F. & K. Electrical & Refrigeration, 1967–83: after 1983 business was moved to High Street.

Mennawartha, ceased trading 1970s
Mr R.H. Gould: haulier.
Mr R. Gould: haulier.

Hall Road

'Cheviott'
Mr B.L. Craddock: builder.

'Marlanca'
Mr A. Trethewey: builder.

Smallholdings have not been included in this list because of the complexity of their histories. Carsella is included in Chapter 3 and Hall is mentioned earlier in Chapter 2. However, certain farms have been incorporated; the following have histories of note:

Menna Farm
Mr A. Yelland: farmer.
Mr J. Crowle: farmer.
Mr F. Mugford: farmer.
Mr E. Stoneman, 1943–57: farmer.
Mr D. Stoneman, 1957–95: farmer.
Mr A. Miller, 1995: farmer.

Little Gothers Farm
Mr R. Retallick: farmer.
Mr Prout: farmer.
Mr C. Barbary, 1968–2001: farmer.
Mr R.C. Hawke, 2001: farmer.

Carnegga Farm
Mr M. Key: farmer.
Mr Morris: farmer.
Mr Woodcock: farmer.
Mr D. Rowe: farmer.
Mrs S. Barker, 1980: farmer.

Domellick Farm
Mr S. Varcoe: farmer.
Mr D. Healey, 1981–86: cider-making farm.
Mrs L. Adams, 1986–2003: animal sanctuary.
2003: kennels and cattery.

Domellick Manor Farm
The Manor House was listed in the Domesday Book (1086) it must be one of the oldest in the parish.
Messrs N.W. & R. Pethick: farmers.
Mr J. Key.
Mr Pascoe: farmer.
Mr Rice: farmer.
Mr G. Smallridge: farmer.
DRS, 1991: demolition, recovery and salvage, including skip- and plant-hire business.

This picture: *Domellick Manor Farm, occupied by the demolition, recovery and salvage firm that also operates a skip- and plant-hire business.* KHR

Inset, above: *Domellick Farm ceased to operate as a farm many years ago. It diversified at first into a cider-processing farm and later was turned into a kennels and cattery.* KHR

Chapter 3

People of Note

Mr William John Blewett

Carsella is mentioned in the Domesday Book as Karsalan, a fortress (the prefix means castle or city). At the time of Domesday it was also a manor under the same baron as Dimelihoc.

The late and lamented Charles Henderson found traces of an ancient village at Carsella dating from between 100BC and AD100. The farmhouse in Carsella is the oldest house in St Dennis, its age being calculated at between 400 and 450 years with the original oak beams being especially interesting. There is reputed to be a secret tunnel connecting Carsella to the church. However, it is so secret that in modern times it has never been found!

Carsella has been farmed in more recent times by five generations of the Blewett family, starting in the nineteenth century with a Mr W.J. Blewett. He was followed by Mr John Blewett who preceded Mr Will Blewett. In 1956 Mr John Blewett took over (well known to many of us), before Mr Paul Blewett took the reins; he still runs the place at the time of writing.

There are records which show that a William Blewett of Carsella, who in 1890 was aged 66 years, was a local preacher and a class leader.

During the Second World War labour on the farm was provided by Italian prisoners of war. These men were based at the POW camp at Whitecross and travelled to and from the farm daily. The Blewett family also accommodated their share of evacuees. The farm and its buildings were used by the Home Guard, auxiliary fire service, civil defence groups and British Army Commandos for respective training exercises.

Mr John Blewett and his wife Freda made significant changes to the farm and practices through a gradual modernisation programme, which also included acquiring additional land, to meet the requirements of modern farming. In 2004 the farm covers approximately 1,000 acres and has 800 head of cattle, which makes it one of the largest in the area. The days of real horse power have been overtaken by mechanical power now provided by seven tractors and a full-time staff of four.

The farm has always attracted attention and has hosted visits from schools, walkers, visiting farmers, some from as far afield as New Zealand, as well as farming bodies. It has also played host to the Cancer Research (UK) Charity Fun Days which have raised thousands of pounds.

John Blewett has served the community and the farming industry well, being involved in various bodies and projects at both county and regional level. This has been recognised and rewarded with introductions to royalty and various radio and television interviews. In 2004 John is president of the St Dennis branch of Cancer Research (UK) and still serves on the Parish Council.

Left: *The Blewett farming family, 2003.* Left to right: *John, Freda, Paul and Helen.* KHR
Right: *Carsella Manor, 2003; the oldest house in the parish.* KHR

Tom Bullock

Born in 1846, Tom started his carpenter's business at Trelavour Square in 1870 after moving from St Stephens, in premises now known as Ontario. He remained there until he built a new carpenter's shop and four houses at the top of Fore Street in 1889.

When he died in 1916 one of his sons, George, took over the business and remained at No. 1 until 1927 when he bought and converted an old barn in Trelavour Road into a larger carpenter's shop. George died in 1935 and the business was taken over by his nephew, also called Tom. In the early days the work involved a fair amount of painting and decorating. Business progressed with general carpentry work, repairing cartwheels, making furniture and undertaking duties. Tom retired in 1985 after being in business for 50 years.

His interests were supporting the Carne Hill Methodist Church and singing in the St Dennis Male Voice Choir for 50 years, during which time he experienced hundreds of concerts, various contests and was even involved in broadcasts on the radio.

Mr Ralph Burnett

Ralph Burnett started his local butcher's shop in Trelavour in 1951 in premises previously used by his father, Mr P. Burnett, and Mr W.J. Yelland. Prior to 1951 Ralph had assisted his father with his farming and butcher's business at Tregoss; they had slaughterhouses at Tregoss and St Dennis. Ralph retired from his butcher's business in 1986.

In addition to his work, Ralph had a proud record of public service. He served on the St Dennis Parish Council for 30 years including a spell as chairman, the St Austell Rural District Council for 31 years and the County Council for 15 years. During these times he served on the County Fire and Public Protection Committee, the Devon and Cornwall Police Authority and the County Rates Appeal Committee. He also assisted in the setting up of the Cornwall Heritage Trust.

It is well known also that Ralph Burnett has been the chairman of the St Dennis branch of Cancer Research (UK) since its formation in 1962. He has also served as chairman of the St Dennis County Primary School governors and in the 1980s was the chairman of the Stannary Parliament.

Mr Ralph Burnett.

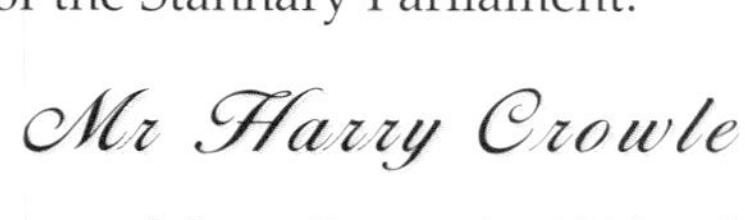

Mr Harry Crowle

After he returned from France in 1919, where he had served as a tank driver during the First World War, Harry Crowle was employed in his father's horse-drawn transport business at Fraddon. Harry believed the way forward was in motor transport, and being the enterprising man that he was he saw the market for motorised public transport in the St Dennis area. In 1920 he set about starting his own business.

He then proceeded to run a small maintenance workshop, with its own petrol pump, a large coach garage plus a house which he named 'Harvena' built in Hendra Road (Lane). A charabanc was purchased to do local hire and service routes, as this proved popular; as the demand increased more vehicles were purchased. Service routes were increased to encompass the St Austell area and by 1934 a dozen buses were being worked, each manned by a driver and a conductor. Weekend and bank holiday private hire was also popular, as was the occasional trip to the London Palladium.

In 1934 the Western National Bus Co. offered to buy Harry's business and he accepted. Although the deal did not include any buildings, all the employees were nevertheless retained, including Mr Crowle, who was made an inspector – a job he did not particularly enjoy.

During the Second World War, in 1943, the American Army, which was encamped all around the village, commandeered the coach garage to use as a repair and servicing workshop for their vehicles. This made Mrs Crowle a popular and busy person as the Americans soon had her making endless cups of coffee (American supplied) throughout the day.

After the war the garage returned to Western National use, which continued until the late 1970s, after which it was sold. In the 1980s the garage was utilised as a vehicle-salvage workshop, then in 1990 it was demolished and had two houses built on it.

Mr F.C. Elgar

A professional photographer and artist who moved to St Dennis in the early 1920s, F.C. Elgar came from London where he had worked in the West End theatres designing and painting scenery.

Apart from his cinema business in St Dennis, Mr Elgar operated a small studio near the Army Yard where he practiced photography, painted and carried out restoration work. He was also a mentor to Mr C.H. Barrett, an electrical engineer, who worked for him in the Plaza Cinema. He passed on all his expertise to Mr Barrett who went on to become a reputable and popular photographer.

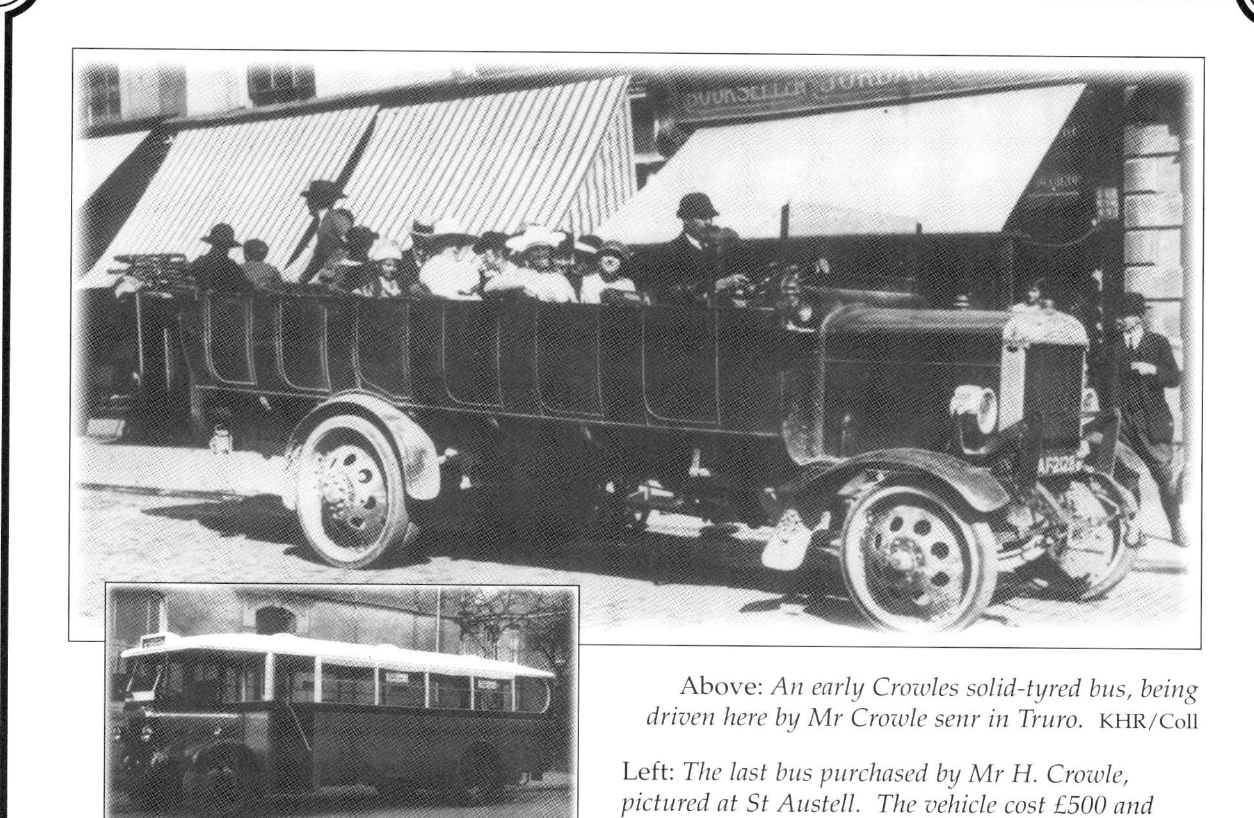

Above: *An early Crowles solid-tyred bus, being driven here by Mr Crowle senr in Truro.* KHR/Coll

Left: *The last bus purchased by Mr H. Crowle, pictured at St Austell. The vehicle cost £500 and increased the number in Mr Crowle's fleet to 12.* KHR/Coll

Harry Crowle ran the occasional coach trip to shows in the West End. Here we see copies of the programme for the first show attended at the London Palladium in 1931. KHR/Coll

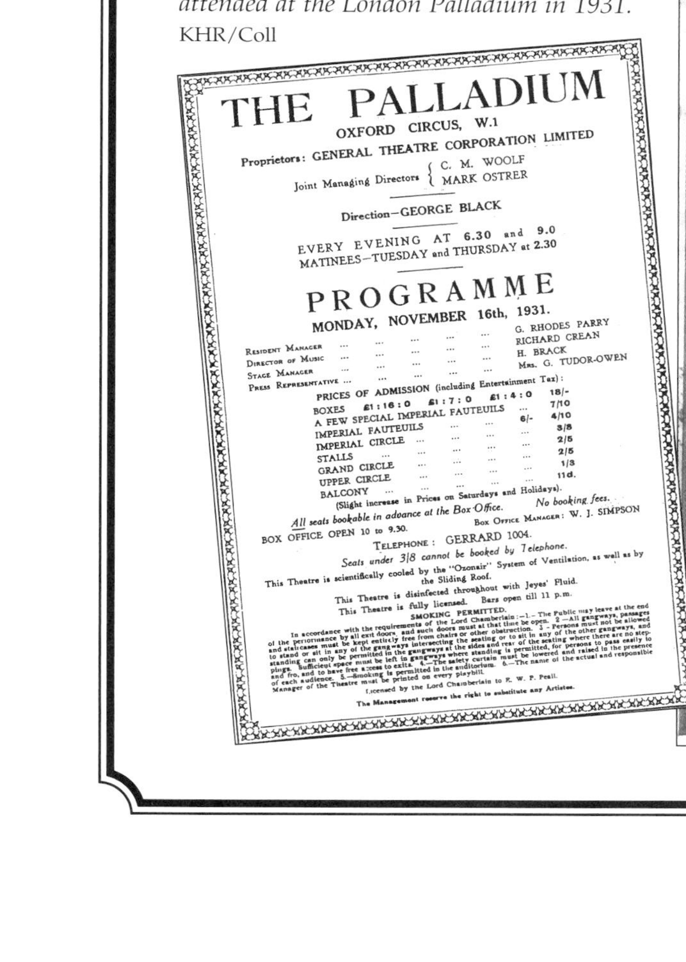

THE PALLADIUM

OXFORD CIRCUS, W.1

Proprietors: GENERAL THEATRE CORPORATION LIMITED

Joint Managing Directors { C. M. WOOLF / MARK OSTRER

Direction—GEORGE BLACK

EVERY EVENING AT 6.30 and 9.0
MATINEES—TUESDAY and THURSDAY at 2.30

PROGRAMME

MONDAY, NOVEMBER 16th, 1931.

Resident Manager ... ... G. RHODES PARRY
Director of Music ... ... RICHARD CREAN
Stage Manager ... ... H. BRACK
Press Representative ... ... Mrs. G. TUDOR-OWEN

PRICES OF ADMISSION (including Entertainment Tax):
BOXES £1:16:0 £1:7:0 £1:4:0 18/-
A FEW SPECIAL IMPERIAL FAUTEUILS ... 7/10
IMPERIAL FAUTEUILS 6/- 4/10
IMPERIAL CIRCLE 3/8
STALLS 2/5
GRAND CIRCLE 2/5
UPPER CIRCLE 1/3
BALCONY ... ... 11d.
(Slight increase in Prices on Saturdays and Holidays).

All seats bookable in advance at the Box Office. *No booking fees.*

BOX OFFICE OPEN 10 to 9.30. Box Office Manager: W. J. SIMPSON

Telephone: GERRARD 1004.

Seats under 3/8 cannot be booked by Telephone.

This Theatre is scientifically cooled by the "Ozonair" System of Ventilation, as well as by the Sliding Roof.

This Theatre is disinfected throughout with Jeyes' Fluid.

This Theatre is fully licensed. Bars open till 11 p.m.

SMOKING PERMITTED.

In accordance with the requirements of the Lord Chamberlain:—1.—The Public may leave at the end of the performance by all exit doors, and such doors must at that time be open. 2.—All gangways, passages and staircases must be kept entirely free from chairs or other obstruction. 3.—Persons must not be allowed to stand or sit in any of the gangways intersecting the seating or to sit in any of the other gangways, and standing can only be permitted in the gangways at the sides and rear of the seating where there are no steppings. Sufficient space must be left in gangways where standing is permitted, for persons to pass easily to and fro, and to have free access to exits. 4.—The safety curtain must be lowered and raised in the presence of each audience. 5.—Smoking is permitted in the auditorium. 6.—The name of the actual and responsible Manager of the Theatre must be printed on every playbill.

Licensed by the Lord Chamberlain to E. W. P. Peall.

The Management reserve the right to substitute any Artistes.

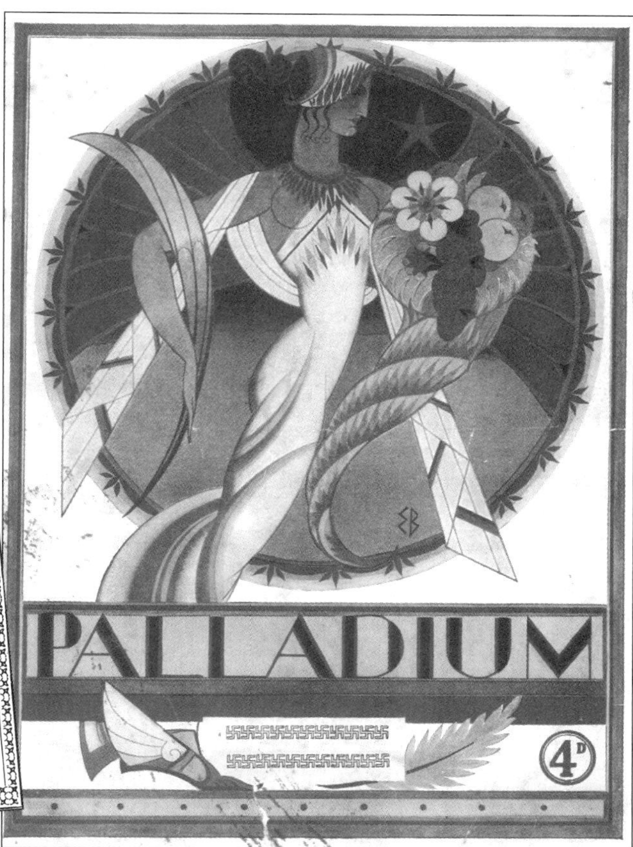

Mr Francis Ellis (left), *self-styled entrepreneur, with the author in 1988.* KHR/Coll

Mr Francis John Ellis

Francis was born at Halviggan in 1916 and later attended school at Nanpean. It was here that Francis sustained an injury to his right leg that remained with him for the rest of his life. On leaving school he trained in the boot- and shoemaking trade with Mr Weether at Lanjeth, then in 1930 he joined the clay works at Halviggan, where he repaired the clay-workers' boots.

From here he joined Mr Trudgeon in his chip shop in St Dennis (which has since become known as the Central Café) where he repaired boots and shoes, and worked in the chip shop. Francis later took over the running of the chip shop from Mr Trudgeon and eventually purchased it. His chip shop was very well known and well patronised. In the 1940s he introduced fish to the menu, and in the 1950s he installed the first jukebox in the village.

The success of the business led to the setting up of a wholesale tobacco business in the 1960s, which led to more success.

Alsation dogs were always part of Francis' life and remembered names are Jana, Ker and finally Tyson.

At one time he also owned and ran a fish-and-chip shop at Foxhole and at certain times operated mobile fish-and-chip carts locally, including one permanently at the Gothers concrete works, and one annually at the Summercourt fair. There was an occasion when one of Francis' chip carts manned by Mr H. McGirl (known to many of us as Mac) caught fire and burnt out at Treviscoe.

Francis leased another chip shop in St Dennis which a lady called Mrs Kay Martin ran for him. At the time of writing this shop is owned by Mrs P. Kellow but still retains the name of 'Kays'.

Francis retired from his business in 1974 and then leased the fish-and-chip business to four different tenants before the Gummow family took over in 1993.

Francis' support and generosity for local organisations was well known, as was his hospitality. Francis Ellis, who died on 16 February 2003 at the age of 87 years, was a popular figure in the locality and sadly his passing closes another chapter in the heritage of St Dennis.

Mr S.H. Estlick

A pharmacy was opened in St Dennis in 1912 by Mr Samuel Henry Estlick who moved to the village from Liskeard where he had been managing a local pharmacy. He took a 14-year lease on a house next to the Church of England School, in 2004 known as 1 Trelavour, and had a large shed built in the front garden. He used this as his pharmacy for 14 years.

Before the lease expired in 1926 Mr Estlick had a large house built by the Lobb brothers of Mevagissey,

Left: *Mr and Mrs S.H. Estlick with their son Harry, outside their new shop in 1927.* C.H. Barrett

Right: *Leslie Lobb, Harry Best, Ernie Lobb and Monty Lobb digging out foundations for Mr S.H. Estlick's new chemist's shop in 1925. The horse and cart belonged to George Angilley.* C.H. Barrett

next to the War Memorial Institute. Here he continued his business with the shop being an integral part of the house. Mr Estlick served on the Parish Council for many years and was an original trustee of the War Memorial Institute.

When he retired on 1 May 1940 the business was handed to his son, Henry Symons Estlick, who had moved to St Dennis with his wife and three-year-old son, Graham, from Stockbridge in Hampshire.

This Mr Estlick, known to all as 'Harry', then ran the business which had become well established and popular in the village and surrounding area.

Harry's reign of 50 years came to an end with his death in 1990. He followed his father's footsteps by becoming a trustee of the Institute and for many years had been a member of the St Dennis Male Voice Choir. He also liked his card games and dancing and regularly attended local events.

Harry's son Graham joined him in the business in May 1965 and worked with his father until 1990 when the business was sold to Mrs Sharon Burgess. Graham Estlick also followed the family tradition of becoming a trustee of the War Memorial Institute; he served many years on the management and development committees. After retiring in 1990 Graham and his wife moved away from the village to settle in the tranquillity of Golant. Sharon Burgess only remained in the business for four years before selling it to Banns Pharmacy, the owners in 2003.

Mr A.C. Gregor

Mr A.C. Gregor learnt his trade as a tailor at a London tailors' school in the 1890s. On returning to Cornwall he set up a 'cutting' shop (tailoring line) making men's trousers, jackets and suits and employing 13 tailors in premises at Bugle. He also opened a gents' outfitters shop in Bugle where he was joined by his son Arthur.

In 1928 a second shop was opened in St Dennis in premises previously used as the Parish Office and a travel agency which did much trade during the industrial slump of the early 1900s when disillusioned miners and clay workers travelled abroad to seek employment.

Arthur John Gregor managed the St Dennis shop with his father managing the Bugle shop. It is unclear when the cutting-shop business in Bugle was closed.

Mr John Austin Gregor was born in 1928 and when he was old enough he joined his grandfather in the Bugle business. When his grandfather died in 1948 John continued with the Bugle shop on his own for many years. In the meantime the St Dennis business was expanded to include the sale of electrical goods. The Bugle business was closed in 1963 when John returned to St Dennis to help his father. After his father died in 1963 John operated the St Dennis business on his own for several years before it closed in 1987.

Mr John Gregor was a keen supporter of the church, being a sidesman and a bell-ringer for many years and a churchwarden for 17 years. He was also the correspondent of the Church of England School managers and a trustee of the War Memorial Institute, as was his father. At one time he was the chairman. In his younger days he took part in many drama and comedy village productions. Sadly John passed away in 1988 aged 60.

Mr Stuart Gregor

Mr Stuart Gregor. KHR/Coll

Born at Fraddon in 1922, Stuart Gregor attended school at Indian Queens Primary. After school he started work in a quarry at Quarry Close.

The Gregor family moved from Fraddon to Gaverigan Manor in 1921. Stuart can remember as a young boy travelling from the farm at Gaverigan to St Dennis with parents on Saturday evenings in a pony and trap selling butter to regular customers.

Being a member of the Territorial Army in 1939, Stuart, then aged 17, was one of the first to be called up into the Army on the outbreak of war. He served for seven years. On leaving the Army in 1946 he returned to his old job at Quarry Close where he remained until 1955 when he left to run a milk round based at Trelavour Prazey. The business was given the name of the Glynn Vale Dairy. This proved a success and later his brother Roy was brought in to help.

In 1976 Stuart obtained employment with the Western Excavating Co., as a driver where he served for six years. In the meantime part of the milk round was being operated by Mr and Mrs K. Durant of Lanjeth. Stuart retired from the milk-round business in 1984, after which he and his wife Manda moved to Polgooth. He had served on the St Dennis Parish Council for 43 years (1956–99) and in the St Dennis Red Cross group for 27 years (1956–83). He was also a parade marshal for the annual Remembrance Day parade for 30 years (1970–2000).

The Gregor family and friends at Gaverigan Manor Farm in 1927. Left to right: *Jim and Elsie Stephens with Stuart in the back and Wilfred, Roy, Rita and children's nanny in the front.* KHR/Coll

Mr Arthur Grigg

Arthur Grigg was born on 2 October 1909 at Prazey, and attended school in St Dennis. On leaving school he worked in the china-clay industry and before 1939 worked in insurance with an agency in St Mawes.

He was called up into the Army in 1940 where he served under General Montgomery in the 8th Army and saw action at El Alamein and Italy. On one occasion his company, while in Italy, was addressed by the Pope.

After demob Arthur returned to the insurance business and obtained an agency in St Dennis, which he retained until he died. He was always a talented singer and it was this ability which enabled him to win several gold medals at local music festivals.

Arthur was a great supporter of Providence Chapel and put a lot of time and effort into its well-being. When it was closed in 1969 he moved his support to Carne Hill Methodist Church.

His concern for the welfare of the village led to him serving a considerable term on the Parish Council, including a spell as chairman. In 1951 Arthur was elected to the St Austell Rural District Council and was honoured in 1963 by being elected as its chairman. During his term of office Arthur and his wife Thelma were invited to a garden party at Buckingham Palace. Sadly Mr Grigg died shortly before he was due to retire in 1974.

Mr Hayward and the Pyramid

The Pyramid was the name given to the site purchased by Mr and Mrs Hayward in 1966. They had a large two-storeyed dwelling and a petrol filling station built. The first floor of the dwelling was used as their home and the ground floor was a café. The petrol pumps had to be manned in those days and there was a small hut to protect the attendant from the elements. The business started trading in 1967 and proved to be a popular and well-patronised village amenity.

After about five years of trading Mr Hayward suffered health problems which prevented him from running the business, so it was sold. Mr and Mrs J. Gristewood then purchased the business in 1972 and ran it successfully for 12 years.

The business closed in 1984 and the property was purchased by Mr K. Hughes who then proceeded to convert the first floor of the building into an independent flat, and the ground floor into a small office and a doctors' surgery. The office was let to a finance firm for a short time and then to a local bookmaking partnership for about two years. The forecourt was let to a Mr M. Kirkham in 1983 for his second-hand car sales. Mr Ted Spragge took this over in 1985 until it closed in 1997. After this the forecourt area was sold to Chapel Developments who proceeded to build three small houses with car parking on it.

Left: *Arthur Grigg with his chain of office, 1963.* KHR/Coll

Pyramid filling station, 1964.

Left: *Arthur Grigg's first parade as chairman of the St Austell Rural District Council in 1963, with PC Charlie Rogers, dignitaries of the Council and various village organisations.* KHR/Coll

Mr Thomas Millard Kellaway

Although born in St Austell Thomas Millard Kellaway spent most of his life in St Dennis, starting with a shop in Trelavour Square. In the 1920s he moved to premises in Fore Street. He was a saddler by trade but 'Jack of all trades' would have been a more accurate description of his activities.

Saddler, as he was known, was the first to introduce chips and ice-cream to the village. His shop sold sweets, tobacco, bicycles and groceries and in his workshop he repaired boots and shoes. All kinds of equipment could be hired from him including bicycles. The workshop was always littered with junk and tools of all descriptions; the village knew that 'if Saddler could not repair it he would make it.'

The workshop was also home to a piano on which Saddler loved to play jazz music and encourage singsongs with customers.

Mr Kellaway owned one of the first motor cars in the village, a Model 'T' Ford which he used as a taxi to convey his business associates to various inns on Saturday evenings where he exercised his well-known taste for Bass No. 1 bottled beer.

Mr Albert Kent

Albert Kent started renting the Wellington Road yard from the Arundel Trust in 1900 from where he started his coal merchant's business. It was only a small yard at that time; it became enlarged in 1950 when Arthur Kent, who had taken over the business from his father in 1946, after Albert's death, negotiated the purchase of the whole area from the Arundel Trust.

Mr Stanley Metherell had a small garage in the yard where he carried out vehicle repairs and maintained the coal-delivery vehicles. This stopped in 1950 when Mr Metherell obtained bigger premises in Trelavour Road. The Kent family purchased Mr Hugh Morcom's newsagent's in 1955 and Penwyn Garage in 1959 which, combined with the coal merchant's, made an impressive company. In 1969 the decision was taken to sell the newsagent's business; it was purchased by Mr and Mrs Raymond Juleff.

Mr Arthur Kent. KHR/Coll

Tragically Arthur died suddenly in 1970 at the young age of 52 years. The business continued until 1974 when the decision was made to sell the coal merchant's and Penwyn Garage business to Smith and Treffry of Par. The sale did not include the coal yard itself, although Smith and Treffry retained the yard on a 14-year lease. When the lease was up in 1988 it was not renewed; instead the site was developed for residential use. The Kent family moved into the first completed building in 1993. In 2003 the site is fully developed with nine quality residences on it.

Mr Stanley Metherell

Stanley Metherell started his own business after the Second World War, when he set up his vehicle repair workshop in property belonging to Arthur Kent in his Wellington Road coal yard. The tenancy agreement involving the servicing and repair of Mr Kent's coal-delivery vehicles in lieu of rent suited both parties. Mr Metherell also introduced a taxi business.

In 1963 Mr Metherell built his own garage in Trelavour Road where he soon established a Land Rover repair and servicing specialist workshop. The utilisation of the facility grew to the extent that extra mechanics had to be employed.

The knowledge gained from the maintenance of the Land Rover prompted Mr Metherell to design and build his own 4x4 vehicle. This proved successful and a production line was started. Once proven the vehicle (now named the 'Landmaster') started to attract interest. On three occasions members of an industrial delegation from Belfast visited Mr Metherell at his Trelavour Road garage, inviting him to relocate his production line to Belfast where they would supply a factory and labour force for 12 months free of charge. Interest from Dubai in the form of a visiting sheik who had a similar offer was also received. Mr Metherell declined both offers, insisting that the Landmaster should be of Cornish design and manufacture.

When this decision was made it was believed that the Government would provide a level of financial support for the project once the production line was working and proven. Vehicles were produced to order and were purchased by the Devon and Cornwall Police Authority, the then Western Excavating Co., and some private buyers. On top of this, British Aerospace purchased a long-wheeled-base chassis and cab, with the aim of

Mr Stanley Metherell, an engineering innovator. KHR/Coll

The Landmaster produced for the Devon and Cornwall Police which after many years of reliable service is back in the custody of Mrs P. Metherell as a vintage keepsake. KHR/Coll

The LWB Landmaster made for British Aerospace to develop as a rocket launcher for the British Army, seen here outside their headquarters in Stevenage. KHR/Coll

developing it as a rocket-launch platform for the British Army.

It was a sad blow when the Government withdrew its promise of financial support, after the production of eight vehicles had drained resources to a point where the project had to be stopped. At this time 21 staff were employed.

When the decline of the Land Rover servicing and repairs started in the early 1980s Stanley decided that the business, apart from the car repairs and petrol sales, had to diversify; the decision was made to start a saw-sharpening workshop. This was initially set up in the carpenter's workshop purchased from Mr Tom Bullock. However, as this arm of the business grew and the Land Rover work had by now ceased the carpenter's shop was abandoned and the saw-sharpening transferred into the main garage workshop.

Since Stanley Metherell's death in 2002, his wife Peggy and son Kevin have successfully maintained his high level of productivity and the standards that he set; at the time of writing the business is one of the premier saw-sharpening operations in Cornwall.

Mr Tom Morcom

Greenwich House was built for Tom Morcom in 1910 after a thatched cottage that had been home to quarry worker, Mr John Trudgeon, had been demolished. Mr Morcom then started a business selling medicines and practising his watchmaking skills.

As the business prospered Mr Morcom's son Hugh was brought in to learn his father's trade. When Tom Morcom eventually retired, Hugh took over the business and, along with his wife Lilian, expanded the trade by introducing a newsagent's, which ran a delivery service.

Hugh Morcom was a musical person and could play several instruments. Along with his wife and Mr and Mrs Raymond White and, at times, others, Hugh formed the very popular White Aces Dance Band which was often in demand. Hugh and Lilian also performed as a musical duo called the Clavatones at concerts and village events.

In 1955 the decision was taken to purchase a jeweller's business in Wokingham and to sell the St Dennis business. The Wokingham business was operated until 1976 when Hugh Morcom retired. As Hugh's two sons had pursued careers in other professions the business was sold.

Mr William Oliver

Born in St Austell in 1912, William Oliver attended school there until he was aged 14 when he left to work in the Teddy Bear clay works. The family moved to Egypt (Trerice) in 1930 and Billy got a job at Wheal Remfry clay works, followed by employment at the Wheal Remfry brickworks.

Marriage to Vera in 1934 was followed by emigration to Canada where he eventually found work in the Trimmins gold fields at the Paymaster Mine, first as a miner and later as an engineer. On returning to St Dennis in 1938, Billy worked again at the Wheal Remfry clay works and later bought a new Morris 8 car.

With the outbreak of war in 1939, Billy was transferred to Charlestown Engineering works to utilise his engineering skills – he was employed setting up munition-making machines for the war effort.

After the war a milk round in St Austell was purchased – he delivered to customers by pony and trap and drew the milk from large churns as required. This business was eventually sold and a milk round and a small farm in St Dennis was purchased. As the business grew a further eight milk rounds were purchased in the St Dennis area. This meant that supplies had to be purchased rather than produced on the farm. Initially milk was purchased in bulk and had to be bottled before delivery. This method improved over the years and eventually milk was received already bottled – it amounted to 100 gallons per day.

By this time Mr Oliver brought his daughter and son-in-law into the business to operate one of the two delivery vehicles. However, in the 1980s the growth of supermarkets and subsidised new businesses eroded the sales to such a level that the company became unviable. It was sold in 1988.

Billy Oliver served on the St Dennis Parish Council for 40 years, the St Austell Rural District Council for 15 years, and with the St Dennis Red Cross group for 40 years, 30 of these as commandant. As a result of this dedication he was awarded life membership of the Red Cross.

A very fit 92-year-old in 2004, Mr Oliver still resides in the village.

Mr W. H. Pascoe

Known to his friends as Mickey, William Pascoe was awarded the British Empire Medal in 1976 as an acknowledgement for his public service.

He was a magistrate from 1972 to 1985 and served as the secretary of the St Dennis branch of the Transport and General Workers Union for 22 years. He also served on the National Joint Industrial Council, the St Austell Postal Advisory Committee, the Bodmin Trades Council, the St Austell Rural District Council for 16 years, and the St Dennis Parish Council.

Mickey was a trustee of the War Memorial Institute and Working Men's Club, and served on the management committee for many years with periods as vice-chairman and chairman. He received his medal from the Lord Lieutenant of Cornwall, Sir John Carew-Pole, at Bodmin military barracks in 1976.

He died in January 2000 after a long illness. In 2004, his widow Barbara, who nursed him through most of his illness, still lives at the family home in the village. Mickey was a friend to many and is sadly missed.

Right: *Mickey Pascoe being presented with his British Empire Medal in 1976 by Sir John Carew-Pole at Bodmin Barracks.* KHR/Coll

Below: *Dr Wilson presenting Mickey with a commemorative tray from the Working Men's Club in recognition of his BEM award in 1976.*

Mr Sam Richards

In the early-twentieth century Sam Richards and his wife Rebecca lived next door to the old Post Office, in the house now known as Violet Cottage. Sam lived by his wits and was reputed to have been a smuggler and poacher amongst other things. It was not unknown for Sam to walk to Padstow by night to pursue his 'interests'. On Saturday evenings Sam and his wife would sell limpets from a stall outside their home. Also on Saturday evenings Sam would parade around the village pushing and playing his hurdy-gurdy (a primitive music machine with shaft-like handles for pushing, two wheels and two legs, with the music being produced by turning a handle); this usually ended with a visit to the Commercial Inn or the Miners Arms.

Mr John Trudgian

John Trudgian was born in Polgooth in 1843 and in his early life worked in the tin-mining industry. When this declined he moved to the china-clay district where he found employment at Hendra Pit as a winderman. At the request of the pit owners, who had learnt of his engineering skills, he joined the tug boat *Treffry* working in and out of Newquay harbour, as the engineer. However, for some reason this was short-lived and Mr Trudgian returned to his previous job at Hendra Pit.

During his days in the china-clay industry he got

One of Mr John Trudgian's creations, the chapel organ at Trethosa. KHR/Coll

Mr Percy Varcoe at work in 1948 in his Fore Street smithy. KHR/Coll

involved in engineering work and often assisted with the installation of Cornish pumping engines including one at Trethosa Pit. Apart from his engineering interests Mr Trudgian was a musical man and at one time played the cornet in St Dennis Temperance Brass Band under the conductorship of Jim Yelland.

His interest in music brought about his building of a small organ for his own use, which led to requests from local chapels to build organs for them. He thus established his Mid-Cornwall Organ Factory in 1889, at the age of 46, and started business as a full-time organ builder.

Mr Trudgian had no formal training in such areas – everything he could do was self-taught. Apart from building organs he would also maintain and tune organs in the locality, travelling to them on his special mode of transport, a tricycle.

There were many fine examples of organs in the china-clay district, which were produced at the Mid-Cornwall Organ Factory in Trelavour Road. These included the St Denys Parish Church, St Dennis Providence Chapel, St Dennis Hendra Road Chapel, St Austell Baptist Church, Trethosa Chapel, plus Stenalees and Mount Charles Methodist Churches. Unfortunately only one of Mr Trudgian's sons entered the business and when Mr Trudgian died in 1925 at the age of 82 the firm closed.

Sadly the church organ in St Denys Parish Church was destroyed in the 1985 fire.

Mr Richard Varcoe

Richard Varcoe had a smithy at Whitepit, now known as Fore Street, where he carried out his blacksmith's business. He taught the trade to his son Percy, which eventually stood him in good stead when his father retired. Percy carried on the trade for many years until he retired in 1973.

In the early- and mid-twentieth century business was good – a blacksmith was an essential member of local industry, making and maintaining quarry and farm equipment, as well as shoeing horses.

By the time Percy retired the demand for blacksmiths' skills was on the wane, which resulted in the smithy being closed, never to operate again.

Percy Varcoe was a prominent member of the Providence Chapel and played an active part in the welfare of the community. He also followed in his father's footsteps by serving a long and respected part-time career as clerk to the Parish Council.

After he retired Percy cared for his sick wife for many years, and in 2003 lives in the village at the ripe old age of 93 years.

The Rowe Family

The Rowes moved to St Dennis from St Just in 1977 to take over the Hendra bakery business, which they have operated ever since. Mr John P. Rowe was a talented cricketer, as were his three sons, Dean, Ian and Jason, all of whom had exceptional cricket careers. John as batsman and Dean as wicket keeper represented the county on numerous occasions. Dean, Ian and Jason all played for the county at various junior levels up to and including the under-19s team. The Rowe family's sporting interests also included football and snooker.

Sadly, John passed away suddenly in 1998 aged 54. The bakery business continues in 2004 under the guidance of John's wife, Mrs Paulyn Rowe.

Madam Maria Yelland

Maria Yelland was a native of St Dennis and possessed an excellent voice which won her a scholarship to the Royal College of Music. She studied there for five years in the early-twentieth century.

Later she sang at Covent Garden Opera House, the Royal Albert Hall, Crystal Palace and before King Edward VII and Queen Alexandra.

In recognition of her Cornish roots, Maria gave an annual concert in St Austell for many years after she had achieved fame.

Adrian Kessell's powers as a grass-track speedway rider are well known; his record of results is second to none, which makes him one of the most successful Cornish riders of all time. Adrian followed in the footsteps of Tommy, his father, and his uncle Ivan – they were both good grass-track riders. Ivan was a speedway rider of distinction in Plymouth in the 1940–50s. Adrian still competes at the time of writing, at the age of 76! KHR/Coll

Left: *Mr Dennis Oliver, born and bred in St Dennis, being presented with his British Empire Medal by the Prime Minister the Rt Hon. Margaret Thatcher on 8 March 1990 at No. 10 Downing Street. Mr Oliver was Mrs Thatcher's personal chauffeur during her term as Prime Minister.* KHR/Coll

Above: *The Queen presenting Mr Brian Skews with his MBE at Buckingham Palace in November 1997.* KHR/Coll

Mr Gilbert Bennetts, a champion Cornish wrestler in the 1930s.

Below: *Mr Monty Best with his prize-winning horse Doxey in Wingfield Yard, 1940s.* KHR/Coll

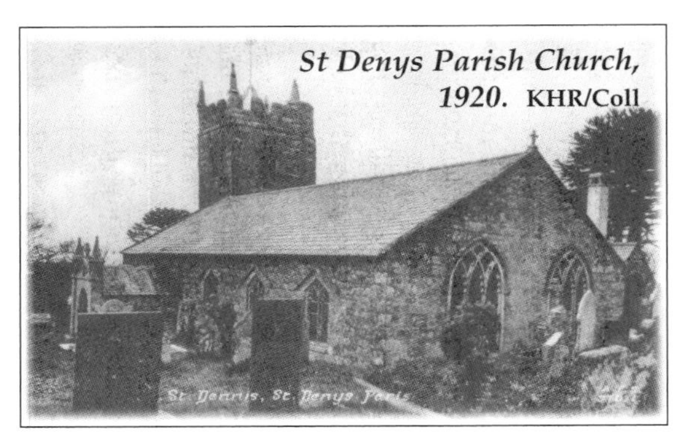

St Denys Parish Church, 1920. **KHR/Coll**

Right: *John Gregor, Barry Nance and Dennis Westlake with new church bells in 1938.* KHR/Coll

Left: *A church bell-ringers' annual coach outing in the 1930s.* KHR/Coll

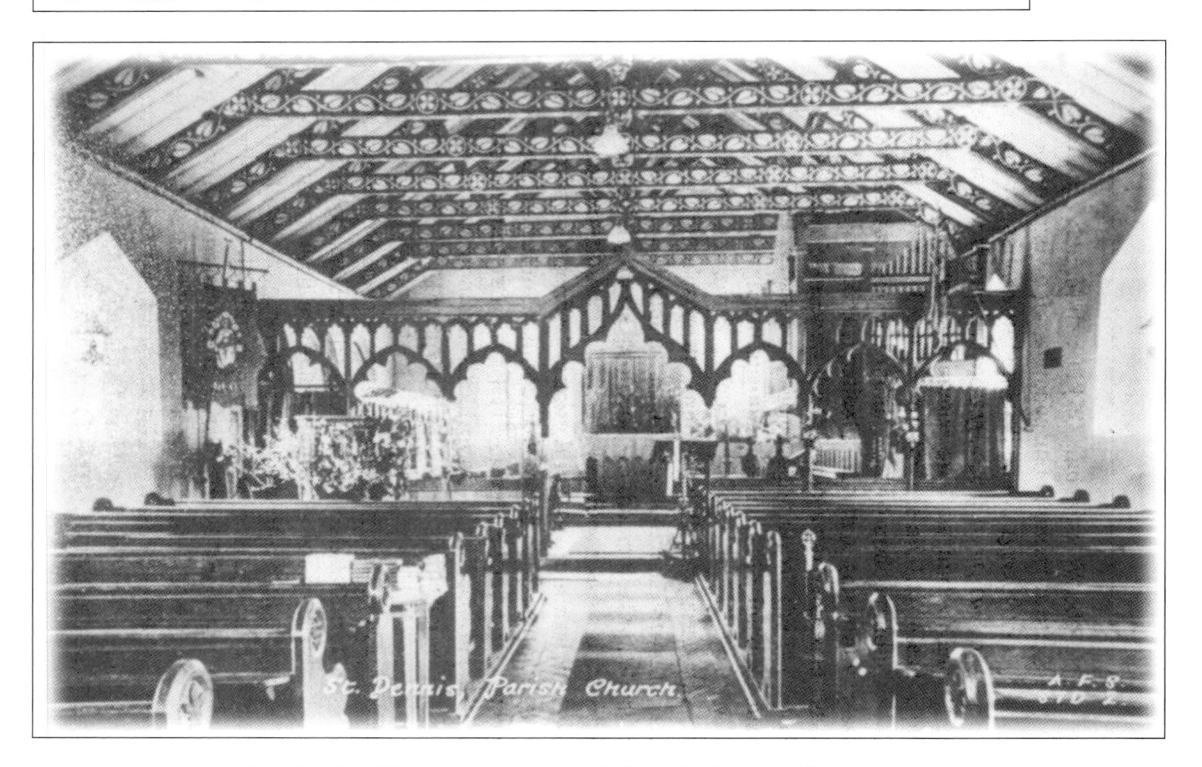

The Parish Church, many years before the fire of 1985. KHR/Coll

Chapter 4

Church and Chapel

St Denys Parish Church

St Denys Parish Church is located at the summit of a hill, and stands on the site of an Iron-Age fort. It was dedicated to St Dionysius (Denys or Dennis) in 1327. The church can be described as a plain structure with a south main porch and a north door.

A church was built on the site by the Normans at the end of the eleventh century, although the present tower dates from the thirteenth century and is on two levels reaching a height of 55ft.

The church appears to have originally been a chantry chapel, and was held by respective families of Cornwall, 'the Hendowers and Tregarthins of Courtrin Brannell', who later appropriated it, together with 'the church of St Stephen-in-Brannel, to the rector of St Michael Caerhayes.'

During the reign of Queen Elizabeth (1558–1603) John Arundel of Lanhorne endowed the church with ten acres of land situated in the manor of Enniscaven. According to Hals the historian, in 1664 a 'shower of blood' fell upon stones covering an acre of ground, and drops the size of a shilling could still be seen on stones 20 years later. In the years following this phenomenon, the Great Plague of London (1665–66) took hold, England was at war with the Dutch (1664–67) and French (1689) and the city of London burnt to the ground (1666).

In early times, when tin streamers made up most of the congregation at St Dennis, a sheaf of rushes was placed in the porch to assist the cleaning of footwear before entering. Until 1826 a perimeter ditch or moat surrounded the church and graveyard, after which time a fine Cornish stone wall was built inside the ditch.

The Parish Church magazine of 1893 states that prior to 1847 the church of St Denys had become very dilapidated and had been rebuilt with the original tower left in place. This resulted in the new building being described as 'ultra puritan' and possessing no architectural beauty whatsoever. It presented a sorry spectacle indeed with its low flat roof that spans the whole building.

The first recorded illumination of the church was probably fuelled by oil or carbide gas, in celebration of the wedding of the rector's niece on 18 September 1895. A weather-vane was erected by Mr John Trudgian in 1898 and the interior of the church was renovated the following year. An organ was installed in 1910; it was built by Mr John Trudgian, and remained in use until the 1985 fire.

The Rectory which was built in 1854 at a cost of £800 was sold in 1978 and a bungalow near the church was purchased for the rector to use as the Rectory.

Mr William Kent, the church sexton, died in 1894 at the age of 75 years. He had been the sexton for 33 years and had attended to 845 burials. He was succeeded as sexton by his son Henry.

One unusual feature of the churchyard was that when graves were dug, water was always present. The presence of water on the summit of a hill is unusual to say the least, but in this case may possibly be associated with the Blue Elvan lode which runs through this part of the parish. There are reports that when Sexton Kent had dug a grave it would partially fill with water and on the day of the funeral he would get his wife and daughter to bale out the water before the burial ceremony took place.

The church, and a font, a cross, the Riddler, Truscott, Varcoe, Gill and one unidentified monument all in the churchyard, are all listed monuments. Unfortunately, in 1985 the church was involved in one of the worst fires ever to occur in the parish. On Friday 31 May 1985 at 10.30p.m. a local lady discovered that the church was on fire. It turned out that it was started deliberately by a young man called Hyde, who then became trapped inside. He was rescued by the fire brigade but escaped the authorities. He was eventually arrested and sentenced to two years' youth custody for his deeds.

Five fire-engines attended the blaze (those from St Dennis, St Columb, St Austell, Bodmin and Fowey) but the efforts of the brigades could not prevent substantial damage to the building, its contents and roof. The latter was completely destroyed, as were the furniture and fittings. The appliances did not leave the site until 4a.m. on the Saturday after the area had been made safe.

On Sunday 2 June the Revd Geoffrey Perry conducted evensong on the church green at 6p.m., after which a united service was conducted on the green by the Revd Shirley Baker with members of all

Left: *Eliza Williams and Eliza Kent, in the trap, and John Keast, outside the Rectory in 1904.* KHR/Coll

Left: *The old Rectory in 2003.* KHR

the village chapels taking part. The congregation numbered some 400–500 and consisted of many residents who had not attended a service for a long time but felt compelled to attend on what was a very sad occasion. St Dennis Band provided the music and the whole event was filmed by Westward Television for the next day's news programme. At the service an appeal for a restoration fund was made.

The actual clean-up started the very next day with all the debris being examined before being removed. Police forensic experts had already made a detailed inspection on Saturday 1 June.

The porch and tower were undamaged except for the first-floor timber which had to be replaced. New walls were also needed, so all the damaged plaster had to be removed, and along with the charred timber and other debris this was stockpiled in the car park. A trench was excavated to enable water and sewerage services to be incorporated during the rebuilding project.

At an earlier Parochial Church Council meeting the architect Mr V. Ellis of St Neot submitted three rebuilding plans for consideration, with plan 'B' being accepted in principle. Detailed plans were drawn up to enable tenders to be sought.

On 23 December a group of archaeologists from the Cornwall Archaeological Unit at Truro excavated the floor of the church interior in an attempt to discover any traces of an early church that they suspected had been built on the site of the Iron-Age hill-fort. The team discovered seven skeletons; their burial positions and measurements were recorded before they were re-buried in the same location. More graves were found but were not opened. Only two were in wooden coffins – others were wrapped in shrouds and laid in the ground 15–18ins below the floor level. The skeletons are believed to be between 300 and 350 years old. No evidence of the Iron-Age hill-fort was found.

In June 1986 a Mr Piper of Liskeard started repairing the stone mullions and surrounds of the windows. At the same time Messrs Dring and Williams of Bath removed the walls and pillars of the vestry in preparation for the building of the new Lady chapel.

The main contractor for the rebuilding work was Sellick Nicholls Williams of St Austell, and the site foreman was a local man, Mr Oswald Pascoe of Gaverigan.

On Monday 10 November new Oregon pine roof trusses made by A.E. Thomas of Ponsanooth and weighing one and a quarter tons each were delivered and off-loaded by a crane hired from MacSalvors of Redruth.

The stone used for the new Lady chapel was from the Polyphant quarries near Liskeard, the stone used for the repair of the west wall was provided by Goonvean & Rostowrack China Clay Co., with the stone for the tower arch coming from their Rostowrack Quarry.

The whole of the church interior was fitted with scaffolding to a height level with the top of the exterior walls. A platform of boards was made on which to lay the roof trusses, which came in three sections, prior to assembly.

On Wednesday 12 November a helicopter hired from Castle Air, Liskeard, lifted the trusses up onto the platform. This was watched by a large number of local people including children from both schools. Once assembled the trusses were hauled into position by a manually operated winch and tackle.

By the middle of January 1987 the roof was timbered and felted. Richards & Rowe of Falmouth then slated the roof with 34 tons of Delabole slate, a task that took about four weeks to complete. The electrical rewiring also started in January and was undertaken by Mr Bryan Camps of Penwithick.

February saw the new concrete floor laid and the task of insulating the roof begin. Mr Nigel Orchard from Probus started the interior plastering on Wednesday 13 February. His working methods were unusual – he only used scaffolding that was 4ft high; and for inaccessible areas higher than this he strapped stilts to his legs!

The external cross by the east gable-end was fitted with a new Delabole quarried base. The old font was positioned and the new surrounds for the chancel and altar were put in place.

On 14 March a party of church helpers removed pews from the Methodist chapel in Belmont Road in

Devonport in readiness for their transfer back to St Dennis – this was carried out on 4 April. These pews were then stored in the ECC Engineering workshops at Drinnick, Nanpean.

A new oak entrance door was fitted, a storm door added to the porch and a new door was added to the north entrance. In June Johnstone & Baxter of Plymouth started the installation of the central heating. Internal decoration continued over a period of months.

On Monday 20 July Mr Peter J. Skirtin from the Lizard installed the right-hand stained-glass window located at the east end of the church. The following day, the laying of the new wood flooring was started by a contractor from Plymouth. On Wednesday 5 August A.E. Thomas of Ponsanooth started work on the oak frame and door at the tower entrance, oak panels to the east end wall behind the altar and the new vestry. Early in August an order was placed with Heles of Truro for a new organ. Two replacement altars were obtained – one for the Lady chapel came from St Mary's Church, Penzance, and the main altar from the Helford Mission Church. Both were cleaned and restored by Mr Gordon Bullen of St Dennis, and finally installed on 8 September. The same day organ builders loaned a pipe-organ for use until the new organ was built.

Scaffolding was erected around the tower on Wednesday 9 September to enable the new weather-vane and standards, including a new ship for the top, (all made by Mr Ted Sparrow, a well-known engineer from St Austell) to be fitted on 30 September along with a new flag-pole and ropes. A new lightening conductor was fitted by Dawsons of Bristol.

Mr Gordon Bullen and Mr John Kellow tidied up the church green by pruning dead branches, etc., then on 9 and 10 October the pulpit, lectern, communion rail and bishop's chair were delivered and installed. The First World War memorial was also fixed at the eastern end.

Sunday 11 October was re-dedication day. The service was held at 9.30a.m. and was conducted by the Bishop of Truro the Rt Revd Peter Mumford, his chaplin and the Revd H. Rich, together with the St Dennis rector, the Revd Geoffrey Perry, and his churchwardens, Michael Fouracres and John Gregor. The organist was Mrs Muriel Barrett and the service was attended by around 100 people, of whom 71 were communicants.

In November Mr and Mrs Michael Fouracres donated new gates which were fitted between the church green and car park. The second week of December 1987 saw the start of the installation of the new organ. After it was completed it was first used at a service on 11 February 1988 with Mrs Muriel Barrett as the organist.

A window given by Mrs Olwen Hawken, dedicated to Thomas Hawken, her father-in-law, and Geoffrey Hawken, her late husband, was installed on 8 March. In May the first nine pews were made and prepared for use by Michael Fouracres.

During September 1988 a window given by William and Hilda Brenton, formerly of Enniscaven, was installed in memory of their son, Police Sergeant Ronald Brenton. October saw the first of the cleaned and renovated pews placed in the church and varnished by Mr Cecil Barrett.

Between the day of the fire and the re-dedication, the church was used for only two services, the first on 5 April 1987 being the christening of Damian, the son of Robert and Debbie Fouracres, and the second on 12 September for the wedding of Sandra Gregor and Mark Crawford. The first regular service following the rebuilding was held on Sunday 13 September 1987 at 9.30a.m., and on Wednesday 16 September the first funeral took place – that of Mr Ken Lagor of Hall Road.

Mr Fred Biddick of Rectory Corner donated a replica of Queen Anne's coat of arms in September 1991 which was installed on the north wall opposite the main entrance door from the porch. The original coat of arms dated 1771 was completely destroyed in the fire. In February 1993 a tapestry of The Last Supper was presented to the church by Mr and Mrs Jason Fouracres of St Dennis. In February the following year Mrs Vera Sampson of Hendra Downs presented to the church a tapestry, which she had embroidered, depicting St Francis of Assisi.

During October 1994 the main gate was widened by 2ft 4ins and the hedge rebuilt. On February 11 1995 100 trees were planted around the church green and graveyard.

Those who attended the commemoration ceremony included Lord and Lady Falmouth, the Bishop of Truro, Michael Ball, our local MP, the Rt Hon. Matthew Taylor and the Mayor and Mayoress of Restormel, Mr and Mrs Brian Higman.

The cost of rebuilding St Denys Parish Church totalled £360,000. A lot of hard work was carried out by a very loyal and dedicated band of helpers who gave their energy and time for no reward other than seeing the final result. These volunteers included: Cecil Barrett, Paul Bullock, Rex Curtis, Jason Fouracres, Michael Fouracres, John Gregor, Eric Hawken, Bill Jenkins, Raymond Johnson, Joe Robson, Archie Snowdon, Ted Sparrow, Jack Trethewey, Paul Trevenna, Bill Trudgeon, Roger Trudgeon, John Varcoe, Andrew Robson, Adrian Wilson, Alan Wilson and Natasha Wilson.

On Wednesday 15 December 1985 the tower was floodlit for Christmas and illuminated until the end of the twelfth day of Christmas. On Saturday 21 December new wheels were fitted to numbers three and five bells. There are eight bells in the church tower with a combined weight of just over two tons. The oldest bell, the sixth, was cast in 1450. The bells were rung for the first time since the fire on

Above and left: *The Parish Church, after the fire-damage debris had been removed, showing the extent of the damage.* KHR

Above and right: *The Parish Church during repairs, 1986–87.* A. Wilson

Christmas Eve 1985, when the ringers were: Jason Fouracres, Michael Fouracres, Robert Fouracres, John Gregor, Eric Hawken, Bill Jenkin, Joe Robson, Archie Snowdon and John Varcoe (captain).

In total, 140 tons of debris were removed from the church shell and eventually disposed of by Goonvean & Rostowrack China Clay Company.

The rectors of St Michael Caerhayes, with St Dennis and St Stephen were:

1536:	*Stevyn Davey*
1643:	*Zacharie Hooker*
1644:	*John Archer*
1676:	*George Tanner*
1704:	*George Hawken*
1719:	*George Rundle*
1719:	*George Parnall*
1719:	*William Sutton*
1720:	*William Stuart*
1771:	*William Leach*
1773:	*Benjamin Foster*
1806:	*Charles Trevannion Kemp*
1852:	*William Willemott*

In 1852 St Dennis became a parish with its own rector:

1852–1904:	*John Glynn Childs*
1904–14:	*W. Bevan Monger*
1914–30:	*John Ching Barfitt*
1931–45:	*Claude George Sara*
1946–56:	*Albert Sykes*
1956–59:	*W. George Ellis Squire*
1961–64:	*William Victor Lambert*
1964–69:	*Frederick John Chase*
1969–83:	*Charles Thomas Cook*
1984–92:	*Geoffrey Perry*
1992–present:	*Timothy Russ*

The last person to be buried in the churchyard was Dora Ann Sheaff who died 28 December 1994, aged 90. The churchyard is now closed for burials.

Since 1987 the church has functioned as normal and has been supported by dedicated worshippers, now led by the Revd Tim Russ. The parish has a beautiful church without the roof problems experienced by many other churches today. The building is a primary place of worship, which welcomes all parishioners for baptisms, marriages and burials.

Regular Roman Catholic Masses are hosted at the church and amongst other activities the local school uses the church and churchyard as a resource for many learning activities. The popular 'Notes and News' booklet is published every month, providing information about all parish organisations and functions, and is free of charge.

The Revd John Glynn Childs, rector of St Dennis for 52 years (1852–1904).
C.H. Barrett

Carne Hill Methodist Church

Carne Hill Methodist Church was formed at a meeting of Bible Christians held in a local house or barn in 1821. The following year a lease was obtained on land at the foot of Church Road on which a church was built some time later.

For how long this building was used as a place of worship is unclear, but we know that the building across the road from the present site was used as a chapel and Sunday school up until 1873. It was around this time that a new building was constructed and given the name of Carne Hill Methodist Church. (During these early days tunes were struck by using a pitchfork tuned for that purpose, then later an harmonium, followed by a manual organ.) The building was enlarged in 1894 to accommodate the increasing congregation. This brought about a temporary closure, and a reopening in 1895.

The Sunday school dates from 1868 and for 24 years it was held in a building across the road where the lighting was provided by tallow candles. During the Second World War the Sunday school was used for a while by the evacuees and their teachers as a classroom. The Sunday school that is used in 2004 was built in 1895.

During the 1920s central heating and electric lighting was installed and powered by electricity produced by an engine-driven generator which was housed in a building that still exists in 2004. Prior to this lighting was provided by paraffin lamps.

Also in the 1920s an adjoining field was purchased on which a tennis-court with a pavilion was built. Tea treats and bus outings were integral to the social aspect of chapel membership. A tree-planting ceremony was held in the recreation field on 12 October 1938 when the first tree was planted by the Rt Hon. Mr Petherick MP. More trees were planted by people of the village.

The tennis-court was neglected during the Second World War, but was utilised again for a while in the 1950s. In 2004 the field is used as a car park. A refurbishment programme of the chapel and Sunday school was carried out in 1951.

Carne Hill Methodist Church has long been a popular venue for choirs and recordings.

The centenary was reached in 1972 with the celebrations being spread over two days. In 1987 extensive repairs and decoration were carried out with the completion being celebrated in July. In 2004 the chapel still functions – it is supported by a loyal but smaller congregation than in earlier times. On the

Above: *Carne Hill Chapel in the 1930s.* KHR/Coll

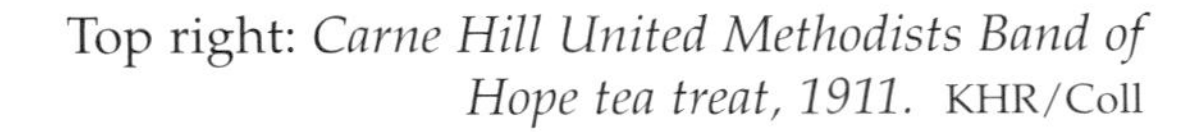

Top right: *Carne Hill United Methodists Band of Hope tea treat, 1911.* KHR/Coll

Right: *Carne Hill tea treat, 1919.* KHR/Coll

Above: *The Carne Hill Chapel Band of Hope tea treat in 1911, with the children enjoying their cups of tea and saffron buns.* KHR/Coll

Right: *Carne Hill Chapel tea treat, 1919.* KHR/Coll

first Thursday of the month an Outreach coffee morning is held in the ClayTAWC building (Clay Training and Work Centre).

Wesleyan United Free Church

Later to be known as Providence Chapel, the Wesleyan United Free Church was built in 1863 and financed privately by an independent trust. At one time the chapel had its own circuit of seven preachers, four of whom were called Giles.

After the Church School upheaval in 1903 Mr John Reed set up his own school in the Providence Sunday School, which he ran with the assistance of teachers until a new County School was built in 1907. How they managed to teach over 200 children at one time is not clear.

In the early days of the St Dennis Red Cross, the Sunday school was used as a training and reporting centre. Up until the 1970s the chapel was very well supported as a place of worship and a social venue. The Young Crusaders used the chapel as their meeting-place, as did the Women's Guild and the Mothers' Union.

However, despite being supported by a band of very loyal and dedicated people, the chapel was condemned by the Cornwall Redundancy Committee in 1969, which led to its closure. It was then sold to Mr Richard Nance for £800. After serving for many years as a carpet sales warehouse the chapel was sold to a developer who, in 2004, is in the process of turning it into a dwelling.

Hendra Road Chapel

Hendra Road Chapel was built and opened in 1904, originally under the North Cornwall Mission. Members of the original trust were: Messrs J. Best, T. Morcom, W.J. Blewett, H. Bunt, R. Arthur, J. Liddicoat, A. Rawlings and O. Coombe. Some time later a larger building was built which included a schoolroom.

An organ with a hymn-number board fixed above it was built and installed by Mr J. Trudgian of Trelavour. The first organist was Mrs W.J. Blewett and the choirmaster was Mr J. Best.

In 1992 the chapel left the St Columb and Padstow (North Cornwall) circuit and joined the St Austell circuit. To mark this change Mr and Mrs R. White made a new banner which is displayed in the chapel.

In the Sunday school hangs the original wall clock which still works accurately at the time of writing. Also hung on the wall are portraits of Charles, John and Susannah Wesley.

A roll of honour is kept of members who served in the First World War, and the old original baptism book is still in use.

The annual Harvest Festival is held on the last Sunday in September. The annual St Dennis Horticulture, Domestic and Craft Show was first held here in 1988; it has been successfully held here ever since. The schoolroom is regularly used by the Good Companions, the Old Cornwall Society and the Rainbow Guides.

Enniscaven Chapel

Although not in the village of St Dennis, Enniscaven Chapel is in the parish. Initial worship was carried out at meetings in various homes, but as the congregation grew, people gathered in barns and such like, until, finally, a chapel was built in 1840. Then, in 1844, a Sunday school was set up in the same building.

Increasing numbers led to the decision to build a new chapel, so land was purchased for the present site in 1906. The building was completed in 1908 at a cost of £500 and was officially opened on Easter Monday. The chapel was originally Bible Christian but later became United Methodist.

Children continued using the old chapel as a Sunday school for many years. It was also used for anniversaries, tea treats, concerts, band practice, Band of Hope meetings, etc. It was even used by the County Council as a library.

Mr J. Trudgian built and installed the organ and Mr Silas Liddicoat was the organist and choirmaster up to the early 1930s. The War Memorial was erected in about 1922.

In 1935 the decision was taken to build a new Sunday school alongside the chapel; this was opened in 1937 with a large gathering of people enjoying the free catering and the children their saffron buns and sugary tea. The cost of the new Sunday school, including a furnace house, was £500. The old Sunday school became a reading-room and Institute and during the Second World War it was used by the Home Guard. Sadly two young men who attended the Sunday school when young, Maurice Grigg and George Hick, lost their lives in the Second World War, and their names were added to the memorial.

Since the 1950s many anniversaries and jubilees have been celebrated and a good social programme maintained. Minor repairs and replacements have been made and generally a good state of repair to the building has been maintained.

Towards the end of the twentieth century and into the twenty-first, in common with other places of worship, congregations have declined. However, there is still a core of people who support this chapel, and none more so than Mr Jack Liddicoat and Mr and Mrs Alan Davey who have been stalwarts for many years. Enniscaven Chapel is still very active and for a small hamlet has a lot to offer its congregation.

Despite the smaller congregations, those that attend all the places of worship within the parish are certainly appreciated. Indeed, it is reassuring to know that they are there along with our ministers to comfort and support people in their hour of need.

Right: *A charabanc trip to Callington for some Carne Hill Chapel choir members in 1926.* KHR/Coll

Left: *Carne Hill Chapel outing in 1924.* Left to right, standing: *Boss Hooper, Cyril Rabey, George Chinn, Jim Rabey, Maurice Bunt, Bob Grigg;* fourth row: *Jimmy Liddicoat, Clifford Trethewey;* third row: *Mr and Mrs George Bullock, Kathleen Penhaligan, Mrs Littean, Mr Goodman;* second row: *Tommy Kessell and his wife, Mrs J. Solomon, Letty and Russell Key;* front: *Revd Dunn, Mr Arnold Kessell, Margery Hill, Captain Jack Hill.* KHR/Coll

Below: *The reopening dedication of Carne Hill Chapel in 1951.* KHR/Coll

Above: *The Rt Hon. Mr Petherick MP planting the first tree at the Carne Hill Chapel tree-planting ceremony on 12 October 1938.* The picture includes: *Henry Bullen, Vinnie Phillips, Mike Grigg, Ray Menear, Rt Hon. Mr Petherick, 'Boss' Hooper, ?, Edwin Bunt, Vian Strongman, Donald Jacobs and Betty Craddock.* H. Nobes

A full house at Carne Hill Chapel for the St Columb and Padstow circuit rally in 1942.

Providence Chapel 1920s. KHR/Coll

Above: *Carne Hill Chapel organ with organist Jimmy Liddicoat, date unknown.* KHR/Coll

The Young Crusaders outside Providence Chapel in 1953. KHR/Coll

Above: *A typical rural scene in 1980; a flock of sheep being driven past the Enniscaven Chapel by shepherd Alan Goudge.* John Blewett

PROVIDENCE METHODIST CHURCH
St. Dennis

HARVEST FESTIVAL

Sunday, October 12th, 1969

Preachers: 11 a.m. MR. L. PARSONS (St. Columb).
6 p.m. MR. J. DYMOND (Grampound Rd.)

2-30 p.m. MISCELLANEOUS PROGRAMME
BY FRIENDS FROM BETHEL.
Chairman: MR. A. GRIGG. Organist: MR. D. W. GILES.

Monday, October 13th

6-30 p.m. **CONCERT**
by LOCAL ARTISTES. Chairman: REV. J. J. LEWIS (St. Columb).

7-30 p.m. PASTY SUPPER

SALE of Fruit, Vegetables, Flowers, etc. at the close.
Collections at all Services in aid of Trust Funds.
Come, one and all, and join in thanking God for all His gifts.

Above: *This poster is advertising the last ever Harvest Festival to be held in Providence Chapel.* KHR/Coll

Above: *Hendra Road Chapel in the 1930s.* KHR/Coll

Right: *Inside Hendra Road Chapel, 2003.* KHR/Coll

A Women's Fellowship group with the Revd Lake outside Providence Chapel in 1950. KHR/Coll

Left: *Nance's carpet showroom after closure, 2003.* KHR

Right: *The old Providence Chapel, being converted into a private residence, 2003.* KHR

This picture: ***Hendra Road Chapel 2002.*** **KHR**
Below left: ***Hendra Road Chapel, 2003.*** **Audrey Blewett**

Right: ***Alan Davey and Jack Liddicoat.***

Right: *Our ministers, Revd Tim Russ and Revd Colin Allen.* KHR

Left: *Children at the Church School performed a 'Washing Day' sketch, at the annual concert, 1910.* KHR/Coll

Left: *Mrs Hancock's Church of England School Group II class of 1911.* Back row, far left: *Miss Gwen Kent who later became Mrs Russell Dyer;* front, third from the left: *Miss Sybil Kent, who became Mrs Eric Trethewey;* second from the right: *Miss Dagmar Hancock.* KHR/Coll

Right: *St Dennis Church School in 1921.* Left to right, back row: *Reggie Rowe, Fred Salter, Cyril Best, Robert Varcoe, ?, Stuart Hore, Donald Trenerry, John Rosevear, ?, Charlie Gregor;* centre: *Mabel Thomas, Gwen Thomas, Joan Harris, Lilian Roberts, Beatrice Martin, Enid Gregor, Flora Pope, Elenor Johnson, Dorothea Nance, Winnie Best, Edith Kent;* front row: *Fred Brenton, ?, Viola Brenton, Florrie Hudson, Margorie Hore, Betty Mennear, Hilda Lewis, Gracie Best, Russell Best, George Kent.* KHR/Coll

Left: *Church of England School class in 1935 with the teacher Miss Harper.* Left to right, back row: *Albert Smith, Monica Davey, Norma Taylor, Doreen Grigg, Phyllis Allen, Joy ?, Frankie Elgar;* centre: *Jack Yates, Peggy Clemmow, Thelma Parkyn, Mabel Brewer, Margaret Whitford, Evan May, Rita Hudson, Ruby Craddock, Freddie Brookes;* sitting: *Saxby Hatton, Jeffery Bragg, Eddie ?, Ronnie Taper.* KHR/Coll

Chapter 5

Schools, the Post Office and the Parish Council

School

There have been schools in the village from 1830 when dame-schools were introduced and held in certain private residences.

In the early-twentieth century there were dame-schools at St Lawrence, at the top of Downs Lane, now known as Trelavour Road, and at the bottom in a property now known as No. 3. These schools, which were privately run, initially had a charge of 1d. per week per pupil.

In about 1848 a Church of England School was built on trust land, near where Trelavour Garage stands in 2003. It remained open until 1860 when a new purpose-built school was constructed on more trust land at Trelavour opposite the Maltsters Arms public house. This school was known as the Church of England School.

Both these schools were built on trust land, with the trust consisting of three registered charities, which eventually became known as the John Arundel Trust. When the second school opened in 1860 the conditions and facilities were primitive to say the least and operated under typical Victorian codes of education and discipline. Punishment was severe and the cane was used frequently on children who disobeyed or misbehaved. Religion played a large part in children's education with Bible studies being regarded as a major subject.

Mr John Reed, headmaster of the Church of England School since 1873, had a good working relationship with the Revd John Childs for 30 years, but when the Revd Childs was succeeded by the Revd Monger, a curate, in 1902, the relationship between church and school faltered. The root of the problem stemmed from a difference of opinion on how religion should be taught, as Mr Reed had Church of England tendencies while the Revd Monger was an Anglican. These differences came to a head in 1903, when the Revd Monger persuaded the school managers to dismiss Mr Reed from his post. This decision proved unpopular with the village parents who had been very happy with Mr Reed's service. Indeed, public opinion was strong enough to force a meeting in an attempt to overturn the school managers' decision. However, this was all to no avail.

The level of public support shown to Mr Reed prompted him to set up his own school in the Providence Chapel Sunday school where nearly 80 per cent of his former pupils joined him. The new school, which had five teachers apart from Mr Reed, was financed by the National Union of Teachers. This fact contributed to it being named the St Dennis National School.

A visit by the HM Inspector of Schools in 1905 brought about the authorisation to build a new school at Carne. This school was built and opened in 1907 and was named St Dennis County Junior Primary School.

In 1907 the Church of England School became the Infant School and the County Junior Primary School became the Primary School. This situation continued successfully for many years as far as administration was concerned but facilities and conditions in both buildings suffered from lack of investment so that they both fell behind in terms of modern standards. A decision by the Government to finance the modernisation of the County School and to build an extension to accommodate all the Infant School children was made in 1994. All this work was completed in 1996 and the transfer of the children from the Church of England School to their new building was celebrated by a grand march that included teachers and the Revd Tim Russ. After the amalgamation the school was renamed the St Dennis County Primary.

Some of the Church of England schoolteachers and head teachers that taught during the twentieth century include: Mr J. Reed, Mr W.T. Harvey, Mr S. Clyma and, in more recent times, Mrs Gladys Curtis (1939–44), Miss Edna Moxey (1945–49), Miss Margorie Alcock (1949–66), Mrs E. Craddock (1958–65), Miss Merle Oliver (1960–96), Miss Joan

Left: *Church of England School, 1936.* KHR/Coll

Below: *Church of England School, 1937.* Left to right, back row: *Clarence Lewis, Doreen Giles, Pam Williams, Doreen Luke, ? Osborne, Mavis Bunt, Dennis Williams;* centre: *Mr Harvey (headmaster), Freddie Brooks, Kate Brewer, Kathleen Davey, Doreen Martin, Dorothy Bullen, Peggy Clemmow, P. Craddock, Ivan Odgers;* front: *Stan Metherell, Den Westlake, Dennis Kent, Albert Smith, Jeff Hawken, Saxby Hatton.* KHR/Coll

Left: *The St Dennis Church of England School, 1937/38.* Left to right, back row: *J. Yates, P. Allen, M. Davey, D. Grigg, R. Craddock, N. Taylor, A. Smith;* centre: *F. Grigg, P. Clemo, N. Bullen, J. Toy, H. Crowle, D. Oliver, P. Craddock, J. Bragg;* front: *H. Colvin, M. Brewer, E. May, R. Hudson, M. Whitford, B. Currah, R. Snell;* cross-legged: *F. Brooks, T. Williams, G. Hudson, S. Hatton.* KHR/Coll

Right: *The Church of England School, 1939.* Left to right, back row: *Peter Taylor, Gwen Davey, P. Kent, Pam Manhire, Joyce Hawke, Ron Juleff;* centre: *Dennis Oliver, Barbara Stephens, Phyllis Bunt, Joy Hawken, Ruby Kent, Ralph Richmond;* front: *Bob Watters, George Tabb, Roy Angilley, Michael Strongman, Peter Strongman, Jack Dunstan and teacher, Miss Trudgeon.* KHR/Coll

Right: *Miss Allcock's Church School class, 1962.* Left to right, back row: *Anthony Warne, David Bunt, Graham Buscombe, Malcolm Roberts, Cyril Harper;* third row: *Robert Dunn, David Parsons, Roy Pentecost, David Burnett, Clive Parkyn, Paul Grigg, Garry May;* second row: *Lorraine Morcome, Jackie Creba, Linda Best, Jennifer Herring, Shirley Couch, Jean Warne, Celia Lucas, Margaret Kessell, Sandra Crews, Linda Davis, Linda Chapman, Lois Brown;* front: *Austin Bond, David Martyn, Nigel Sands.* KHR/Coll

Left: *Miss Oliver's Church School infants' class, 1967.* Left to right, back row: *Peter Nance, Steven Tabb, Ian Rowe, Robert Fouracres, Kevin Hemmings, Miss Merle Oliver;* centre: *Cheryl Harper, Elizabeth Chapman, Anita Crowle, Sharon Allen, Peter Hawken, Andrew Magor, Gary Rickard, Steven Harvey, Terry Chapman;* front: *Mark Crocker, Peter Costello, Timothy Collett, Charles Hancock, Jane Stead, Valerie Kent, Karen Thorne, Carol Craddock.* KHR/Coll

Right: *The old Church School now occupied by ClayTAWC, 2003.* KHR

May (1968–71), Miss Lemon, Mrs Blacklock and Miss Carole Gardner (1972–96). In 2004 Miss Oliver is one of 12 governors of the County Primary School.

No doubt when the school closed in 1996 many former pupils reminisced about their introduction to learning and preparation for life's journey in the Church of England School in St Dennis, with Victorian standards and attitudes not acceptable in modern times.

The Church of England School, which belonged to the John Arundel Trust, was leased to a newly formed company named the Clay Training and Work Centre (ClayTAWC), an initiative formed to provide training, employment, administration and room-hire facilities for the clay-district villages. Alterations and modernisation of the building were carried out in 1997/8 which enabled the centre to be equipped and opened in 1999.

The following is a comprehensive list of headmasters who have served at the County Primary School:

1903–10:	*Mr J. Reed*
1910–20:	*Mr J. Radcliffe*
1920–31:	*Mr A.W. Jenkin*
1932–56:	*Mr W. Pellymounter*
1956–73:	*Mr R.S. Lewis*
1973–84:	*Mr O.S.J. Giles*
1984–88:	*Mr R.C. Maunder*
1989–95:	*Mr G. Walker*
1995–2000:	*Mr P.M. Saich*
2001–present:	*Mr M. Lindfield*

Many fine teachers have taught here and contributed to the school's efficiency and popularity, none more so than Mr George Jacobs of Nanpean who served here for 30 years before retiring in 1978. Mrs B. Craddock also a local person, taught here from 1971–88 after teaching in the Church of England School from 1958–65. Other local teachers have included: Mrs E. Best, Miss I. Kent and Miss O. Williams.

An additional facility was created in 2002 when a new library was built at a cost of £80,000, giving pupils

Left: *The managers of the Council School on 13 March 1907, seen outside Carne Hill Chapel.* Left to right, back row: *John Gill, James Grigg, John Reed, W.G. Tremain, William Pollard, Allan Bettison, Albert Grigg;* front: *R. Hooper, Tom Bullock, John Hooper, John Tremain, John Bunt, Harry E. Bullock.* KHR/Coll

The parade and dedication of the new Council School at Trelavour on 13 March 1907. **KHR/Coll**

Souvenir Programme

OF EVENTS IN CONNECTION —WITH THE—

ST. DENNIS COUNCIL SCHOOL

Opening Ceremony

March 13th, 1907.

COMMITTEE—

J. HOOPER, CHAIRMAN,
T. BULLOCK,
R. HOOPER,
J. GILL,
W. G. TREMAIN,
W. POLLARD, } Managers of the Council School.

J. GRIGG,
A. GRIGG,
J. TREMAIN,
A. BETTISON,
J. BUNT,
H. BULLOCK,
J. REED,
REV. ALFRED EVANS,
DR. T. B. BROADWAY.

Left: *The souvenir programme for the official opening of the new Council School in 1907.* KHR/Coll

Below: *The St Dennis Council Primary School, 1920.* KHR/Coll

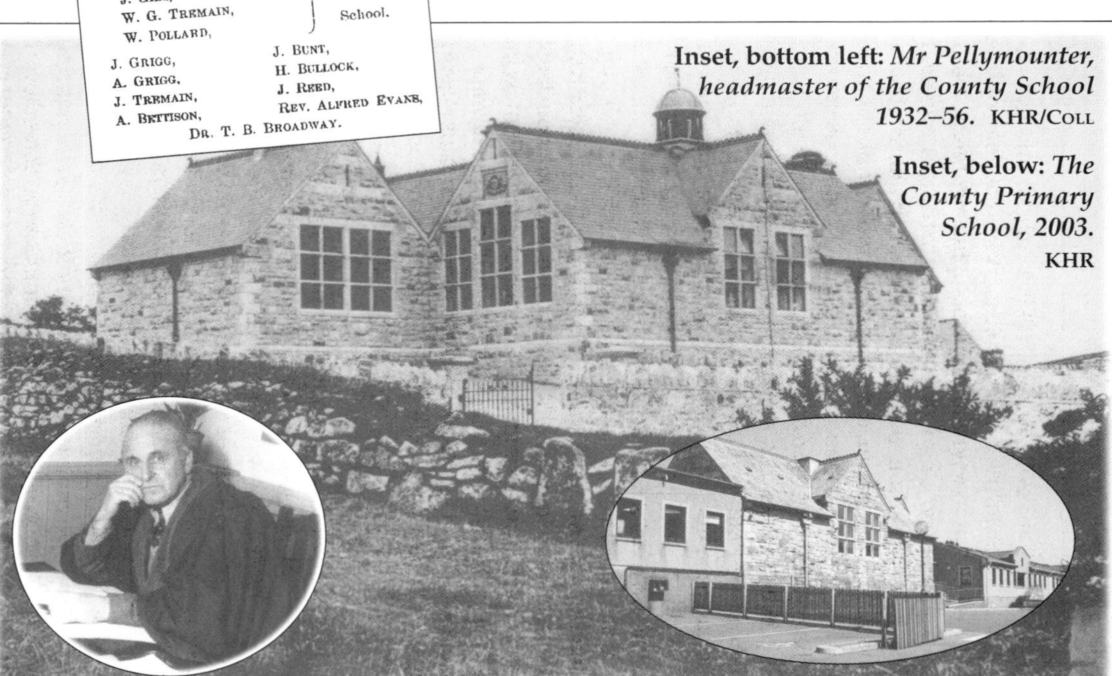

Inset, bottom left: ***Mr Pellymounter, headmaster of the County School 1932–56.*** **KHR/Coll**

Inset, below: ***The County Primary School, 2003.*** **KHR**

Left: *A Council School infants' class of 1922.* KHR/Coll

Right: *A Council School Group I class of 1922.* Left to right, back row: *Narcissa Angilley, Jenny Robins, Amie Giles, Hazel Common, Loretta Bunt, Flossie Keast;* third row: *William Coombe, Hartley Richard, Clarence Allen, Maurice Bunt, Leonard Greenslade, Paul Snell, John Edwin Kessell, Raymond Varcoe;* second row: *Rosa Craddock, Maisie Curtis, Muriel Bunt, Lilian Roberts, Mavis Kent, Vera Honey, Flossie Bullen, Susie Phillips, Ida Kent, Verlie Gill, Gladys Hawke;* front: *August Greenslade, Humphrey Brewer, Willie Yelland, Leslie Harrie and Leslie Lobb.* KHR/Coll

Left: *A Council School class of 1925.* Left to right, back row: *Miss Donithorne, Freda Pethick, Hazel Coombe, Violet Richards, Ruby Hick, Mavis Best, Gwen Coon, Amy Hicks, Vera Docking, Sylvia Greenslade;* centre: *Melville Osborne, Tom Bullock, Sylvester Bunt, Chris Underwood, Maurice Knight, Stuart Key, Will Runnalls, Donald Taylor, Ewart Coombe, Wilfred Giles;* front: *Chester Gill, Arthur Rowe, Edwin Davies, Joyce Endean, Lilian Sweet, Will Pethick, Roy Bennett, Gilbert Trethewey, Cyril Kellow.* KHR/Coll

Right: *Mr Harris' Council School class, 1925.* Left to right, back row: *Charlie Penhaligan, Mervyn Kent, Reg Leverton, Melville Brewer, Will Mellow, Reuben Runnalls, Robert Grigg;* centre: *Eunice Key, Hester Richards, Gwen Davey, Myrtle Stoneman, Mabel Best, Arnie Diamond, Doreen Davey, Mr Harris;* front: *Albert Kessell, Stuart Watters, Ethel Hicks, Ethel Trethewey, Millie Grigg, Les Brenton.* KHR/Coll

Left: *Council School class of 1925, with the teacher Miss Gladys Grigg.* Left to right, back row: *Christopher Endean, Dennis Underwood, Reg Rabey, Reg Snell, Maurice Grigg, Basil Broad, Roy ?;* centre: *Ada Bunt, Eva Matthews, Marjorie Dickins, Hazel Thorne, Ruby Keast, Pearl Keast;* front: *John Giles, Dudley Coombe, Esme Chapman, Glyn Giles, Maudie Greenslade, Mowbray Alford, Bernie Snell, Claude Bunt.* KHR/Coll

Right: *A St Dennis Council School football team, 1927.* Left to right, back row: *Mr Jenkin, Maurice Knight, Frank Brewer, Roy Bennett, Mr Clyma;* centre: *Jim Roberts, Jack Liddicoat, Bill Mellow, Arthur Best, Vic Treloar;* front: *Charlie Penhaligan, Rex Curtis, Melville Coon, Arthur Rowe, Bill Pethick.* KHR/Coll

Left: *A County School class in 1926.* Left to right, back row: *Lenox Drown, Joyce Endean, Iris Grigg, Kitty Matthews, Madge Tucker, Mavis Best, Ruby Kent, Iris Martyn;* centre: *Ken Penhaligan, Stan Grigg, Ivy Brenton, Gwen Grigg, Donald Taylor, Chris Stribley, Alwyn Bunt, Mirriam Solomon, Ray Bennett;* front: *Cyril Rabey, Fred Greenslade, Ewart Coombe, Melville Keast, Richard Grigg, Clifford Tonkin, Chester Gill, Gerald Poad, Stan Penhaligan, George Truscott.* KHR/Coll

A Council School class of the 1920s. KHR/Coll

A Council School class of the 1920s. KHR/Coll

Left: *Council School class of 1930, with teacher Miss Bertha Grigg.* Left to right, back row: *Cora Stephens, Clarence Watters, Bernard Bennetto, Eric Kelly, Stanley Diamond, Ken Rickard, ?, ?, ?, ?;* third row: *Hilda Davey, Doreen Grigg, Phylis Leverton, Emmy Cammon, Joan Thorn, Meta Common, Muriel Coombe, Joan Bennett, Inez Alford, Viola Grigg, Nina Broad;* second row: *Ruby Best, Rosa Giles, Dorothy Angilley, Joyce China, Nora Varcoe, Ida Underwood;* front: *Willie Grigg, Hailey Brewer, Reggie Bunt, Mervyn Keast, Stanley Greenslade, Greta Tabb, Donald Hawke, Robert Coombe.* KHR/Coll

Right: *Council School class with teacher Mr John Reed.* KHR/Coll

Left: *The School Band in 1936.* Left to right, back row: *Betty Bunt, Elsie Diamond, Dorothy Trudgeon, Sheila Yelland, Edna Varcoe, Betty Truscott;* centre: *Joan Tucker, Audrey Blewett, Ron Westlake, Amy Chapman, Betty Rouse, Ken Rickard, Clarenda Rowe, Joyce Common, Geoff Runnalls, Ken Kent, Margorie Yelland, Marion Chapman;* front: *?, Fred Greenslade, Ron Kent and Stan Bullen with conductor Doug Stoneman.* S. Hatton

Council School group, 1935. Ronald Kent is in the front, sixth from the left. KHR/Coll

access to 4,000 books. In 2004 the village has a fine school with modern facilities and a record of excellent reports from OFSTED; at the time of writing the most recent of these followed an inspection in July 2002.

The high standard of the school, its staff and the children was acknowledged in 2001 and 2003 by the winning of the Department of Education's Skills and Achievement Award.

A unique statistic regarding the caretaking duties is that, at the time of writing, these have been carried out by the local May family for 56 years. Mr and Mrs Sammy May led the way by starting in 1947 and continuing for 22 years. They were followed by Mr and Mrs Colin May who did the job for 11 years and finally Mr and Mrs David May, who retained the post for 23 years until they retired in 2003 for medical reasons.

Post Office

There is evidence that in 1879 a Mrs Betsy Cock ran the village Post Office, although from which premises it is not clear. In the late 1800s the Post Office was run by Thomas Bullock; he was also a tailor who made working clothes for the village men. Mr Bullock died in 1907, and in his memory a memorial plate was placed in the church.

Thomas' son, Charles Bullock, a well-known local historian, operated the Post Office until 1922 and kept the tailoring business going until he eventually died in 1930.

Old photographs show that at least from 1900 the St Dennis Post Office was part of a cottage next door to the Post Office that exists in 2004.

In the very early days of the twentieth century, before the introduction of the wireless, a service which the Post Office provided was the practice known as 'time setting' which provided the village with the correct time. This was obtained by the postman when collecting the mail from St Austell Railway Station – each day he would adjust his watch to the time on the station clock which previously had been set according to the clock on the early-morning mail train. On the postman's return to St Dennis the Post Office clock would be set to match that at St Austell.

A new Post Office was built in 1922 and it was about this time that Mr Wilfred Jenkins became postmaster, a position he held until he retired in 1961. Mr Raymond Bunt then took over the business and combined his Post Office duties with that of his other work as an undertaker. Both sides of the operation continued to grow. After the death of his father in 1988, Robert Bunt took over the family business. In more recent times the retail side of the firm has been increased and the premises equipped to modern standards.

In 2004 this village Post Office must surely be one of the busiest in the county. It is of some interest to note that when the premises were built in 1922, it was the first building in St Dennis to incorporate cavity walls.

St Dennis Parish Council

The first public meeting, held under the National Local Government Act of 1894, took place on 4 December 1894 in the National School with an agenda to form a Parish Council. Mr Thos Mason Hocking [sic] was elected as chairman, and the following as the council members: Messrs J. Blewett, T. Blewett, J. Bunt, T. Bullock, J.H. Dyer, R. Hooper, Caleb Key, James Key, W. Menear, T. Morcom, J. Tremain and C. Varcoe. The council was charged with the task of looking after the general well-being of the parish.

Meetings were held in the Primary School until 1932 after which they were held in the Infant School. In 1992 the meeting venue was switched to the Red Cross centre in Boscawen Yard and remained there until 2000 when the venue was changed to the

The original Post Office, 1910. **KHR/Coll**

Right: *St Dennis mail was collected from St Austell by a postman with a horse and trap. This picture, taken in 1910, also shows the shed on the site of the present-day Post Office, which housed the vehicle when it was not in use.* KHR/Coll

Left: *Today's Post Office when it was first built in 1922.* KHR/Coll
Right: *The Post Office, 2003.* KHR

ClayTAWC building which includes more modern facilities, including wheelchair access.

A contribution to public service which deserves a mention is that made by Mr Percy Varcoe, who retired from the post of clerk to the Parish Council in 1977. He served in this capacity for 31 years. Mr E. Cocks then served as the clerk for four years, after which Mrs J.E. Salmon was engaged, a position which she still retains in 2004 after 23 years of service.

A successful project was started in 1949 when the Parish Council purchased land from Lord Falmouth at a cost of £350 to provide the village with a playing-field. Over the years this area of land has been progressively equipped and improved. In 2004 it consists of a large children's play area, tennis-courts and a football pitch with changing facilities.

The millennium sundial on Trelavour Prazey, 2003. KHR

Other notable achievements are the provision of traffic lights at Domellick Bridge, the steady increase in street lighting, and as part of the millennium celebrations, a Celtic cross was erected at Carne, a sundial was erected on Trelavour Prazey, five public seats were positioned around the village and every child in the parish was given a commemorative medal.

Until recently the council employed its own sexton which was reflected in the excellent condition and tidiness of the cemetery.

Some notable people who have served the parish with distinction during the twentieth century are: J.T. Best, T.F. Biddick, John Blewett, George Bullock, John T. Brewer, P.R. Burnett, Phillip Coon, Frederick Greenslade, S.A. Gregor, Arthur Grigg, Richard Hooper, William Jenkin, Mrs M.H. Kent, J.J. Liddicoat, Dr Robert H. Manson, Mrs I. Meagor, E.R. Mennear, William Minnear [sic], C.J. Miller, William F. Oliver, Percy Parker, William ('Mickey') Pascoe, William Pollard, George Reed, A.C. Rickard, Mrs J.E. Salmon, Revd G.C. Sara, R.A. Stribley, Richard H. Tabb, Hart Trevenna, Timothy Trevenna, Charles H. Underwood, Percy Varcoe, Revd P. Williams, Richard Yelland and William Yelland.

In 2004 the Parish Council's powers and duties include providing and maintaining the cemetery, bus shelters, public footpaths and bridleways, roadside verges, litter receptacles, recreation-grounds and parking areas and to provide lighting for roads and public places. It is also obliged to provide and equip buildings for the use of clubs with athletic, social or educational objectives, as well as to fund crime-prevention measures and to financially support traffic-calming techniques and community transport schemes.

There have been three chairmen since the 1980s: Mr George Reed (1983–92), Mr John Blewett (1993–97) and Mr Fred Greenslade (1998–present).

The millennium Celtic cross at Carne. KHR

Left: *Dr R.H. Manson, to whom a tribute was paid in 1948 when part of the new council-housing estate, Manson Place, was named after him*

Above: *Dr Wilson in his surgery at 'Harvena' in 1975.* C.H. Barrett

Right: *Dr Wilson and Dr Crabtree at Dr Wilson's retirement party in 1976.* C.H. Barrett

The purpose-built (1972) doctors' surgery in Fore Street, 2003. **KHR**

Chapter 6

Doctors and the Red Cross

Doctors

In about 1919 Dr Harper was the village practitioner who when making house calls would travel to visit his patients on horseback. Dr Robert Henry Manson, who was from Broomhill in Glasgow, started practising in the village in 1921. He purchased land in Hendra Lane and had a house named Broomhill built on it where he set up his surgery. Dr Manson had a consultancy partnership with Dr Bradshaw of St Austell and a private telephone line was installed that connected the two doctors.

Dr Manson immediately showed an interest in the organisations of the village and was soon elected to various committees. He served on the Parish Council for many years including a period as chairman. He was also a founder member of the War Memorial Institute, where he served as chairman, as well as serving as a founder member of the Tennis Club.

Dr Manson supported village life and often gave trophies for competitions, some of which can still be seen at the Wheal Martyn China Clay Museum at Carthew. In 1934 Dr Manson brought his nephew, Dr Charles Montgomery Wilson MBchB, down from Scotland to join him in his practice and to prepare him to take over when he retired in 1936.

Dr Wilson practiced on his own until 1940 when he was called up into the Army and given the rank of captain. Dr Manson then brought in Dr Theodora Crabtree from the hospital in Bristol to replace Dr Wilson. She ran the practice on her own until 1945 when Dr Wilson returned, after which he and Dr Crabtree formed a partnership which was to become a popular and respected practice for many years.

Their surgery and dispensary was in Robartes Road at a site that went on to be a base for part-time dentists and opticians. A gentleman called Mr Burnett from Nanpean manned the dispensary and was well known for his military abruptness and character.

Dr Manson died in 1954 and left his estate to Dr Wilson. However, in the 1960s Dr Wilson developed cancer, which he successfully overcame after having treatment in Plymouth. In 1963 he purchased 'Harvena' in Hendra Road and brought in Mr and Mrs William ('Mickey') Pascoe to live there and maintain the place for him. He proceeded to set up his surgery there with Mrs Pascoe's assistance.

Dr Crabtree, who retired in 1968 after serving the village for 28 years, was a remarkable woman – she had was an old-fashioned doctor and foster parent. She started fostering children in 1937 while in Bristol when she was in her twenties and continued to do so throughout her time in St Dennis. In fact when she came to St Dennis in 1940 she brought three foster children with her. In total she fostered 37 children, seven of which were long term. One of them, Michael Fouracres, became a well-respected parishioner and a dedicated member of the church who served the local fire brigade for many years. Sadly Michael, who contributed to this book, passed away before it was completed.

When Dr Wilson broke his hip in 1972, he was out of action for two years. This development led to the introduction of a locum called Dr Peter Brady as cover. Dr Wilson returned to the practice in 1974, where he continued to work until 1976 when he retired. His retirement was acknowledged with a grand social occasion held in the football club – it was was attended by all his friends and patients who presented him with various gifts and accolades.

In his role as village doctor, which spanned 42 years, 'Monty', as we all knew him, built a reputation for his excellent medical skills. He was a qualified surgeon, who often carried out minor operations at St Austell Hospital. His skills were put to the test in 1935 when 'Mickey' Pascoe was involved in an accident and received a serious head injury which resulted in him being rushed to St Austell Hospital. Dr Wilson diagnosed that an emergency operation was needed. However, the hospital did not possess the necessary instruments, so a list of carpenter's tools was sent to Hodge's ironmongers in St Austell – these were quickly supplied and sterilised before being used by Dr Wilson to successfully carry out a life-saving operation. Needless to say after Mickey's recovery the pair went on to become lifelong friends.

Dr Wilson liked an active social life and enjoyed sports such as rugby. He even played tennis and squash with the old Prince of Wales, Edward VIII, when the latter stayed at the Carlyon Bay Hotel. In later years of practising Dr Wilson was recognised by his green Morris 1000 traveller.

After Dr Wilson retired Dr Brady returned to the practice and, as the tenancy of the old practice surgery in Robartes Road had been terminated, Dr Brady started his surgery days in a caravan on the Pyramid forecourt, where he stayed until a new surgery was constructed in the Pyramid building in 1976. He remained in practice until he retired in 1993 when it was taken over by the partnership of Drs Francis Burke and John Cecil of St Stephen who continue to work there in 2004, along with a new partner Dr Jay Purohit.

Dr John Therwell started another practice and leased the old surgery premises in Robartes Road. A partnership was formed in 1967 when Dr Therwell was joined by Dr John Winslade. A new purpose-built surgery was built in Lower Fore Street in 1972 on a site created by the demolition of four cottages. After Drs Therwell and Winslade, who both practiced for many years, came Drs Pierman, Side, Foster, Robinson, Shanks, Jenkin, Kurth and Brown. There has been a practice nurse in the surgery since 1982 and in 2004 the practice consists of five doctors. The surgery's receptionists, both of whom have recently retired, were well known, with Mrs Jennifer Fouracres serving 29 years and Mrs Malvina Higman serving 19 years.

St Dennis Red Cross Detachment

This group was first formed in 1937 when a group of ten interested ladies got together and took a St John Ambulance first-aid examination. By 1939 the group had grown to include 24 members. They studied for and took a Home Nursing examination which they all passed to become fully-fledged Red Cross members. Training continued locally, including at St Austell and Truro City Hospitals. Mrs Cooper-Hore from Whitemoor was nominated as the first commandant.

During the Second World War members helped in the doctors' surgeries at Broomhill and Lower Fore Street, collected items for POW parcels and carried out duties at the Castle-an-Dinas Isolation Hospital.

Practice and lectures were carried out in the vestry of the Providence Chapel, with the garage being turned into a first-aid post and being used as a call-out mustering point.

In 1944 the US troops encamped around the village gave the Red Cross a field ambulance which the ladies manned and men of the village volunteered to drive. Later the County Red Cross replaced the field ambulance with a county ambulance.

The men of the village who were interested in first aid formed a Red Cross group in 1939 which was initially deemed to be part of the St Austell Detachment. These founder members were: Messrs F. Biddick, D.W. Giles, H. James, T. Kessell, W. Key, P. Magor, W. Oliver, J. Truscott, A. Williams and P. Varcoe. The men's group amalgamated with the St Dennis Detachment in 1946.

For about 31 years the St Dennis Red Cross covered the county ambulance night and weekend duties. This involved teams of drivers and nurses being organised on a rota basis which, as with all Red Cross duties, was purely voluntary. At a time when telephones were few and far between, Mr Gordon Richards agreed to receive all call-out messages on his business telephone. The ambulance duty had to be covered 24 hours a day with each call-out requiring a personal visit to the duty ambulance driver. Mr Richards carried out this public-spirited duty for many years without complaint or reward – a fine example of the community spirit.

Dr Wilson was the medical officer up until 1940, at which point the post was assumed by Dr Crabtree. She was later followed by Dr Oates.

After Mrs Cooper-Hore, Mr Munday became the commandant and filled the post for many years. He was followed by Mr W. Oliver who was the transport officer before taking over the post which he retained until he retired. By this time the title had been changed to centre leader, a title by which Mrs M. White was known in her short reign. Mrs V. Lagor then occupied the post for a few years before handing over to Mrs L. Stoneman who fills this position in 2004.

In 1958 a team of six ladies won first prize of the Beatrice Williams Silver Bowl at the County Nursing Competition. The winning team was: Mrs O. Grigg, Mrs A. Pethick, Mrs O. Toy and Mrs M. White, with Mrs V. Brewer and Mrs M. Rickard as reserves.

At one time there was a group of girl cadets trained and controlled by Mrs M. Rickard. She was followed as cadet leader by Mrs J. Andrews. Later a boys' cadet group was formed under the guidance of Mr G. Kelly who did excellent work with the youngsters.

In the 1950s the Boscawen Yard building was adopted as the Red Cross centre, where training and social events took place for many years. A luncheon club for pensioners was formed in 1978 to provide hot meals twice a week for a nominal charge; this was a popular and well-supported facility. Sadly the club has since closed because of the withdrawal of funding by certain official bodies. This was a big disappointment to the old people of the village, who had come to depend on this opportunity of a hot meal.

In 1991 the building was modernised with improved facilities, a venture celebrated with a grand opening performed by HRH The Prince of Wales. Mrs M. White has achieved the honour of becoming the longest-serving member of the local detachment and in 1987 she was presented with the Badge of Honour and life membership of the Red Cross for distinguished service. In 1994 she was awarded the 50 years' service medal.

Since the mid-1900s the group has organised a Christmas party for all the parishioners that are over 70 years of age (for many years prior to this it had been held in the Church of England School). The party, including transport, is given free of charge.

Left: *The first St Dennis Red Cross detachment, 1938.* Left to right, back row: *Mrs O. Toy, Mrs W. Willcox, Mrs B. Yelland, Mrs P. Hawke, Dr C.M. Wilson;* front: *Mrs H. Dunstan, Miss J. Richards, Mrs Lewis, Mrs R. Cooper-Hore (commandant), Miss C. Bunt (secretary), Mrs F. Blight.* KHR/Coll

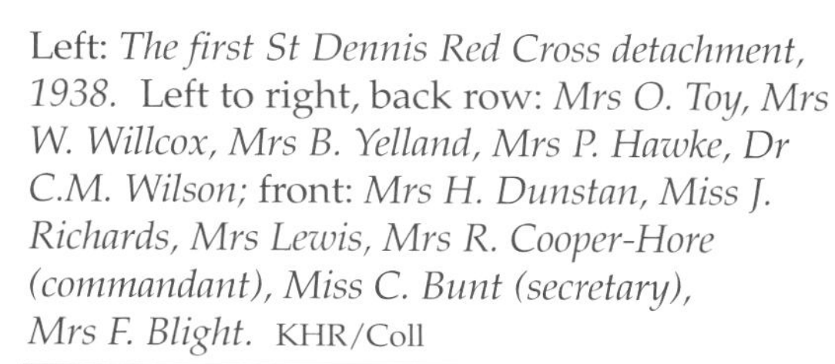

Right: *Dr C.M. Wilson (Major), home on leave in 1943, presenting certificates to* (left to right) *Mrs W. Willcox, Mrs H. Dunstan, Miss W. Curtis, Mrs Crago, Miss P. Hawke and Mrs M. White.* M. White

Left: *A 1949 group of Red Cross members.* Left to right, back row: *Mrs M. Jay, Miss R. Job, Miss W. Curtis, Mrs Brewer, Miss G. Trethewey, Miss D. Bunt, Miss D. Trudgeon, Miss W. Meagor, Miss A. Pethick;* centre: *Mrs F. Blight, Miss R. Brokenshire, Mrs R. White, Mrs T. Grigg, Mrs T. Crago, Mrs M. Sara, Miss Williams;* seated: *Mrs P. Hawke, Mrs H. Dunstan, Mrs W. Wilcox, Mrs Lewis, Mrs Cooper-Hore, Miss E. Bunt, Mrs O. Grigg.* KHR/Coll

Right: *The winning Beatrice Williams Rose Bowl team in 1958.* Left to right: *Mrs V. Brewer, Mrs M. Rickard, Mrs O. Grigg, Mrs O. Toy, Mrs M. White, Mrs A. Pethick.* KHR/Coll

Left: *The St Dennis Red Cross Detachment group in 1967 at the dedication of a new ambulance.* Left to right, back row: *Mr Ern Matta, Mrs Liddicoat, Mr Ernest Keast, Mr Percy Pethick, Mr Eric Davis, Mr Ronnie Trudgeon, Mr Percy Commons, Mr Morley Chapman, Mr Roy Trelease, Mr Stuart Gregor;* centre: *Mrs Barbara Sands, Mrs Joyce Allen, Mrs D. Heaman, Mr Trevor Tregenza, Mrs Maud Rickard, Mrs Ruby Truscott, Miss Kellow, Mrs Vi Lagor, Mrs Thelma Grigg, Mrs Maureen Hodd, Mrs Dorothy Trudgeon, Mrs M. Varcoe, Revd Chase;* front: *Miss Gladys Trudgeon, Mrs Phyllis Luke, Miss Goudge, Miss Reed, Mr William Oliver (commandant), Mr Hedley Mundy, Mrs A. Pethick, Mrs Sheila Andrews, Miss Olive Grigg, Mrs Mavis White, Mrs B. Sweet.* KHR/Coll

Right: *The 40th Red Cross Christmas party for the over-seventies, 1987.* Left to right: *Mrs M. White, Mrs T. Grigg, Mr D. Harris (Deputy Mayor of Restormel), Mrs V. Lagor, Mrs O. Dunstan* (cutting the cake), *Mrs M. Harris (Deputy Mayoress), Mr W. Oliver.* KHR/Coll

Left: *Old building at Trelavour, which in the past was used as a fire-tender garage, for firemen's training and as a Cubs' meeting-room.* G.K. Rickard

Below: *Firemen Fred Crews, Jack Michael, Stan May and, in front, Jim Williams and Raymond Stribley pose with their Austin water tender in 1958.* KHR/Coll

The village fire brigade in 1956. Left to right: *Fred Crews, Jim Williams, Arthur Best, Bill Williams, Cyril Rabey, Raymond Stribley, Stan May, Doug Stoneman, Jack Michael, Geoff Hawken.* KHR/Coll

Chapter 7

The Police and Fire Service

Police

In the first half of the twentieth century the village policeman was well respected, and was even feared by some inhabitants. People would have been desperate or fearless to offend or misbehave, and people believed that the younger element being caught and punished, by way of a clip around the ear or a boot up the backside, served as a deterrent.

The village policeman was responsible for his designated village, plus special duties, and he would have been acquainted with virtually every household. This knowledge assisted in the apprehension of many offenders.

During the Second World War PC Taylor had the luxury of 12 Special Constables to assist him with the additional duties involved. The trusted bicycle was the only form of transport issued until 1972, after which the Morris 1000 'panda' cars were introduced. St Dennis Police Officers:

Date?	*PC 'Bobby' Knight*
Date?	*PC Pill*
Date?	*PC Trebilcock*
1922–46:	*PC 'Bobby' Taylor (No. 145)*
1946–52:	*PC Tom Willey*
1952–59:	*PC Brice Ward*
1959–67:	*PC Charlie Rogers*
1967–69:	*PC Jack Benny*
1969–72:	*PC Dave Coe*
1972–79:	*Community policing from St Austell (panda cars)*
1979–92:	*PC Alan Best*
1992–99:	*Community policing from St Austell*
2000–03:	*PC Alan Lenton*

From 1922 to 1926 the police house was in Hendra Lane, off Hendra Road in an area known today as Delabole. To give the local police constable an improved standard of accommodation the police authority were allocated No. 26 Robartes Road in 1926 which was retained until 1969 when community policing was introduced and manned by St Austell-based policemen.

From 1969 policemen used an office in the old fire station as a reporting point, but this facility was transferred to the ClayTAWC building in 2000.

Mrs E. Solomon with her small son arriving at court in St Austell for the trial of her attacker who was charged with her attempted murder, 1924. The inset is of PC Taylor who, thanks to his knowledge of first aid, had saved her life when he arrived at the scene of the crime. KHR/Coll

St Dennis Fire Brigade

The first fire brigade was formed during the Second World War when St Dennis and surrounding villages were covered by the auxiliary fire service. When the Cornwall County Fire Brigade was formed in 1948, St Dennis became part of that group.

In the early days the brigade was equipped with an Auxiliary Tender Vehicle and a Coventry Climax trailer pump. The latter was kept in a small barn behind what was then Mr Stanley Pope's shop in Trelavour. Unfortunately there was not enough room for the ATV van so it was parked a few hundred yards away in Arthur Kent's Wellington Road coal yard. Meetings, drills and training lectures were held in the first floor of the barn.

The first sub-officer was Mr Raymond Stribley who remained in charge for many years. When telephoned about a fire he took a hand-held siren into the street and cranked the handle to raise the alarm. Firemen answering the siren hitched the van and trailer pump together then proceeded to the incident.

Left: *The Glamorgan Constabulary in Boscawen Yard – here to police the clay-workers' strike in 1913.* KHR/Coll

The brigade's reputation for efficiency and commitment has always been held in high esteem by the public and is a credit to the team's training and commitment. In 2004 the unit consists of 13 firemen bringing together a mixture of youth and experience. In the past, invariably most of our firemen have obtained a long-service award for 20 years' service and have remained in post until reaching compulsory retirement age. Fireman Brian Skews had his 25 years of service and his charity work acknowledged in 1997 when he was awarded an MBE, presented to him by the Queen at Buckingham Palace. Mr Skews went on to complete 29 years in the fire service, which included the post of station officer, before he retired in 2001. Other firemen who have served as station officer include: Norman Crews, Wilfred Jenkin, Stanley May, Jack Michael, Cyril Rabey and Raymond Stribley. Roger Best holds the post in 2004.

The brigade moved to the Robartes Road site in 1951 where the premises were much larger and able to accommodate recently acquired newer vehicles, a Green Goddess NYB33 and an Austin water tender MAF 948. The Green Goddess remained at the station until 1959, after which time it was replaced by a heavy road vehicle, GXH 966, which was in turn replaced in 1964 by a L4P fire-engine. The official opening of the Robartes Road station was held on Saturday 18 April 1964 and was performed by F. Dann Esq., OBE, HM Inspector of Fire Services.

In those days there were no doors on the front of the building yet no incidents of theft or vandalism were ever experienced – a sign of the times.

During the 1970s and '80s the St Dennis crew regularly entered the Fire Brigade Quiz and achieved much success, often winning the 'B' Division and representing the county. In the 1980s the brigade won the Efficiency Shield five times and the Kingsley Memorial Cup three times.

With the increasing number of vehicles on our roads and with St Dennis being situated near the A30, a large number of call-outs were to road traffic accidents. Consequently, a decision was made by station personnel to purchase Black Hawk hydraulic rescue equipment costing £2,000. Funds were raised by various ventures organised by the brigade personnel plus a large donation from the Royal Ancient Order of Buffaloes (RAOB) at Nanpean. The new equipment was purchased in 1983. In 1992 a Crash Rescue Equipment Fund was set up to enable more modern equipment to be bought. The proceeds of darts marathons, sponsored walks and support from local business reached £7,000 within six months. This was enough to purchase the new equipment and an emergency lighting kit.

In 2002 a new fire station, complete with training tower and parking space, was built on Hendra Downs and brought into use in December of that year.

Perhaps one of the biggest fires ever attended by the brigade was in St Dennis on 31 May 1985 when the church became a victim of arson.

The old fire station in Robartes Road, 2003. KHR

The new fire station on Hendra Downs, 2003. KHR

Chapter 8

Bands, Choirs, Cinema and Pantomime

Enniscaven Fife and Drum Band, 1906. KHR/Coll

The St Dennis Band

Thought to have been formed in 1836 as part of the festivities staged to celebrate the coronation of Queen Victoria, up to 1921 the band was known as the St Dennis Temperance Brass Band. After 1921 the name was changed to the St Dennis Silver Band.

A band committee was formed in 1912 led by the Hooper brothers – John Hooper, local businessman and manager of a clay work, became the first chairman.

From 1906 practice was carried out in a barn in Gulley's Lane. Between 1922 and 1938 the band qualified for the National Brass Band Championship at Crystal Palace and Alexandra Palace on ten occasions, winning the second section in 1928 and 1938.

Both during and after the Second World War the band suffered for various reasons and the period was one of instability. However, the players struggled on with the few men available and endured a succession of bandmaster changes. Finances were poor because of a lack of income from engagements.

During the early 1950s, with the effects of the war and the rebuilding of the band overcome, a gradual recovery started to be made. Mr W.D. Lawton was appointed musical director in 1949, which benefited the band and resulted in some success. By 1958, however, the band was still in a relatively unstable position and had not reached the heights of success to which it had been formerly accustomed. That year saw the start of a new era with the appointment of Mr E.J. Williams as musical director, a Cornishman who had returned to his native county.

Mr Williams, who retained his position for 25 years, was responsible for one of the most successful periods achieved by the St Dennis Band. He was a musician of great ability, and went on to become a well-known and highly respected tutor and musical

St Dennis Temperance Brass Band, 1908. Left to right, back row: *?, Jim Bunt, W. Juleff, Charlie Coombe, Mr Snell;* centre: *Lewis Bunt, Mr Coombe, Alf Varcoe, Mr Snell, A. Snell, Mr Coombe, J. Best;* front: *Jack Docking, ?, ?, George Coombe.* KHR/Coll

The St Dennis Temperance Brass Band in 1910. Bandmaster Mr W.H. Juleff is fifth from the left in the front row, holding the baton. KHR/Coll

Left: *The Temperance Brass Band, 1910.* KHR/Coll

Below: *St Dennis Band, 1924.* KHR/Coll

Left: *The St Dennis Silver Band, winners of the Royal Trophy at Bugle in 1920.* KHR/Coll

Right: *The St Dennis Band returning from Callington by charabanc in 1937.* KHR/Coll

Left: *The Dunstan family band members, 1949.* Left to right: *Roy, John, Steve and Harold.* KHR/Coll

St Dennis Silver Band in 1950, with conductor Mr W.D. Lawton. **KHR/Coll**

Above: *The St Dennis Silver Band in the 2003 carnival parade led by Brian Minear.* KHR

Above: *The St Dennis 'Celestian' Ladies Choir with choirmaster Charles Baker in the mid-1930s with the Doctor Manson Shield.* Left to right, back row: *Joan Thomas, Nora Varcoe, Gwen Bunt, Muriel Varcoe, Lily Sweet, Ethel Yelland, Mavis Best, Joyce Giles, Norah Thomas, Joyce Crowle;* front: *Muriel Coombe, Hazel Coombe, Olive Crowle, Evelyn Baker, Charles Baker, Ada Thomas, Nellie Jacobs, Avis Goodman, Lil Bunt.* KHR/Coll

Left: *The St Dennis Silver Band, winners of the championship section Royal Trophy at the Bugle contest in 1963.* Left to right, back row: *R. Richards, M. Strongman, D. Angilley, K. Trethewey, C. Barrett, L. Trethewey, G. Hitchins, T. Hitchins, R. Craddock, F. Northey, F. Arthur, N. Glasson, M. Bazely, B. Goudge, T. Willcock, M. Brewer;* front: *H. Dunstan, H. Camps, B. Minear, P. Minear, K. Tucker, D. Williams, E.J. Williams, F.H. Grime, D. Hambly, P. Strongman, M. Faro, J. Yelland, M. Yelland, V. Hawkey, J. Dunstan. Absent through illness was M. Hawkey.* KHR/Coll

The St Dennis Silver Band – which achieved sixth place in the National Championships held at the Royal Albert Hall in 1978. **KHR/Coll**

director not only in Cornwall but the brass band movement at large. This was recognised in 1981 when he was awarded the Medal of the Worshipful Company of Musicians of the City of London, an honour reserved for only a select few in the brass band movement.

It was during Mr Eddie Williams' directorship that qualification for the national finals at the Royal Albert Hall was achieved on no less than 15 occasions.

In the 1950s and '60s practice was carried out at the Commercial Inn public house, the Institute and the old Institute at Whitemoor. A new band room was built in 1966 just off Hendra Road, to which a bar was added in 1985 to help raise the financial support needed to meet the ever-increasing running costs.

In 1972 the youth band won the Championship of Great Britain, a major success which was repeated the following year. The year 1978 saw the senior band being placed sixth in the National Championships, which was the best result ever achieved.

Disappointment followed in 1981 when nine members of the senior band resigned. The band was consequently relegated to the second section the following year. The band suffered another blow in 1983 when Eddie Williams died.

After these setbacks, the band gained promotion to the championship section in 1985. The Royal Trophy was won at the Bugle contest in 1994 – the first time since 1979.

Difficulties were experienced again in 1997 when the senior band nearly ceased to exist and a reconstruction plan had to be established to revitalise the whole organisation. By 2001 the reconstruction had resulted in senior, youth and learner bands as well as a beginners' class being established. It was then that Mr Brush retired and Brian Minear took over as musical director.

Under Brian Minear's leadership in 2002 the band won the West of England Regional Championship in the fourth section and the Cornish Championship's fourth section, the West of England Bandsman's Festival, second section, and the National Championship's fourth section. These achievements were rewarded when the band was promoted to the third section for 2003. Past bandmasters and musical directors include:

1870–85: *Jim Yelland*
1885–90: *Henry Richards*
1890–1905: *John Best*
1905: *Elijah Bunt*
1906–23: *William H. Juleff*
1923–24: *R.W. Davidson*
1925–26: *E. Calverley*
1926–39: *C.H. Baker*
1939–43: *William H. Juleff*
1943–46: *Horace Bennett*
1946–48: *R. Polmounter*
1949–55: *W.D. Lawton*
1955–56: *John Harrison*
1957–58: *George Thompson*
1958–83: *Edwin J. Williams*
1983–86: *John Brush*
1987–90: *Seth Appleton*
1990–91: *Derek Greenwood*
1991–93: *Mike Cotter*
1993–95: *Gwynne Price*
1995–97: *Colin Togill*
1997–2001: *John Brush*
2001–present: *Brian Minear*

The people of St Dennis have always been very proud of their band, which has, over its 165 years of existence, built up a reputation which has been second to none. It is a credit to everyone who has been involved with it. Towards the end of the twentieth century and into the twenty-first, the band has started to regain earlier standards – as a result of the hard work and dedication of the musicians, committee and supporters.

St Dennis Male Voice Choir

The choir was formed in 1922 when Mr Marsh Kessell was appointed as the musical director, or choirmaster as some prefer to call it. Mr Kessell carried out his duties for many years until Captain Hedley Martin took over and led the choir until the outbreak of the Second World War when it was forced to suspend its activities.

The choir was re-formed in 1946 under the directorship of Stanley Treloar. Two years later his son Harold took over and proceeded to reshape the choir with a completely different approach. New arrangements of popular songs of the day meant a change from the traditional choral singing. It was during Harold's musical directorship that the choir won the 1948 County Festival.

In 1993 David Tidball assumed the position of musical director, a role he successfully filled until his retirement in 2002. Clive Jago was appointed as the new musical director to succeed Mr Tidball and this proved to be a popular choice with a good relationship soon developing between himself and the singers.

Since its existence the choir has always been in demand and has performed in concerts and competitions around the country. In 2002 the group celebrated its 80th anniversary.

Miss Doris Bullock, as the choir's accompanist, had the proud record of over 50 years' service, during which time she played more than 150 different organs, pianos and harmonicas in Cornwall and Devon.

Cinemas

In the mid-1920s a Mr Elgar decided to open a cinema

Above: *The St Dennis Male Voice Choir outside the Foster Hall at St Lawrence's Hospital, Bodmin, after they had made a radio broadcast in 1937.* Left to right, back row: *Will Lewarne, Wesley Tucker, Leslie Yelland, W. Trembath, Scott Banfield, Harold Treloar, Charlie Penhaligan, Victor Treloar, Stanley Treloar, Clifford Hancock;* centre: *Jack Salter, Johnny Bunt, Tom Bullock, W. Hopper, John Edwin Kessell, Melville Coombe (accompanist), Edwin Stoneman, Harry Cory, Fred Crews, Reg Bray;* front: *Will Yelland, Ken Yelland, Arnold Best, George Arthur, Albert Kessell, George Harris, Captain Hedley Martyn (choirmaster), Tommy Evans, Kenneth Penhaligan, Billy Bennett, Ivor Bunt, Chester Gill, Will Trethewey.*

Above: *Mr Eddie Williams, the musical director of the St Dennis Silver Band from 1958–83.* KHR/Coll

St Dennis Male Voice Choir with their musical director Mr Harold Treloar, winners of the County Music Festival in 1948. Left to right, back row: *Harry Cory, Fred Crews, Norman Crews, Donald Williams, Charlie Dean, Frank Arthur, Jack Bunt, Garfield Craddock, Stan Penhaligan, Ewart Rowse, Maunder Cocks, Roy Magor;* centre: *Hugh Stephens, Tommy Lobb, George Hawken, Russell Gummow, Bill Dunstan, Marsh Docking, Alf Bunt, Mamphy Allen, Bert Jenson, Edward Smale, Claude Grose, Dick Tucker, Stan Best, Stan Tabb;* front: *Ivor Bunt, Albert Goudge, Arnold Best, Ken Penhaligan, Vanice Pethick, Bill Trethewey, Revd Albert Sykes, Harold Treloar, Richard Yelland, Margaret Treloar, Ken Mitchell, Reuben Runnalls, Stan Hawken, Stan Treloar.* KHR/Coll

in the village. He purchased a surplus Army hut, erected it near the Boscawen Hotel on the site of the modern Barclays Bank and equipped it as a cinema. When it opened, it was the only cinema in Cornwall.

Only silent black-and-white films were available in those days, and music was provided by someone playing the piano (usually Mrs Hilda Rickard or Mrs Snell) who did their best to create the appropriate music for each film. Sometimes when the audience's behaviour was too boisterous Mr Elgar entered the hall, rang a hand-bell and called for order. At the end of each performance people often visited one of the five chip shops in the village to purchase a bag of chips and peas to eat on the walk home.

In 1931 Mr Arthur Trudgeon, known locally as 'Whiskers' because of his hair-cutting and shaving skills, decided to build a new cinema on land opposite his business premises, known as the Army Yard. The cinema was completed in 1931 and given the name 'Plaza'. Mr Elgar then closed his own cinema and arranged to lease the new cinema from Mr Trudgeon, which he ran for six years before 1938.

The lease was then purchased by Cornwall Cinemas, which was owned by Mr J. Taylor. He employed a Mr R. Bauress to manage it. In the early days the cinema proved a popular and well-used village amenity which also attracted people from outside the village. A Mr and Mrs Davey were next to purchase the lease; they ran the cinema for a few years before they eventually sold the lease to Mr Ronald Hill of Duchy Cinemas. The cinema's popularity started to decline in 1960 as various forms of alternative entertainment started to emerge. This situation reached a point where the cinema was losing money and it was forced to close in 1962.

Staff who worked at the Plaza included: Mr C.H. Barrett, Mr T. Kellow and Mr C. Hill (projectionists), Mr H. Truscott, who assisted with the bookkeeping for many years, Mrs Burt (usherette) and Mrs Thelma Stoneman (ticket sales and usherette).

Mr Trudgeon, the owner of the cinema, also owned other property in its vicinity, namely a small shop, three cottages and a garage. He sold the lot in 1964 to a property developer, who demolished all the buildings and sold the land to Mr and Mrs R. Hayward.

Pantomimes

The performance of pantomimes in St Dennis started in the late 1930s. The shows took place in the cinema and Church of England School. At one time the St Dennis Variety Company, the St Dennis Players and the Hot Spots were performing their own shows.

Miss Dagmar Hancock was always involved in some way with many of the productions, as was Mrs Hilary Crowle and later Mrs D. Osborne (née Crowle). Casts were made up from village talents, as were the orchestras.

It would be virtually impossible to record all pantomime titles along with the names of the cast members and production teams. However, it is obvious that they were all talented and dedicated people. For example, it is difficult to recall these earlier shows without remembering the ever-popular antics of Arthur Best and Jack Michael.

The production of pantomimes ceased in 1963 as a result of limited support and finance. Then, after a break of 30 years, the village pantomime was revived by a group of people, namely: Mrs Pam Kelly, Mr Jack Michael, Mr Melville Hicks and Mr Rex Harvey. A calculation by Jack Michael highlighted that £2,500 would be needed to get the project off the ground. A committee was formed called the St Dennis Variety Company, which proceeded to implement a fund-raising programme which eventually generated sufficient funds. Preparations were made in 1992 for a 1993 production of *Robinson Crusoe*. This proved a great success and paved the way for the further nine shows that have followed in its wake.

Lots of people, young and old, have performed to a high standard over the years and have entertained the public admirably. There have been many stalwarts as far as the acting goes – none more so than John Keast and Brian Skews who have been involved in most productions. The organisation and fund-raising team has also included a number of dedicated volunteers, who over the years have given a tremendous amount of time and effort to support the productions.

The committee believes that the St Dennis Variety Company will continue to go from strength to strength, with the village talent being endless. Indeed, at the turn of the twenty-first century, the annual pantomime is performed for six days in the War Memorial Institute and Working Men's Club.

Miss Madge Varcoe, the village singer who had made recordings and was reputed to be called the Cornish Nightingale. Sadly Madge died of TB at the young age of 26. KHR/Coll

The following is a list of people from the village who, up to 1951, had made broadcasts on the radio:

Madge and Nora Varcoe, vocalists
Jack Soloman, young vocalist
Lawrence Goudge, young vocalist
Marjory Bunt, vocalist
Betty Bunt, vocalist
Mrs Solomon's children's choir
St Dennis Male Voice Choir
The Silver Band
The White Aces Dance Band
Mr J. Best, trombone
Mr Harold Dunstan, cornet.

During St Dennis Feast Week the annual hunt was held with the Fowey Harriers usually meeting at the Boscawen Hotel. This picture was taken in 1912. **KHR/Coll**

Right: *The Plaza Cinema (1932–64).* C.H. Barrett

Below: *The Plaza Cinema in 1951 where children are waiting for the doors to open for a matinée.* KHR/Coll

Left: *The White Aces.* Left to right: *Mr Desmond Snell, Mr Jack Morcom, Mr Hugh Morcom, Mr Gordon White, Mr Stuart Hore and Mr Raymond White.* KHR/Coll

Right: *The Noveltones Dance Band (1930–50).* Left to right: *Mr B. Stephens, Mr Hugh Morcom, Mrs Lily Morcom and Mr Raymond White.* KHR/Coll

Left: *St Dennis Pantomime Group in 1951, with orchestra members* (left to right) *M. Brewer, L. Goudge, P. Strongman, D. Osborne, B. Kessell, M. White and P. Lawry.* KHR/Coll

The cast of the play The White Sheep of the Family *in 1953.* Left to right, standing: *Mr Desmond Ronyane, Mr Cyril Rabey, Mrs Sylvia Rabey, Mr Raymond Stribley, Miss Dagmar Hancock, Mr Harry Truscott, Miss Jennifer Wilson;* sitting: *Mr Colin Kneller, Miss Barbara Currah, Mr Melville Hicks, Mrs Chris Ronyane, Mrs Gwen Harris, Mr Geoffrey Hawken, Mrs Hilary Crowle.* KHR/Coll

Above: *The whole company of the* Jack and the Beanstalk *pantomime performed in 1955.* KHR/Coll

Right: *The whole company of the 1993 pantomime* Robinson Crusoe. KHR/Coll

Below: *The cast of the* Dick Whittington *pantomime which was performed in 1958.* KHR/Coll

Chapter 9

Leisure and Social Groups

The War Memorial Institute's original trustees in 1920. Left to right, back row: *J. Kessell, S.A. Estlick, T. Varcoe, S. Kessell, R. Veall, G. Bullock, W. Kellow, C. Bullock;* front: *H. Truscott, Dr Manson, R. Hooper, E. Allen, J. Best, the Revd Barfitt.* F.C. Elgar

The War Memorial Institute

This group was formed at a parish meeting held on 6 January 1919 when a proposal was carried to build a non-sectarian and non-political institute as a war memorial. The meeting was chaired by the chairman of the Parish Council, Dr R.H. Manson. The offer from Lord Falmouth to donate land was accepted, and funds were raised by donations, local events and by a parish collection. A loan was also arranged from Lloyds Bank.

A Mr J.H. Lobb of Mevagissey was engaged to build the Institute for an agreed price of £1,520. An offer from the ex-servicemen of the village to provide an external clock was accepted. The building work commenced in 1920 and was completed in 1922.

A committee of trustees was formed in 1920 and given the overall responsibility for the premises and its upkeep. This committee consisted of: Messrs E. Allen, the Revd J.C. Barfitt, J. Best, C. Bullock, G. Bullock, S.H. Estlick, R. Hooper, W. Kellow, J. Kessell, S. Kessell, Dr R.H. Manson, H. Truscott, T. Varcoe and R. Veall.

A Delabole slate memorial plaque was inscribed with the names of the 49 parishioners who had fallen in the First World War. It was positioned externally on the front of the building.

A stone-laying ceremony was held on 17 May 1922 and carried out by the Revds Barfitt and Dunn, the Rt Hon. H.D. McLaren, MP, Mrs Bowling and the village schoolchildren. The grand opening and unveiling of the memorial plaque was carried out by the Lord Lieutenant of Cornwall, Mr J.C. Williams on 18 February 1923. The official opening ceremony was held on Wednesday 20 June 1923 at which the key was presented to chairman Dr Manson by Mrs McLaren, the wife of the local MP. The celebrations started at 1.30p.m. and continued well into the evening.

In May 1925 the local Women's Institute and the British Legion were invited to join the Institute in the planned extension that was scheduled to be built. The Women's Institute accepted the invitation, but the British Legion declined. The building was extended by some 40ft at the back on both floors in 1926, which provided increased facilities and a room for the WI.

Above: *The War Memorial Institute's grand unveiling of the memorial plaque ceremony being carried out on 18 February 1923 by the Lord Lieutenant of Cornwall, Mr J.C. Williams.* KHR/Coll

Above: *Dignitaries at the opening of the extension to the War Memorial Institute in 1926.* Left to right: *Mr Harry Truscott, Dr R.H. Manson, Lord and Lady Falmouth, Captain R. Hooper.* P. Taylor

Right: *The War Memorial plaque, 2003.* KHR

The trustees managed the Institute until 1926, when they formed a management committee. It was to be elected annually, and was responsible for the day-to-day administration of the Institute.

After the Second World War a further 12 names of those who had fallen in that conflict were added to the memorial plaque. For many years the Institute survived on members' subscriptions and income from events held in the hall, such as its own music festivals, etc. During the 1940s and early '50s income was generated by holding weekly dances, which, in those days, were very popular. However, times changed and the dances lost their appeal.

Finances reached a critical level in the mid-1950s and at a special meeting of members and the committee the decision was taken to form a registered club and install a bar to generate the much-needed funds for the Institute's survival. The club was approved by the trustees and the local magistrates, and opened in 1959 (the business was amended to the St Dennis War Memorial Institute and Working Men's Club). The bar work was carried out by volunteers from the committee, notably Stan Barron, Donald Bray, Derek Brewer, Charlie Hugh, Roy Juleff, Jethro Kellow, Peter Nobes, Michael Pearce, Kenneth Rickard, Dudley Wade and Les Warne. Dudley Wade, in particular, was the instigator of the club and expended a lot of time and effort to get it 'off the ground'; he should always be remembered for that.

It is interesting to note that church magazines written by the Revd Childs record the existence of a Working Men's Institute that was formed in 1851, which was still in existence in 1894. It is not clear where it was situated.

The bar soon proved popular and generated enough income to enable bar staff to be employed which eventually progressed into the employment of a full-time steward. Its success also enabled the loan from Harry Estlick, which had kept the Institute afloat, to be repaid.

Success generated success and in the 1970s a second bar was installed on the first floor to serve members attending entertainments on Saturday and Sunday evenings. As a games venue the club excelled, with darts, snooker, pool and euchre teams playing their part alongside the entertainment and bars. From the very early days up to the time of writing, the standard of the billiards, snooker and darts teams has been very high and has brought much success and recognition to the Institute/club.

Many individuals have had the honour of being selected to represent the county. Of the home-grown snooker players, Malcolm Hugh, Carl Boundy and Kenneth Rickard have played for the county at senior level, and David Grigg and Malcolm Roberts at youth level. Of the darts players, Nigel Morford, Ian Hugh, Michael Hugh and Paul Chaffe have played.

Over a period of years the profits from the bar sales have been invested in major projects such as enlarging the lounge, building a new toilet block and committee room, improving bar and cellar facilities, building a car park (for which land had to be purchased) and various refurbishment programmes. Apart from all these changes, the property has been kept in a good state of repair including modernising the appearance of the front of the building.

During its lifetime the external clock has been overhauled three times, twice by Mr Bernard Broad of St Austell and once by a firm called David Jones, when the mechanism was converted from manual to electrical working.

Unfortunately, as a result of the decline in employment in the china-clay industry, the addition of two more social clubs in the village, and the general economic state of our county, since 1990 the club has had to live on its investments accumulated during the good years. Without doubt, the officers and committee members at the time of writing have a more difficult time in managing the club than did their counterparts of the 1980s.

The War Memorial Institute's trustees, 1972. Left to right: *W.H. Pascoe, K.H. Rickard, T. Rowe, S. May, F. Watters, C.H. Barrett, H. Trevenna, Dr C.M. Wilson, S. Hore, S. Barron, L.G. Docking, H.S. Estlick, J.A. Gregor, D. Bray, A.J. Best.* C.H. Barrett

The War Memorial Institute and Working Men's Club, 2003. KHR

At the time of writing the first-floor function room is used by local organisations and charities regularly with events taking place virtually every day. The club has a reputation second to none and is registered under the Friendly Societies Act. It has been a member of the Club and Institutes Union since 1960.

Kenneth Rickard has been associated with the Institute since 1952 when he was first elected to the management committee. He remained as part of it until 1987, during which time he served 26 years as the secretary. Kenneth was elected to the trustees in 1964 and was honoured with the chairmanship in 1978, a position which he still holds in 2004.

The following people have been honoured by being elected to the position of chairman of the trustees: Revd J.C. Barfitt, A.J. Best, C. Bullock, R. Dyer, H.S. Estlick, S.H. Estlick, G. Goodman, A.J. Gregor, J. Hooper, W. Julian, Dr R.H. Manson, J. Radcliffe, K.H. Rickard, T.J. Skelton, T. Varcoe, Dr C.M. Wilson and W.J. Yelland. Club secretaries since 1959 have been: Roger Best (in post in 2003), Charlie Hugh, Alan Martin and Ken Rickard. Chairmen of the club have included: Donald Bray, Les Docking, Alan Martin, William ('Mickey') Pascoe, Michael Hill and Dudley Wade. Presidents have been: Mr Francis Ellis, Mr T.J. Skelton and Dr C.M. Wilson.

Other members who have been stalwarts of the club in some way over the first 25 years include: Raymond Allen, Stan Barron, Cecil Barrett, Roger Barrett, Joe Best, Graham Estlick, Charlie Gee, Cleon Harvey, Graham Hugh, Roy Juleff, Jethro Kellow, Garnet Knight, Les Knight, John Martin, Sam May, Colin May, Percy Nobes, Michael Pearce, Trevor Rowe, Fred Watters, Tom Willey and Albert Williams.

In the days of various music festivals many trophies were donated by supporters. In 2004 these cups and shields are on permanent display at the Wheal Martyn China Clay Museum at Carthew.

The St Dennis Women's Institute

The St Dennis WI was formed at a public meeting held on 3 April 1922 when a committee emerged from those present. The first committee meeting followed on 25 April 1922 at which Mrs S. Barfitt, the rector's wife, was elected the first president and a decision was made to hold committee meetings on a monthly basis. The first of such meetings was held on 4 May 1922 in the Church of England School when Ingeberg Lady St Aubyn attended and 53 members were enrolled. The second monthly meeting was held in the grounds of the Rectory.

During the first year dressmaking and choral classes were introduced and a dramatics society was formed. Following an approach to the trustees of the War Memorial Institute requesting the hire of a room for monthly meetings, the WI was invited to join the Institute and have its own room in an extension planned to the building. This invitation was accepted with the undertaking from the trustees that the War Memorial Institute would be responsible for all running costs and the WI would be expected to pay an annual rent of 22d. per member. When the extension to the building was completed the grand opening ceremony was held on 7 October 1926.

St Dennis Women's Institute at the Rectory, 1926. Left to right, back row: *Gladys Stribley, ?, Mrs W. Jenkin;* third row: *Mrs Hill, Mrs Strongman, Mrs Pedlar, ?, Mrs Gordon Richards, Mrs Estlick, Ada Thomas, Audrey Estlick, Mrs Bert Stephens, Beattie Key, Mrs Tucker, Mrs Florrie Stephens;* second row: *Mrs Ball, Mrs Rickard, Lily Menear, ?, Miss Donithorne, Kathleen Penhaligan, Mrs Tom Varcoe, May Bullen, Mrs Angela Trudgian, Nurse Rickard, Mrs E. Osborne, Mrs A. Tucker, Mrs Hancock;* front: *Mrs Percy Magor, Mrs G. Varcoe, Mrs Hilda Barfitt, Mrs Lily Bunt, Mrs Kent, ?, Mrs Kelloway, Mrs J. Best, Gladys Angilley, Mrs Stribley, Mrs Annie Wilson.* KHR/Coll

Opening of the new Women's Institute room in the War Memorial Institute in 1926. C.H. Barrett

Above: *Women's Institute group in 1953.* Left to right, back row: *Mrs T. Bullock, Mrs B. Jenkins, Mrs Ruby Best, Mrs Mabel Hugh, Mrs Hazel Bray, Mrs Mary Trevenna, Mrs Winnie Varcoe, Mrs G. Knight, Mrs Davis, Mrs Joan Kent, Mrs Gertrude Buckingham, Mrs Tucker, Miss Williams, Mrs Hawkey, Mrs J. Tucker, Mrs M. Allen, Mrs Doris Best;* front: *Mrs Muriel Barret, Mrs Vera Oliver, Mrs Lily Pearce, Mrs Winnie Greenslade, ?, Mrs Pat Common, Mrs Doris Kemp, Mrs Phylis Higman, Mrs Vi Brewer, Mrs Betty Bell, Mrs Dorothy Trevenna, Mrs W. Williams, Mrs Flo Truscott.* KHR/Coll

WI group photo taken in 1965.

With the formation of the Working Men's Club in 1959, to generate needed funds to maintain the building, the WI was asked by the management committee to consider moving to another room within the building, to make way for the proposed bar area. The WI agreed to the move, which resulted in the old reading-room being renovated. It was also agreed at this time by the Institute's management committee that the first-floor hall be reserved for the WI's use on the first Monday of every month.

In February 1947, it was agreed to seek links with other WIs overseas. A link was established with a WI in New Zealand, and the St Dennis WI started exchanging correspondence with their New Zealand counterparts on a monthly basis, as well as at Christmas. For many years Miss F.O. Williams was the correspondent, although in 2004 Mrs C. Gregor carries out this task.

In May 1966 an embroidered tablecloth was made with the help of several committee members. It was designed by Mrs Muriel Barrett and the linen was given by Mrs Best. In 1948 a picture incorporating the song 'Jerusalem' written in old verse by Miss Allcock was presented in a frame given by Mrs Knight. The picture was then hung in the WI room where it remains in 2004. A scrapbook recording WI and village events has been kept for many years.

St Dennis WI membership figures have varied over the years (1922: 53; 1927: 63; 1952: 86; 1975: 30; 2003: 20) and at the time of writing are at an all-time low. The longest-serving member is Mrs Muriel Barrett who joined in the late 1930s. During her time as a member Muriel has served as secretary and president. Over the years the WI presidents have been:

1922–29:	*Mrs S. Barfitt*
1930–32:	*Mrs S. Kent*
1933–34:	*Mrs Sara*
1935–36:	*Mrs Estlick*
1936–48:	*Mrs S. Kent*
1948–55?:	*Mrs P. Varcoe*
1955–56:	*Miss W. Truscott*
1956–58:	*Mrs W. Williams*
1958:	*Mrs V.S. Williams*
1961–67:	*Mrs D. Kemp*
1967–70:	*Mrs P. Commons*
1970–73:	*Mrs M. Docking*
1973–77:	*Mrs M. Barrett*
1977–79:	*Mrs M. Docking*
1979–82:	*Miss F.O. Williams*
1982–84:	*Mrs M. Docking*
1984–88:	*Mrs M. Key*
1988–89:	*Mrs M. Docking*
1989–92:	*Mrs M. Hore*
1992–97:	*Mrs M. Key*
1997–2001:	*Mrs D. Thompson*
2001–present:	*Mrs K.J. Truscott*

The WI celebrating its eightieth birthday in 2003. Mrs Muriel Barrett, the longest-serving member, is cutting the celebration cake. Left to right: *Mrs A. Hemmings, Mrs P. Dunn, Mrs Williams, Mrs Hobba, Mrs Hewitt, Mrs M. Hore, Mrs Fugler, Mrs P. Bilkey, Mrs D. Thompson, Miss J. Luke, Mrs M. Barrett, Mrs L. Brenton, Mrs E. Trevenna.*

Reading and Recreation Society

A reading and recreation society was formed in 1892 and used the old Salvation Army hut which had fallen into disuse. The society was given one year's subscription to the *Western Daily Mercury* by a Mr Willis of Wadebridge, and an anonymous person gave a bagatelle table.

This contribution was gratefully received and bagatelle matches with other villages and between the young and old members were a regular activity.

The Salvation Army hut was positioned in an area which later would have been roughly behind the Plaza Cinema. This area was known for many years as the Army Yard.

Girl Guides

The first St Dennis Girl Guides troop was formed in September 1931 when a meeting was held in the Church of England School at which 16 recruits aged between 11 and 16 were enlisted. The troop later registered as the St Dennis Church School Company.

Miss D. Hancock, formerly of Ramsgate, was elected as the captain with Miss Sara and Miss Osborne as her lieutenants. The company then divided into three patrols: Blue Tit, Robin and Kingfisher.

The enrolment ceremony was held on 24 November 1931 and was attended by the District Commissioner, Mrs R.C. Treffry of Porthpean. The first camp was attended at Harlyn Bay in 1932 and later camps were attended at Bodrigan Farm, 1933, the Scilly Isles, 1936, Reigate, 1937, and Mannabilly Barton in 1938.

The Hot Spots, as the Guides' acting group was called, produced their first pantomime *Snow White and the Seven Dwarfs* in 1934, and went on to produce many more. In 1933 the Guides won the District Shield and the Bolitho County Shield which was contested by the six district winners at the county final

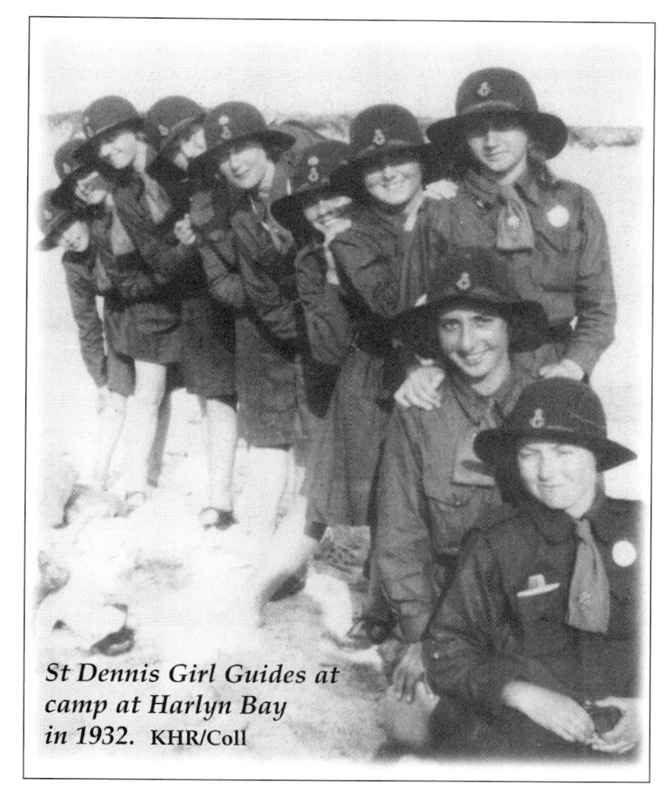

St Dennis Girl Guides at camp at Harlyn Bay in 1932. KHR/Coll

in St Austell, a feat which was repeated again in 1939. There are records showing that the Girl Guides had a hockey team in 1934. At their ninth birthday party in 1940 the Guides were joined by guest of honour, Mrs Michael Rogers, the Cornwall County Commissioner.

During the Second World War the St Dennis Girl Guides contributed stirling work to the war effort. During 1941 the Hot Spots performed several concerts in Newquay to entertain the convalescing troops stationed there. They also performed at RNAS St Merryn entertaining the sailors, and did one concert at Grampound Road to raise funds for the local Red Cross, travelling there and back in vehicles supplied by the American Army. Many concerts were performed in St Dennis, all to raise funds for the war effort and local charities. In addition, woollen garments were knitted for the Royal Navy, food parcels were made up for DCLI men on active service, and funds were raised for the Plymouth Air Raid Victims Fund and the Russian Fund. In March 1944 the St Dennis Guides were chosen to provide the colour party and to carry the chief standard for the visit to St Austell by the Chief Guide, Lady Baden-Powell.

Sadly, Miss Hancock left in 1946, and Lieutenant B. Wilson took over the captaincy. The order of events is rather unclear during the postwar years, although it is known that the company folded in the early 1950s. Miss Carole Gardner, headmistress of the Church of England School, revived the troop in the 1970s, which unfortunately only survived for two years.

Brownies

A Brownie pack was started in 1938 for girls aged seven to ten. Miss M. Stephens was Brown Owl and Misses Dorothy Currah and Joyce Crowle were Tawney Owls. However, this group probably folded with the Guides in the 1950s.

The Brownies were re-formed in 1970 by Mrs Peggy McCaughan who became Brown Owl to a pack of 24 girls known as the 2nd St Dennis Carne Hill Brownies, with Miss Gloria Bicknell as Tawney Owl. When Mrs McCaughan retired in 1982, Miss Bicknell took over as Brown Owl and retained this position until 1985 when another person filled the position for 12 months. Mrs Janice Grose took over as Guider-in-Chief in 1986 and continued as such until 1990 when the group had to close.

In March 1996 the district commissioner for this area, Mrs N. Coombes, assisted by Miss C. Gardner, head of the Infant School, re-formed the Brownies again, with Caroline Rogers and Corinne Jenkin agreeing to stand in as leaders. Eventually Janice Grose took up the post of Guider-in-Chief.

The Brownies' base was in the Infant School until 1998, after which they transferred to the County Primary School. Since 1996 they have entered a float in the village carnival. In 2004 the pack, led by Janice Grose and assistant guider Corinne Jenkin, has 24 Brownies. The troop has a waiting-list to join and appears to be going from strength to strength.

Rainbows

A Rainbow group was started in March 2003 for girls aged between five and six, with a room in Hendra Road Chapel being used as their base. The Rainbows are led by Helen Tomlin and Sarah Boulter.

Rangers

A Ranger company was formed in 1932 with Mrs E. Barker as captain. In 1940 the captain was Miss H. Lewis who during the war served in the WAAF.

Cubs

In 1926 there was a Wolf Cub pack led by a Mr Pank, a captain at Gothers clay works. Mr John Varcoe of Wellington Road remembers attending meetings held in the old barn at No. 10 Trelavour where access to the meeting room was via external stairs.

A Cubs group was re-formed in 1980 by Mrs Jackie Salmon and Mrs Jean Amos who successfully ran the group for four years before handing over to Mr Ivor Johns in 1984. Mr Johns was the Cub Master for two years before handing over to Mrs M. Cobble and Mrs M. Lorimor who ran the group until it folded in 1989.

Boy Scouts

There was a Boy Scout group in the village in the late 1930s but unfortunately research has failed to turn up

The first Girl Guides company which was formed in 1933. Left to right, back row: *Muriel Coombe, Joyce Crowle, Pat Wilson, Margery Stephens, Doreen Hawken, Joan Menear, Joan Cowling, ?, ?, ?, Gwen Currah;* centre: *Roma Varcoe, Nora Varcoe, Joan Goldsmith, ?, ?, officer Hilda Lewis, Miss M. Hancock (captain), Mrs R. Treffry (commissioner), Eileen Richards, Dulcie Angilley;* front: *Dorothy Currah, ?, Mavis Arthur, ?, Clarissa Goldsmith, ?, Shirley Wilson, ?, Margaret Treloar.* KHR/Coll

Left: *The St Dennis Girl Guides company in 1936.* Left to right, back row: *Pat Wilson, Dorothy Currah, Hilda Crowle, Gwen Currah, Joan Cowling, Margorie Stevens, Nora Varcoe;* centre: *Ruby Brenton, Roma Varcoe, Muriel Coombe, Dagmar Hancock, Hilda Lewis, Joan Stoyles, Nadja Sara;* front: *Thelma Brown, Gladys Smith, Connie Willcox, Shirley Wilson, Doreen Stoyles, Clarissa Goldsmith, Barbara Wilson.* KHR/Coll

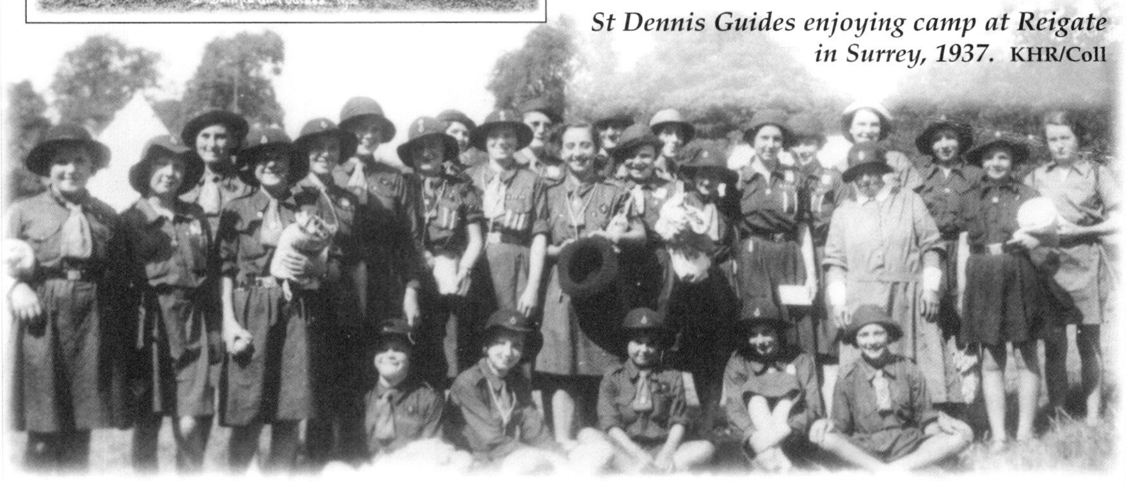

St Dennis Guides enjoying camp at Reigate in Surrey, 1937. **KHR/Coll**

Left: *The whole Girl Guides company, including Brownies, at their ninth birthday party on 17 October 1940, along with the Cornwall County Commissioner Mrs Michael Rogers and the district and county shields won in 1933 and 1939.* Left to right, back row: *Mary Yelland, June Davey, Iris Miners, Betty Hawke, Delphine Allen, Sheila Yelland, Margorie Yelland, Shirley May, Marion Truscott, Pansy Parker;* fourth row: *evacuee, evacuee, Monica Davy, Pamela Roberts, Gladys Smith, Barbara Wilson, Shirley Munday, Ellen Knight, Nancy Knight;* third row: *Connie Willcox, Winnie Pethick, Josie Toy, Dorothy Bullen, Olwyn Grigg, Freda Halford, Zelda Bunt, Phyllis Allen, Nancy Keast, Hilary Crowle;* second row: *Joyce Crowle, Doreen Stoyles, Roma Varcoe, Dagmar Hancock, Mrs Michael Rogers, Hilda Lewis, Joan Stoyles, Dorothy Currah, Margorie Stephens;* front: *Thelma Truscott, Betty Bunt, Lorraine Gilbert, Barbara Currah, Nancy Bullen, Gladys May, Yvonne May, Daphne Rowse, Dorothy Trudgeon.* KHR/Coll

The St Dennis Scouts at a jamboree at Falmouth in 1938. Mr Arthur Kent, who drove the Scouts there, is on the left, and others in the picture are, left to right: *Terry Chapman, ?, Ken Cundy, ?, Reggie Arthur;* centre: *Popsy Ford, Roy Mortimer;* front: *Willie Tapper, Norman Crews, Dennis Hawke, Saxby Hatton, Ken Rickard.* J. Kent

any detailed records. Mr S.H. Estlick was the Scoutmaster some time in the 1940s.

One thing that is known is that the St Dennis Scouts attended a jamboree at Falmouth in 1938. Mr Arthur Kent drove them to Falmouth in his lorry.

The British Legion

A branch of the British Legion was formed in the village after the First World War to raise funds for the benevolent support of ex-servicemen in need.

One of the main fund-raising events was the annual horse show and sports day held on 1 July in the Whitegate football field.

Some of the early organisers were: Mr A.W. Jenkin (teacher), Jack Rogers and Reg Metherell. Roy Andrews was the organiser in the 1950s and '60s and for many years Stan Best was the standard-bearer on the Remembrance Day parade.

The Remembrance Day poppy and wreath sales co-ordinators have been: Fred Bennetto, Roy Best, John Gregor and Martyn Best, the last of whom performs this duty at the time of writing. The branch ceased to function in the 1960s.

Right: *St Dennis AFC pose for a team photograph at their Trelavour ground in 1902.*

Below: *The St Dennis football team in 1924. In the middle of the centre row is Mr Edwin Stoneman.* KHR/Coll

Below right: *St Dennis AFC team in 1920.* KHR/Coll

Left: *The St Dennis football team (reserves), 1933/34.* Left to right, back row: *Percy Varcoe, R. Bray, A. Roberts, S.M. Kent;* centre: *Charlie Penhaligan, R. Bunt, G. Bennetto, W. Grigg, Charlie Underwood;* front: *S. Kent, K. Richards ('Rip') and A. Mitchell.* KHR/Coll

Right: *The St Dennis Minors football team, winners of the St Austell and District Minor League in 1937/8.* Left to right, back row: *Mervyn Keast, Claude Bunt, Jack Rowe, Fred Friend, Mowbray Alford, Stuart Kent, Ronnie Allen;* front: *Roy Best, Raymond Best, Jack Solomon, Arthur Angilley, Donald Martin. Stan Huddy could not attend.* KHR/Coll

Left: *St Dennis AFC team and officials, 1927/8 – winners of the County Charity Cup.* Left to right, back row: *Len Seymour, Bert Currah, Fred Richards, Bill Polland, Sylvester Kessell, Fred Dyer, Albert Williams, Stuart Best;* centre: *Harry Truscott, G. Menear, Mr Alcock or Spriggett, D. Hambly, Bill Blewett, Garfield Giles, Reg Mather, Jack Tucker;* front: *Harry Estlick (senr), Will Brenton, 'Darky' Colvin, Fred Andrews, R. Hooper ('Boss'), Alfie Chamberlain, Edwin Stoneman, Harold Tucker, Stanley Clemo, Reg Martyn.* KHR/Coll

Plantation area on the most northern part of the moor – the site of an American Army field kitchen prior to D-Day in 1944. KHR

Above: *The site of an American Army fuel dump prior to D-Day in 1944.* KHR

Pitsmingle–Tregoss road. However, once the Tregothnan estate heard about this it was stopped.

In 1989 Ken Abrahams, who was processing the old railway waste tip contents and producing ready-mixed concrete at the time, obtained permission from Tregothnan estate to prospect for tin in an area of the moor where the River Fal flowed to the bridge under the railway embankment. The aggregate produced a low percentage of tin ore which it was eventually deemed not commercially viable to pursue. However, the extraction process created large pits which quickly became filled with water and left the River Fal unrecognisable. Long gone are the days when this area of the moor, including the river, was a favourite spot for visitors who enjoyed bathing, fishing and picnics.

In 1989 a bungalow was built on the moor beside the access road that served the block-and-sand works many years ago. A 20-acre site adjacent to the bungalow was used as a waste-spoil and rubble tip after the bungalow was occupied.

The moor, both then and at the time of writing, was a Site of Special Scientific Interest (SSSI), which is managed by English Nature and afforded legal protection. It is thus debatable whether the local authority should have given planning approval for the bungalow. In 1996, after difficult and lengthy negotiations between the owner of the bungalow, English Nature and other authorities, the dwelling was vacated and demolished. No approval was ever given for the waste tip and even in 2003 this ongoing problem remains with English Nature to resolve. It is not as straightforward as one would expect, as the contents of the tip are unknown and may be hazardous. No attempt to remove the offending materials can be made until they have been sampled and analysed (the removal of hazardous materials could lead to the contamination of the watercourse, so it may be safer to leave them where they are).

When new electricity pylons were erected in 1965 rough hardcore roads were constructed across the moor for access to each pylon site. Unfortunately they were constructed without any consideration or provision for adequate drainage. Many years later one of these roads has resulted in the natural drainage from the Toad's Hole and Enniscaven areas being restricted, with fields being waterlogged and the growth of rushes taking over from grass.

The Register of Common Land Act (1965) required County Councils to be responsible for maintaining a register of all common land within their own counties and for enforcing the Act. Cornwall County Council started compiling a register of common land by inviting applications to register in January 1967. The Goss Moor area was divided into numbered blocks and each application had an objection period before being accepted and registered. This process started in 1967 and was completed in June 1979. Today six different people have commoners' rights, although only two choose to exercise them. In addition, there are ten different owners of various parts of the moor, with four different parties owning mineral rights.

Towards the end of the twentieth century, the moor was subjected to unwanted controversy because of the A30 trunk road which is built upon it. Prior to the nineteenth century the present A30 across the moor was known as the turnpike, a name still used by local people up to the mid-twentieth century. The turnpike (usually incorporating a toll-gate or barrier) on the Goss Moor was part of the main coaching route between Jamaica Inn on Bodmin Moor and the Indian Queens coaching inn. In modern times, this section of the A30 has two poorly designed and dangerous junctions, a restricted-height railway bridge, and is near an unmanned railway level crossing – all accident black spots with above-average accident figures.

Successive governments have staggered along a path of financial and bureaucratic restraint regarding any improvements to this road, ignoring the requests from industrial leaders, heads of respective county organisations, the Devon and Cornwall Police, commuters and local people, all of whom have campaigned for this section of the A30 to be made into a dual carriageway and the railway bridge removed or avoided.

One restraint which inadvertently assisted the Government's policy was the fact that in 1988 the Goss Moor was designated a Site of Special Scientific

Left: *English Nature erected five of these signs around the moor in 1996. Today the top part of these signs, which contains the words English Nature, have been removed to prevent continued and costly vandalism. This picture is of the sign positioned near the River Fal bridge at Tregoss and was taken in 2003.* KHR

Below: *Cattle-grids were installed around the moor in 2002; this one is at Pitsmingle.* KHR

Inset below: ***Another cattle-grid, this time near Tregoss, which also shows the warnings and signs of an unmanned level crossing.*** **KHR**

The old cattle arch near Domellick as it looked in 2003. **KHR**

Interest. This brought special attention to the marsh fritillary butterfly, a species that has declined in Europe by 60 per cent since the 1980s. Goss Moor is one of only ten breeding sites in England to be afforded European protection.

In January 2002 the Government gave the go-ahead for a new A30 dual carriageway to be built from Innis Downs roundabout to Indian Queens where the A30 is already dualled. The transport minister at that time decided on a route which would pass around the northern edge of the moor avoiding the low railway bridge and the sensitive SSSI moor. At the time of writing no physical progress had been made but a public enquiry is imminent.

Goss Moor NNR: Past Nature Management and the Road Ahead

A total of 1,100 acres of Goss Moor were leased by the Nature Conservancy Council from Tregothnan estate in 1987. At the time, there were no on-site staff available and until 1991 the moor remained under the watching brief of the site manager based on The Lizard National Nature Reserve.

In 1991, the Nature Conservancy Council, which formerly covered England, Scotland and Wales, metamorphosed into English Nature, Scottish Natural Heritage and the Countryside Council for Wales; Government agencies with the remit to provide both nature and conservation advice to Government and to conserve and manage a network of nature reserves across the UK as examples of the best wildlife sites in Britain – 'the jewels in the crown of the collective countries' natural heritage'. In wildlife terms, Goss Moor became a Cornish gemstone of national importance largely because of its past involvement in tin streaming and grazing.

A full-time site manager was appointed in 1992 and a management plan was drawn up for the site which identified four main areas of work that would improve the wildlife interest of the site: clearance of some willow scrub, increased cattle grazing and the reinstatement of pony grazing as practised by former commoners, a rotational programme of swaling or burning, and the raising of the water table on parts of Tregoss Moor where the River Fal had been channelled in the late 1970s. The latter was to be performed under an agricultural improvement grant to assist in the removal of clay waste from the river and reduce the risk of subsequent flooding.

Through much of the 1990s limited internal funding prevented many of these works from being achieved, though it was possible to progress some projects through external funding. Plymouth University undertook a seven-year study of water-levels on the moor and as a result of their findings, in 1996, the Environment Agency funded the first phase of a river reclamation project to install weirs in the Fal in a move to reinstate former water-levels.

In the late 1990s, via funding from the Cornwall Heathland Project (financed by the Heritage Lottery Fund), 70 hectares of scrub were cleared and, in 2002, seven cattle-grids and roadside fencing were installed, which will assist in stock-proofing the moor, enabling existing commoners to safely exercise their grazing rights if they so wish.

Three major Government initiatives have had an irreversible impact on the moor since 2000: firstly, the need to improve the existing A30 across Goss Moor; secondly, the recognition from Brussels that Goss Moor is a site of European importance for its unique wildlife features (dry heath, wet heath and the marsh fritillary butterfly); and thirdly, through the so-called 'public right to roam' provision in the Countryside and Rights of Way Act (2000). Although a potentially hazardous site, Goss Moor will enjoy open public access within a few years.

The coincidence of these initiatives occurring at the same time led to the development of a partnership between English Nature, the Highways Agency, Cornwall County Council and the Environment Agency to use the re-routing of a major trunk road as a catalyst for local change. Frequently, when a bypass is constructed to ease congestion in a town, that town receives funding for pedestrian precincts and the like. Why couldn't the same rationale be applied to a rural area that in planning terms had been severely afflicted for many years? To what extent can the re-routing of a road be a catalyst for changing a landscape? We will be watching with interest.

A panoramic view of the southern part of the moor. **KHR**

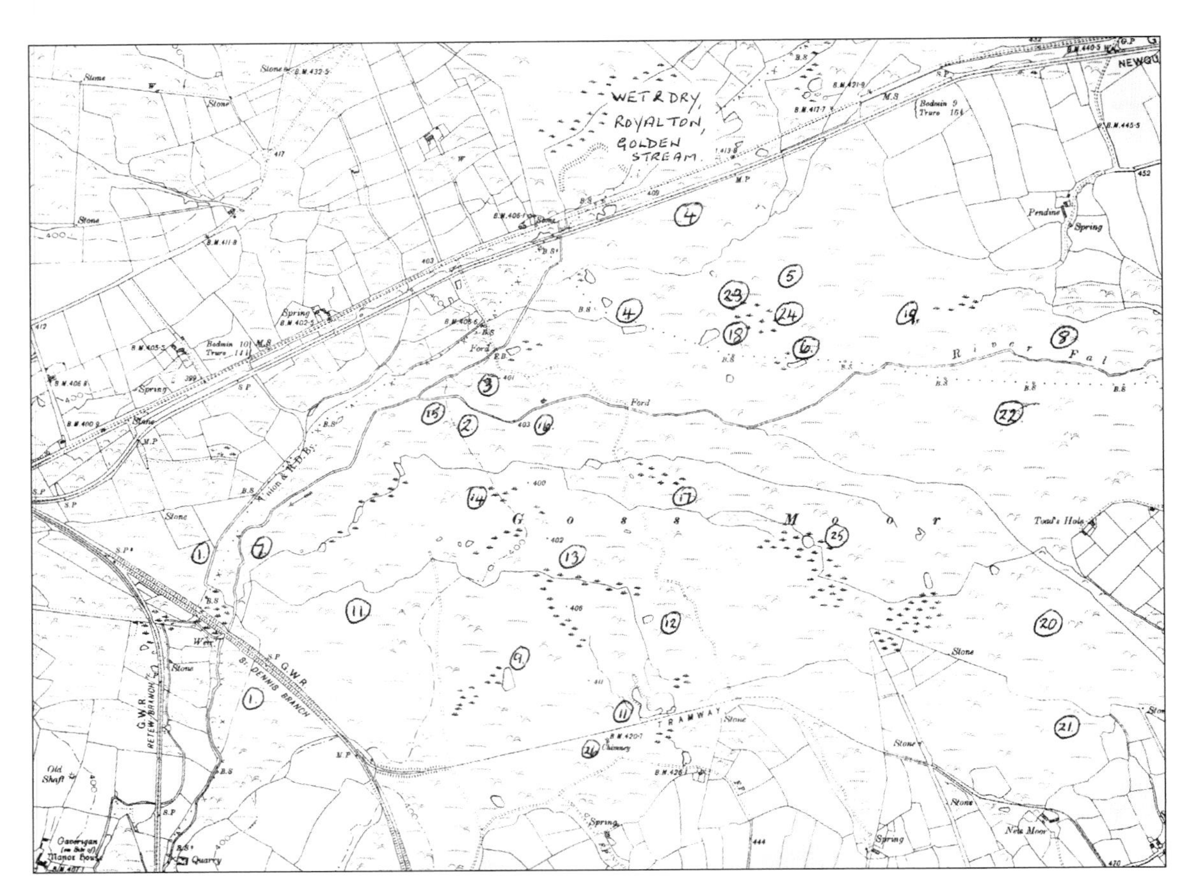

Above: *A mining map of 1854.*

Left: *Tin-recovery dredger belonging to the British Alluvial Tin Syndicate working on the moor between 1925 and 1928.* Bullen/Trounson

Below: *This pool near the centre of the moor was one of the last sites of the tin-dredging operations still referred to today as 'Tin Mine'.* KHR

Right: *The ruins of the old Wheal Penrose engine house, built in 1860. This picture was taken in 1961, four years before demolition for safety reasons.* M. Cole

Chapter 13

Mining

Early Times

Goss Moor, one of the largest of the upland basins in Cornwall, has been extensively worked for tin from time immemorial up to the 1920s. The tin industry was so important as a source of revenue for the Crown that in 1201 tinners were given their own charter, with William of Wrotham becoming warder of the stannaries. He later drew up laws to form the basis of the jurisdiction of stannaries and tinners had their own courts to deal with stannary affairs.

From early times and until the nineteenth century Cornwall was the main source of the world's tin, with the Goss and Tregoss Moors playing their part. Prehistoric tin streaming required a lot of hard labour as it involved deep digging, with the 'streaming' referring to the washing of the ore after it had been dug up.

The only local discovery dating from the Dark Ages that might be connected with the tin industry is a little penannular brooch, probably fifth century in origin. In addition, it is recorded that in 1772 an ancient wooden shovel was also found and about the same time a slab of tin weighing some 20lbs was discovered, although the latter was deemed to be of earlier origin. At the time of writing, the wooden shovel can be seen in the County Museum at Truro.

Goss Moor has traditionally been streamed for its alluvial tin. There is little doubt that in the course of these operations the backs of many lodes were revealed, both in the moor itself and in the upper reaches of the Mawgan stream which rises on the northern flank of Castle-an-Dinas. Two such lodes were referred to in Carnsewe's notes of c.1580: 'one in the north side of Castell Dennyse and riche by Burchard's [Burchard Kranick] report' and 'one other great loade before John Merefields doure' [door].

The Merefields were an ancient St Columb family whose place of residence in 1623 was Halveor (Great Moor), a name which suggests it was on Goss Moor. From this one may assume that the 'greate lode' before their door was the well-known stanniferous elvan which has been worked sporadically from the southern foot of Castle-an-Dinas for a distance of two miles to the east. (However, Halveor is situated to the west of St Columb Major and has no mining history, neither does it overlook Goss Moor. As such, the Merefields' home may have overlooked the Goss Moor but it was certainly not from Halveor. It is worth noting that the Merefields' home was not the Castle-an-Dinas manor-house, a monstrosity built in 1860 for the American Consul in Falmouth.)

The position of the other lode mentioned by Carnsewe is more conjectural. The Castle-an-Dinas wolfram lode is generally regarded as a late discovery, first developed as a mine in 1916. No record exists of any other mines nearby apart from Royalton iron mine.

On Goss Moor a poorer band of tin lay nearer the surface of the ground, resting on what the tinners called a 'false floor' with the profitable tin lying on the valley floor. Any stream coming off the granite and coursing lodes will pick up cassiterite, while shallow basins such as the Goss and Tregoss Moors were rich in much of their extent with coarse cassiterite.

In 1780 the Revd John Swete described a small working that employed about a dozen men somewhere on Goss Moor.

Mines called Wheal Grose, Be Lovely, Fat Work and The Gilley were worked in a small way in 1777. The Goss Moor Mining Company was formed in 1817 to consolidate these rich tin mines. They were up to five fathoms deep and 100 fathoms in length in open-cast situations, but as a result of a 'great accession of water' one day which drowned a miner, the mines were abandoned. The locations of these mines is unclear, although Gilley and Be Lovely may have been in the Dyehouse and Belowda areas respectively.

A report in the *Mining Journal* of 7 November 1835, which quoted from the *West Briton*, read:

> *In 1835 two tin streamers both called Paddy working near the parsonage at Roche came across an enclosure of stones, inside they found a block of tin of peculiar shape, nearby lay several ancient coins, it is not known whether they were Roman or Mediaeval. They were sent to London for assessment but there is no known result.*

The two tinners opened up a barrow some 200 yards away where they unearthed several pickaxes and spearheads of brass. This report also states that 'the moor has been called from time immemorial Attal Surazin', which, according to Carew, means Jews Offcast. The deposits on the Goss and Tregoss Moors

Old Mining Sites

Tin Streaming:

1. *Goss Moor Stream Works (three sites)*
2. *British Tin Syndicate*
3. *Water Meet Tin Pits*
4. *West Pendine Stream Works (two sites)*
5. *Upper Fal Tin Pits*
6. *Pendine Stream Works*
7. *Tregoss Stream Works*
8. *Tregoss Stream Tin Mining Co.*
9. *Hal Dhu Stream Works*
10. *Dye House Stream Works*

Opencast Tin Mining:

11. *Hopewell*
12. *Gazen*
13. *Britton*
14. *Rock Work*
15. *Lower Three Johns*
16. *Chance*
17. *True and Honest*
18. *Marsh Work*
19. *Fair Play*
20. *Gun Deep*
21. *Quibble*
22. *Bold Venture*
23. *Green Banks*
24. *Starye Harry*
25. *Good Luck*

Underground Copper Mining:

26. *Wheal Penrose*

lay in a marshy tract (the name Goss is local dialect for the phragmites reed).

The stream deposits around Wheal Gasson are typical of Goss Moor. The overburden (rock that must be removed prior to mining the mineral deposit beneath it) was described by Collins as consisting of clay, sand, gravel and stent. The tin ground varied in thickness and rested on an irregular surface of bedrock. Much of the best tin lay in pits or pockets within the bedrock, perhaps 9m deep, and it was the tinners' custom to search for these.

A report by Henwood in 1873 states that 40–50 years previously Tregoss Moor exhibited an almost countless succession of low stoney hillocks and deep weedy pools, the abandoned scenes of earlier operations. Amongst them many small tin-stream works were run by speculative workmen, either on ancient unworked deposits or on matter imperfectly gleamed by their predecessors. The works were drained by deep open cuttings or by water-wheels. Drainage would have caused a problem in earlier times, as did the lack of water in the summer. These problems, coupled with the need for cheap removal of overburden, brought all such operations to a close by 1880.

Tin streaming on the Goss and Tregoss Moors was actively carried out on a large scale during the early part of the nineteenth century with a few areas surviving until the 1880s, notably at Golden Stream and Wet and Dry near the base of Castle-an-Dinas.

One of the last areas to be worked was a site north-east of the railway girder bridge over the A30, which was worked by two men called William Tellam and John Moss during the 1870s and '80s. The last known tinner there was a Jim Tellam.

Dredging For Tin

The Goss Moor Alluvial Syndicate was founded in 1907, when the moor was evaluated on its prospects for tin recovery. The company was founded by Collins, a mining engineer, and his associates to work an area around the Great Gasson (Gazen) pool near St Dennis.

Overburden at this site was at an average of 30ft in depth with a return of 3lbs of tin per ton, a better return than expected. However, in September 1909 this company was taken over by Goss Moor Ltd which had its registered office in London with a capital of 60,000 £1 shares and five directors, Messrs Collins, Storey, Burnard, Lush and Field.

The company ordered a Tasmanian type suction dredge (also referred to as 'Australian'), which was delivered and commissioned in May 1910. It had three Crossley gas engines which powered a 40psi pressure monitor, a 12ins gravel suction pump and lighting for night work. The raw material was pressure washed from the bank face then pumped into sluice boxes to separate the tin from the residue. This dredge was very similar to the Alfa dredge which worked on Breney Common.

It is estimated that 16.5 tons of tin were produced per month – not enough to provide a profit. In the later part of 1910 moves were made to reduce production costs by converting to steam power. However, this did not improve the financial situation and the company continued to operate at a loss. The firm was re-formed in 1911 as Goss Moor Tin Alluvial Ltd. The new company had J.H. Collins, C.G. Lush and O. Wethered as directors with capital of £75,000 (300,000 shares of 5s. each).

On 17 August 1911 the *Cornish Post* and *Mining News* both reported that:

> *A meeting was held in a bungalow on or near the moor, the location of which has never been established, apart from the directors there were others present who were introduced to a new production concept by way of a steam powered plant positioned on a pontoon which would operate as a kind of dredge to recover tin from the moor. Two 250 hp engines would drive a pressure pump, a suction pump, and sixteen head of stamps for crushing. The steam plant was supplied by Messrs Marshall, Son and Co. Ltd, of Manchester and the whole plant was designed by Mr Frank Lush.*

There was much optimism regarding future tin production and financial success. Indeed, during October 1911, after 26 days of working, it was recorded that nine tons of black tin had been recovered. The plant could deal with 70 tons of material per hour but with operating costs still excessive the company was not yet profitable. Further modifications were made to the plant in 1913 including the installation of a Victoria hydraulic pump.

With the company still not in profit operations were stopped in September 1914. It was finally struck off the register in 1922.

Mining interest resumed in 1924 with the formation of the British Alluvial Tin Syndicate who obtained licences from Lord Falmouth to work the Goss and Tregoss Moors including areas near Royalton and Belowda. By the end of 1925 a new tin dredger had been assembled, launched and equipped at a site on the western side of the moor. For the launch, which took place at a pool now known as 'Tin Mine', many people came to witness the memorable event. The commissioning was carried out by Mrs Clark, the wife of the chairman of the board. The pontoon and plant was built by a Mr Werf Conrad and was named Number One. It was said to have weighed 200 tons.

This was the first time that this type of dredger had been used for the recovery of tin. It had 40 buckets on its dredge belt which could work to a depth of 20ft. The complete plant was powered by four engines, two to power the recovery and processing, one to work the generator and one to serve as a reserve. During the three years of this tin-dredging operation, which worked the western side of the moor, the plant had a resident engineer from St Dennis called Will Soloman.

There were a few incidents involving the operators – including one fatal when an Irishman drowned. His body is buried in the church graveyard in St Dennis.

Records show that this dredging for tin operation which commenced in 1925 ceased after three years. The pontoon and plant, which originally cost £15,000, was broken up and sold for scrap.

It appears that none of the large-scale dredging operations were financially successful and it was the small streaming and mining operations that made the profits.

Underground Mining

The Wheal Gasson Mine, situated on the moor near the Penrose Veor smallholding, was started in 1846. Collins states that small quantities of very rich copper ore were obtained from the mine, on which a small engine with a stamping (crushing) mill was erected. The remains of the engine house can still be seen in 2004, adjacent to the old Gothers tramway trackbed.

This mine was also known as Gorgan, Penrose and possibly Wheal Alfred James. Penrose was a copper mine on the Goss Moor alluvial tract half a mile north-west of the church in St Dennis. The name Penrose was taken from the property on which it stood.

According to Collins the mine was sunk a short way into the killas (a Cornish term meaning the greenstone that was created during the formation of the region, some 400 million years ago) underlying the alluvials and raised small quantities of rich chalcocite (copper) ore.

Wheal Alfred James, adjoining the base of the Carne Hill of St Dennis, was a short-lived adventure. The sett was granted in February 1862 and was reported to contain four tin lodes and one of copper. Two of the tin lodes intersected at 10 and 20 fathoms and proved payable, even in the broken and unsettled ground at that depth.

As the mine was equipped with a 40ins cylinder pumping engine and a 30ins rotary stamps engine, it was considered advisable to sink the shaft another 20 fathoms. As funds were not immediately available for this purpose, it was decided to transfer the property to another company in which many of the former adventurers (investors) expressed a willingness to take shares. The project, however, seems to have failed, and in 1872 Spargo refers to the mine as being idle for seven years, and only being worked for a short time (1862–65).

It is well known locally that the copper lode in the vicinity of the mine still attracts lightning during a storm, often with spectacular results.

In 1965, the ruins of the old engine house had become unsafe after over 100 years of exposure to the elements with no maintenance. The ruins were made safe by engineers of the Goonvean China Clay Co., who used explosives to complete their task. The engineers were Basil Coad, 'Stachie' Grigg and Roy Julian – all local men. As there was no electricity supply in the vicinity of the old ruins, power needed for the drilling of the holes to hold the explosive charges was provided by a compressor mounted on a Massey Ferguson tractor belonging to Rex Davey, a local contractor. At that time Goss Moor and the Goonvean China Clay Co. were part of the Tregothnan estate, as they remain at the time of writing.

Right: *The tunnel which brought the tramway from street level down to the harbour. The GWR metal-bodied wagon with a wooden chassis, No. 31076, is loaded with coal for use in the production of china clay, etc. The engineering materials were carried in the other wagon. The lower entrance of the tunnel can still be seen today; after serving for several years as part of an aquarium, it is now used as a boat store.* KHR/Coll

Left: *A rake of five empty wagons being pulled by horses to the Newquay Station terminus passing a site which in later years became the bus station.* KHR/Coll

Above: *The 96-yard-long inclined tunnel had steam-powered winches to lower and raise the wagons.* KHR/Coll

Above: *Originally the infamous girder railway bridge over the A30 on Goss Moor was constructed of wood. In 1930 this structure was replaced by iron girders. Here we see the two giant steam cranes being used to position the new girders, watched by some locals from Roche.* M. Dart Collection

Left: *The loading of china clay from tramway wagons onto schooners at Newquay harbour was carried out manually, as this picture shows. The vessel shown here is the* Mary Wrighton. KHR/Coll

Chapter 14

Treffry's Tramway

Treffry's Tramway reached the Newquay harbour via a tunnelled incline. The harbour's central pier was accessed by a wooden trestle-like bridge which was constructed by the Cornwall Minerals Railway in 1872. The rail tracks on the right-hand arm of the harbour were built in 1845 as the final part of the tramway linking St Dennis and East Wheal Rose with the harbour. This picture was taken in 1890. KHR/Coll

In c.1838 Mr J.A. Treffry of Fowey purchased Newquay harbour from the executors of a gentleman called Richard Lomax. He also purchased china-clay and china-stone works near St Dennis the same year. Treffry had plans to link the two by a standard-gauge horse-drawn tramway which would pass over two and a half miles of Goss Moor.

The 12-mile long tramway was very complex and took six years to complete (1844–50). Apart from embankments and cuttings, there were road crossings at Bodmin Road Junction, Halloon, Quintrell Downs, Trencreek and three in Newquay. There were also tunnels at Toldish (the largest at 530 yards long and 8ft–8ft 6ins high – it took over two years to build), Coswarth (44 yards long, built in 1849) and Newquay harbour (96 yards long, 14ft 6ins wide, 17ft high and with gradients of 1 in 4 and 1 in 6), a 147-yard-long viaduct with 18 wooden arches, each with a span of 25ft and based on granite pillars, over the narrowest part of the Trenance Valley, plus loading wharves at Hendra Prazey and sidings at Halloon and Newquay. Most of the construction work was carried out by Irish labourers with the exception of the Newquay harbour tunnel, which was built in 1844 by a contractor and miners from St Dennis. In December 1849 Treffry laid the last brick in the Toldish tunnel, this was also to prove his last contribution to the tramway as he died of pneumonia in January 1850. The tunnel enabled wagons to gain access to the loading and unloading quays on the harbour; they were let down and hauled up by a steam-powered winch housed at the top of the incline.

The Hoytes family ran a Newquay-based carrier company with stables near the harbour tunnel entrance and sidings. The firm had the sole contract to haul the wagons to and from the terminus at Cliff Road and the sidings at the top of the harbour tunnel incline. The Hoytes were also responsible for operating the points. Loaded wagons were moved through the town one at a time and the empty wagons in rakes of five or six.

In J.A. Treffry's will his entire estate was left to the Revd Willcocks, who had been a chaplain on the Scilly Isles. However, there was a condition – that he adopt the name of Treffry. Willcocks did so; he became known as the Revd Treffry.

The St Dennis–Newquay tramway was officially opened on 1 May 1857 with two of the newly acquired trucks, each drawn by a single horse carrying the dignitaries. The Revd Treffry, his son and two other trustees, Messrs Head and Lambert, were in one truck, and in the second was the Revd Childs, rector of St Dennis, and a Mr Ellery of St Dennis Consuls and China Clay Company, a prospective customer. When the procession arrived in Newquay it was met by the St Dennis Band playing a march, the firing of cannons and with the streets decorated with flags and bunting.

For many years after its opening the tramway carried china clay and stone, the produce of local clay works and quarries, to Newquay harbour for shipping to buyers on a daily basis.

One prominent haulier from St Dennis called Thomas Varcoe provided horses and drivers for the tramways. It was normal practice for a single horse to pull one truck loaded with seven tons of clay or stone. The carrier at St Dennis would hire horses from various local farmers as required to work the tramway. A blacksmith's shop at Lower Bodella was kept busy every evening, and sometimes at night, shoeing horses in preparation for the following day's work. There was a steep gradient on Polywin Hill which needed additional horsepower to climb. This was achieved by stationing additional horses at the bottom of the hill to assist with the climb.

As the line was horse drawn, with very little speed involved, accidents were rare. However, a local paper reported in May 1872 that:

> *... last Saturday a 14-year-old boy, the son of the carrier, Mr T. Varcoe of St Dennis, while driving a horse-drawn truck loaded with seven tons of china clay, alighted from the truck to lead the horse through the Toldish tunnel, when getting back on the shafts, slipped and fell which resulted in a wheel passing over his leg above the ankle. The boy's brother coming along behind with another horse and truck heard his brother's screams then hastened to St Columb for assistance from Messrs Norman and Fowler, surgeons.*

A narrow-gauge tramway was laid in 1853 from Hendra Prazey, St Dennis, on an incline to Treffry's clay works on Hendra Hill. It had gradients of 1 in 9 and 1 in 20 and was worked by a steam engine which operated a winch drum with a wire rope to pull up and let down the small wagons. A dispute between Treffry and engine owners Edward Stocker and William Best of St Blazey Foundry, settled by the High Court, resulted in Stocker and Best being made responsible for the narrow-gauge tramway's working and Treffry being responsible for supplying the cable and keeping the winding drum in good condition.

This tramway was first used in 1857 to carry china clay and stone from Hendra Hill to the loading wharf at Hendra Prazey, where it was transferred into the horse-drawn wagons of Treffry's Tramway for transporting to the harbour at Newquay. A stone slab bridge at the bottom of the old inclined tramway can still be seen.

In 1871 a gentleman called William R. Roebuck set up a company called the Cornwall Minerals and Harbour Railway Ltd, with the objective being to improve Treffry's Tramway system. An agreement was reached in 1872 for Cornwall Minerals Railway, as it was by this time known, to lease all Treffry's Tramways. In 1872 an Act of Parliament specified the building of, among others, new lines from Bugle–Bodmin Road Junction and Bodmin Road Junction–Retew.

The Cornwall Minerals Railway's objective of improving the tramways included introducing steam-powered locomotives and new services. The project involved building and improving embankments and the trackbed, installing new rails and signalling systems, strengthening the Trenance viaduct, building bridges at Bugle, Victoria, Holywell, the Goss Moor (3), Bodmin Road Junction, Halloon and Whitecross, and bypassing the Toldish tunnel, which was not high enough to allow locomotives to pass through. This was carried out from 1872–74, as was the building of a terminus at Newquay, including a turntable, building platforms at halts and the appointment of stationmasters and crossing keepers. A new stone jetty was built in 1872 to increase the harbour's loading capacity and in the same year the railway was extended to Parkandillick and the branch to Retew was started. By 1874 sidings had been laid at Newquay, Quintrell Downs, Halloon and Bodmin Road Junction, and bridges at St Dennis and Domellick had been enlarged. Most of the new bridges were built of stone except those at Whitecross, Halloon and Goss Moor, which required the inclusion of girders.

However, there was a delay in the building of these bridges in 1874 and records show that the girder bridge over the A30 on Goss Moor was originally made of wood, which was replaced by girders in 1931. Over half a century later, this bridge is still known by locals as 'girder bridge'. The bridge carrying the A30 at Bodmin Road Junction, renamed St Dennis Junction in 1878, replaced the original road crossing. At Halloon, later renamed St Columb Road, the new bridge replaced the old road crossing with the A39 road being lowered to pass under it. The level crossings at Quintrell Downs and Trencreek are still in use.

The new Bugle–Newquay track which crossed over part of Goss Moor was officially passed for use by a Government inspector on 20 June 1874. The first locomotive to traverse the new line was a light steam engine on 7 April 1874, and the first passenger train made up of six open wagons ran on 1 May 1874. The first passenger train with real coaches ran on 26 June 1874 and was witnessed by cheering crowds at every vantage point. This service ran twice a day, seven days a week, which raised objections from the Indian Queens Methodists and others about the Sunday trains; they were eventually stopped in 1877.

To operate the new system 18 new steam-powered 30-ton 0-6-0 side-tank locomotives were purchased from Sharp, Steward Co. of Manchester, second-hand coaches were purchased from the Midland Railway and over 500 mineral wagons and 12 brake vans were purchased from unknown sources.

In 1877 the Great Western Railway reached an agreement with Cornwall Minerals Railway to operate their system and to pay the CMR a fixed sum of money annually for the privilege.

As the tramway from the Newquay terminus to the harbour incline was not up to the standard required to obtain a Board of Trade certificate to allow locomotives to use it, the hauling of full and empty wagons still had to be carried out by horses.

One relevant action required was for the GWR to return CMR locomotives and rolling stock to manufacturers, in order to pay off CMR debts. GWR practices were gradually introduced and improvements made. Integration with other GWR rail systems and rolling-stock followed. This arrangement continued for 19 years until 1896 when another agreement was reached for the GWR to purchase the CMR system outright, with the exception of the Newquay harbour tramway and the Hendra Hill incline.

Passenger and goods traffic steadily increased with Newquay harbour playing its part in the shipping out of minerals and the shipping in of coal and other goods. However, the decline in seaborne traffic at Newquay harbour started in 1914 and continued until it virtually ceased when the terminus to the harbour tramway was closed in 1926. Horses were last worked on the actual harbour in 1922.

The Par–Newquay branch proved increasingly successful in the 1920s when passenger traffic and the 'shipping' of china clay and stone continued to expand, although it took place at Fowey and Par Docks. In 1931 the tramway from Newquay Station to the harbour was conveyed to the GWR. The engine house and winch-house area was purchased by Newquay Town Council from the British Transport Commission in 1953 and later demolished. Today the site is part of a supermarket complex. The tunnel has been partially filled in with the lower part being used as an aquarium.

A passenger train at Newquay waiting to depart for Par in 1920. **M. Dart**

Above: *A Metro 2-4-0 tank engine with a passenger train from Par, 1920.* M. Dart

Left: *Rolling-stock used by the GWR between Par and Newquay in 1920.* M. Dart

Newquay Station, 1920. **M. Dart**

Above: *This rare and excellent photograph shows the old Pochin's Tramway loading wharf and lengthmen's cabin on the St Dennis mineral branch line, 1960.* M. Cole

Above: *Pochin's Wharf in reasonable condition in April 2003.* KHR

Above: *The shutes used to unload coal from GWR wagons into tramway wagons after they had been emptied of china clay, 2003.* KHR

Above: *A train of loaded wagons leaves the Higher Gothers Clay Dries.* J.C.R. Key

Above: *One of Pochin's 'Puffing Billies' with wagons loaded with bags of china clay about to leave Gothers Clay Dries for the journey to the GWR branch loading wharf.* KHR/Coll

The Gothers clay-drying complex of seven separate drying units, 1920s. **H.D. Pochin**

Chapter 15

Pochin's Tramway

In 1879 H.D. Pochin, who owned the clay works of Lower and Higher Gothers and Wheal Frederick, was aware of the benefits of rail transport which could carry coal and timber to, and china clay from, his clay works. This resulted in the construction of a 3ft 1ins-gauge tramway from Gothers to a siding and loading wharf near Domellick on the Cornwall Minerals Railway branch line that ran from St Dennis to Newquay. The tramway replaced the original system of shipping clay by horses and wagons to the sidings at Drinnick and Whitegate, St Dennis.

The tramway was just over two miles long, travelling over the south-west edge of Goss Moor then climbing to the Gothers village and works area. Construction took a few months, with timber sleepers coming from broken-up naval warships at Devonport, and materials for the trackbed and embankment construction coming from the clay works.

Initially horse-drawn wagons were used, but the horses were soon replaced by two second-hand 0-4-0 saddle-tank steam locomotives. During the course of the tramway's working life four locomotives were known to have been used; their names were 'Dinah', 'Crockfoot', 'Greenfold' and 'Brooke'. Greenfold was a Hunslet-type locomotive built in 1922 and numbered 1423. These small locomotives, which had the nickname of 'Pochin's Puffing Billies', were only capable of pulling six trucks, each carrying three tons of clay to the wharf, and only four trucks of three tons of coal on the return journey to Gothers because of the gradient. Crockfoot and Dinah were the first two locomotives to be used, with only one working at a time, while the other stood by in case of a breakdown and to cover for maintenance and repairs. Crockfoot was the favourite with the drivers because it was the most powerful, but it was also the first to become unserviceable for track work. When this occurred the old loco was installed as static power to operate the pump which pumped water from the dries back to the Gothers pit reservoir. Eventually electric pumps were used for this task and the old loco was used to raise steam for the pickling of timber for use in the Gothers complex.

Driving these old locomotives was not very easy. On wet days, or mornings with heavy dew, the locos would slip and slide on the gradients, so keeping them under control was a tricky job. With only one truck at the rear of each train having brakes, there were times when this was not enough to assist in controlling the train when going down a gradient. It was then that the home-made emergency braking system would be brought into use. This consisted of using a 3ft length of old rail to jam through the spokes of a truck's wheels – this stopped them from turning.

There was a locomotives' shed and workshop at Gothers where the locomotives and wagons were maintained and repaired. In 1920 Pochin built a branch line from the tramway to a nearby mica works owned by C. & J. Varcoe. This line crossed the Gothers road with the crossing being manned by an elderly gentleman whose job it was to ensure that nothing or no one obstructed it. There was also a crossing on the St Dennis road which had gates on it, which were manned by a young man who had the luxury of his own 'cuddy' (hut) for protection from the elements; inside he also had his own 'crib'.

The tramway, which served six of Pochin's clay dries and one mica kiln owned by C. & J. Varcoe, had, for 52 years, transported china clay to Pochin's wharf for shipment to Melangoose Mill for milling and to Newquay and Fowey for shipping to buyers. It finally closed in 1931 as a result of the general decline in the demand for china clay.

The track groundwork and loading wharf, which is still known as Pochin's Wharf (although some people's memories have highlighted the fact that the wharf siding was also known as Melangoose Siding), are still much in evidence today, as are the St Dennis road crossing gateposts and part of the engine house near the entrance to the Gothers experimental works. In the early days of the tramway clay was transported from Gothers via the wharf to Melangoose Mill in the Fal Valley. This may be why the name Melangoose was also associated with the siding.

The number of persons who were normally employed on the tramway operation were: six loaders at Gothers, three loaders at the wharf, three linesmen maintaining the track, two crossing keepers, an engineer who maintained the rolling-stock, a guard, and a locomotive driver. Known employees were: Bill Gill and William Liddicoat, locomotive drivers, Russell Kessell, shunter/guard, John Kendal, Mr

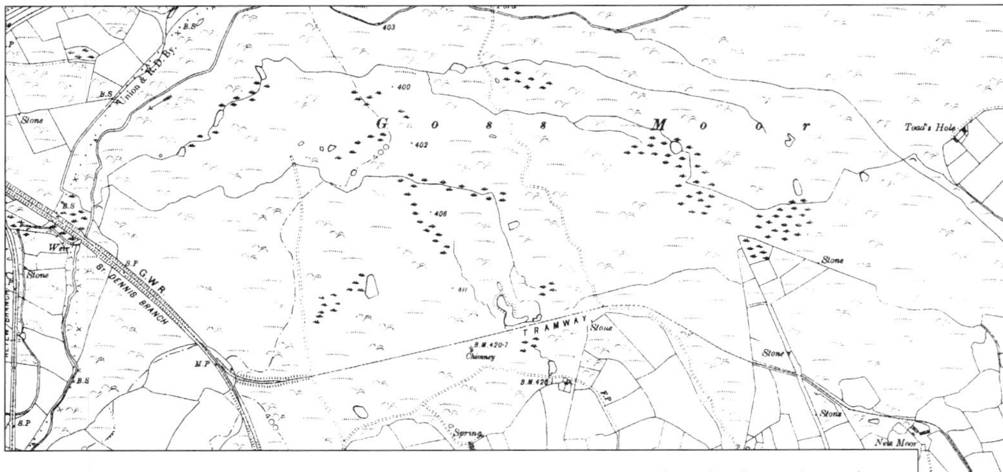

Left: *A 1908 map showing Pochin's Tramway. Reproduced from the 1908 Ordnance Survey Map.*

Minnear, Billy Best and Mr Soloman, track gangers.

In around 1920 a young manager from Manchester, Frank Grime, joined the Pochin team. He became a popular figure with the St Dennis football team and with a local concert party. Along with his motorcycle Frank was a well-known sight in the locality. In the 1950s he joined ECLP & Co. Ltd as an engineer and eventually went on to become a director.

Once a year during the St Dennis Feast Week, when the Fowey Harriers would meet at Trelavour Square then proceed to Goss Moor to hunt for hares, a gala day would be held at the Pochin's Wharf siding where people would congregate to watch the hunting; the wharf provided a suitable elevation for a panoramic view across the moor. As part of the festivities, children were given rides on the tramway train to and from Enniscaven.

Varcoe's Mica Clay Dry at Gothers

In 1869 Cornelius Varcoe (1834–1913) was persuaded by his grandfather, Captain James Best of Nanpean, to set up workings to catch and wash the mica cleanings flowing away from the Pochin's clay dries at Gothers. This he did and started his workings in 1870. The liquid clay cleanings were purified and held in a settling pit before being pumped into drying pans made of sand. The pump was made from a young elm tree bored out by a manually operated auger.

Isaac Grigg, a carpenter from Menna, St Dennis, made wooden launders to convey the liquid clay. He may have also made the elm pump. This method was in general practice at that time – in fact the 1838 Tithe Book of St Stephen-in-Brannel listed certain enclosures of land as clay pans. With fine and dry weather the clay would solidify in the pans and crack, which would facilitate its removal by hand.

John Varcoe (1866–1931) of St Dennis, a haulier, carried dried clay by horse and cart with a donkey in the pulling chains, to the Drinnick Mill railway sidings at Nanpean where 'Nellie' Varcoe had a storage shed. Martin Snell of Whitemoor was employed to load the clay from the shed into trucks. In about 1920 Tom Crabbe, a GWR shunter at Drinnick Mill, lost a leg in an accident involving some trucks carrying Varcoe's clay.

Mr Pochin would sometimes meet Mr Varcoe in the dark coal shed of No. 3 clay dry to agree terms for the purchase of mica dried clay. In reality he was buying his own waste. In later years Cornelius Varcoe had a drying kiln built, complete with a stack, by Jim Yelland of Rees Hill, Roche.

Some time before 1908 some mica clay was hauled to railway sidings at Whitegate, St Dennis. Also in 1908 Mr Varcoe's two sons, John and Charles, succeeded him in the business. By this time most of the mica clay was taken to Newquay harbour by railway, and was sent by coasting vessels to Runcorn, Warren Point and Bristol. A well-remembered vessel was the *Katie* which would carry 150 tons of Varcoe's clay.

The family business experienced fair trade until 1929 when the lease expired and it had to close down.

The St Dennis farmers listed below supplemented their income by using their horses and wagons to carry for Varcoe's and other clay-work owners such as C. & J. Varcoe, John Hayle and Messrs Beale, J.Y. Crowle & Sons, A.W. Varcoe & Sons, J.D. Thomas, Fred Stephens, James Brokenshire & Son, Dan Bunt & Son, T.J. Angilley and Almond Stephens. They brought back coal, tiles and bricks for the clay dries.

Bottom: *Pochin's Tramway track across Goss Moor with the ruins of the Wheal Penrose engine house nearby and Wheal Remfry clay works in the background, 1910.* KHR/Coll

Chapter 16

St Dennis GWR Junction and the Waste Tip

The St Dennis Junction was and still is positioned in the south-western corner of Goss Moor and was first used in 1849 as a crossing over the A30 by Treffry's Tramway, which ran from St Dennis to the harbour at Newquay. The crossing at that time was called Bodmin Road Junction.

When the Cornwall Minerals Railway took over Treffry's Tramway in 1872, steam locomotives were introduced, the track was extended to Bugle, a road bridge was built over the railway, and the name was changed to St Dennis Junction.

The Great Western Railway took over from the Cornwall Minerals Railway in 1896 and then introduced their own working practices and rolling-stock. The St Dennis branch was extended to Drinnick Mill in 1874, the same year as the Retew branch was built, which was extended to Meledor Mill in 1912. Both these branches served 14 separate china-clay and china-stone sidings.

The first through passenger train from Paddington to Newquay passed through the Junction in May 1906.

To accommodate the increase in traffic and to enable efficient and safer work to take place, the track from Tregoss level crossing to St Dennis Junction was doubled for about two miles in 1921 to form a passing loop. To assist with the signalling and control of the loop a signal-box was built at Tregoss which remained in use until it ceased operating as such in 1965. However, it continued with ground-frame (unmanned) signal-box status until 25 May 1973 when it was finally closed. Pochin's Tramway and loading wharf on the St Dennis branch which opened in 1879 ceased working in 1931.

During the later 1930s the increase in mineral and passenger traffic made the junction an important part of the GWR system, and although it was called a junction, it was also a marshalling yard.

It had a signal-box, two water columns, three large water-storage tanks, one of which was below ground and fed by springs, a shunters' cabin, a coal compound, an oil store, a pump house, a small wooden platform on the main 'up' line, one ground-frame hut, two lengthmen's huts, a double track throughout, four sidings, two waste-tip sidings, and a very complex points system. The configuration of the track layout was designed to enable various shunting manoeuvres to be carried out.

The sidings on the tip were not stable enough for engines to fully traverse them and shunting was carried out by using a rake of wagons in front of the engine. This was not perfect as there were occasions when wagons were pushed over the end stop block and had to be recovered from the embankment. There were only one or two occasions when recovery was not possible.

Shunting the long mineral trains always involved the use of the main Par–Newquay branch line and had to be carried out as and when the track was available between passing passenger traffic. Incoming empty clay wagons and loaded goods and coal wagons were marshalled at the junction into delivery order prior to despatch, as was the loaded china-clay and china-stone wagons and empty wagons brought back from the clay branches and other stations. The latter were all assembled as a train ready for despatch to St Blazey, Par, Fowey and destinations further afield.

Normally the train would be hauled by two engines but there were many occasions when excessive tonnage was brought back from the clay branches. This was left in sidings until the next day when an additional train would be organised to move it.

Engines had their tonnage limits for level and normal gradients, but the steep gradient on the Goss Moor embankment reduced these limits considerably. This resulted in most mineral trains requiring two engines to haul them. Any engine assisting at the rear of a train was called a 'banker'. The Goss Moor embankment gradient was so severe that trains of empty clay wagons had to stop before descending to enable guards to apply the brakes of a certain number of wagons to assist the engine in controlling

Left: *A view of the western side of the St Dennis Junction, seen in 1922, shows the old wooden signals, a water-tower on stone piers housing a water column, a short access platform which also contains an underground water-supply, a pump house and an inspection pit.* KHR

Right: *A general view of St Dennis Junction in 1947, including the waste-tip sidings.* KHR/Coll

Left: *A 'Grange' class 4-6-0, No. 6809 'Burghelere Grange' leaves Goss Moor on 8 July 1955 on its journey from Newquay to Par.* R.C. Riley

Above: *Having operated for 39 years, the Tregoss signal-box was closed as such in 1965 when the double-track length to St Dennis Junction was lifted.* KHR/Coll

Left: *A 2002 photograph, taken from the same spot as the top photograph, captures the level of decline which has overtaken the once-busy junction.* KHR

The top six pictures record what used to be an everyday occurrence at the junction – the afternoon mineral train, made up of loaded wagons brought back from the Drinnick and Retew Mineral branches, being prepared for and starting the home run to St Blazey on 11 July 1955. The Prairie-tank engine, a 2-6-2 '4500' class No. 4526 coupled to the guard's van will act as a banker while the Pannier-tank engine, a 0-6-0 '5700' class No. 3635, will head the train. One scene is of the assembled train waiting for the main branch to be cleared of a passing Par–Newquay five-coach passenger train headed by a Hall-class engine, No. 5969. The bottom two scenes show the 'pinning down' procedure being applied before a train of empty clay wagons descends the girder bridge gradient, and its arrival at St Dennis Junction.

A Prairie-tank '4575' class 2-6-2, engine No. 5557, heads a Newquay passenger train just entering the Goss Moor near Roche. Weatherill Photomatic

Right: *This is an interesting scene from June 1958, taken at St Dennis Junction and showing a Pannier tank 0-6-0, No. 9755, standing by while a Par to Newquay passenger train passes through on the main branch. The oil and lamp store on the left, the signal-box and shunters' cabin are seen from an unusual angle.* Norman Simmonds

This picture: *Pannier tank, No. 8719, shunting its china-clay load at St Dennis Junction on 15 August 1960.* M. Cole

Inset: *Pannier tank 0-6-0, No. 8719, passing the Retew level crossing on 15 August 1960. The then Heavy Transport lorry was being driven by a local man, Mr Jim Pinch.* M. Cole

Below: *'Cardigan Castle' No. 4087 passing through St Dennis Junction on its way to Newquay on 24 April 1961.* M. Cole

On 21 June 1962 a Diesel Multiple Unit (DMU) approaches the junction, after travelling from Newquay, and is just about to pass one of the redundant water tanks. **R.C. Riley**

Right: *The same DMU passing through on the 'up' line on the same day. The junction, the waste tip and the junction track layout can be seen.* R.C. Riley

Left: *A busy scene on 20 September 1979 at the junction. Locomotive No. 50030, 'Repulse', is heading for Newquay from Paddington. It is starting to move off after waiting for a class 120 DMU No. 557 to pass through on the 'up' line from Newquay.* John Vaughan

Right: *Locomotive 37411 propelling its load of CDA clay wagons to a siding for de-scaling on 24 December 1991. The aggregate and ready-mixed concrete plant can also be seen.*

the train during the descent; this practice was called 'pinning down'.

The normal daily work programme included up to eight passenger trains travelling through in each direction, with the earliest starting at 5a.m. It brought in the daily newspapers to each station on the Par–Newquay branch. Obviously the summer season was the busiest with through trains from Paddington and Liverpool consisting of 15 coaches being regular on Saturdays. Normal services and main-line connections to and from Par operated all year round.

The movement and shunting of goods and minerals accounted for most of the junction's daily workload. All this kept the junction busy from 8a.m. to 5.30p.m. each day. Whereas china clay proved to be by far the highest mineral tonnage handled at the junction, coal (being a major fuel in those days) was the second highest.

The permanent workforce consisted of two signalmen and two shunters, who worked a two-shift system for six days a week, and 15 lengthmen who worked a day shift, five-and-a-half days per week in gangs of five each with a 'ganger'. Each gang was responsible for the everyday maintenance of its own length of track. The main branch line length was from Tregoss level crossing to the Kelliers bridge, the St Dennis branch length was from the junction to Drinnick Mill Station and the Retew branch length was from the junction to Meledor Mill.

Major track repairs and improvements were carried out by specialised gangs based at St Blazey and Plymouth, usually on Sundays when there was little or no traffic. On the main branch line it was the ganger's or his deputy's duty to walk the length every day to replace loose keys and tighten loose fish-plate bolts. Keys were small blocks of hardwood that held the rail in the metal chair bolted to the wooden sleeper, and fish-plates were pieces of metal used for holding the ends of rails together.

An inspector was responsible for the whole Par–Newquay branch and he would visit each gang on a regular basis. The lengthmen had certain times to complete various duties, such as weeding the track, cutting grass and undergrowth, and cleaning drains, etc. The inspector would check to see if the times were being adhered to.

The main branch line gang had a lengthmen's hut, or cabin, which was always kept clean and tidy and situated in an area opposite the signal-box. During the summer it was a colourful picture as it was virtually covered in rose bushes, as was the archway leading to it. Outside was a rotating circular wet stone used by the railwaymen to sharpen their axes, pruning hooks and other tools; it was also much appreciated and utilised by local people.

There were two other cabins on this length, one by the sand road crossing to the old block- and sandwork sites on the moor, and one by the entrance to the old Toldish tunnel. All these cabins were made entirely from old wooden railway sleepers except for the stone-and-brick fireplace and chimney. Available ground around these cabins and at the junction was planted with lupins, which soon became an integral part of the railway scene.

Two of the remaining railwaymen who had worked for the GWR at St Dennis Junction, Messrs Ken Hannaford (left) *and Bill Edyvean.* KHR

Some of the men employed by the GWR at St Dennis Junction from the mid-1930s onwards were: Arthur Ackford, Bert Alford, Ernie Barkwill, Ned Roberts and Jack Rundle (signalmen), Mr Burgess and Owen Lean (shunters), Percy Ackrell, Charlie Billing, Bill Common, 'Ces' Common, Percy Davies, Bill Edyvean, Art Greet, Phil Greet, Nip Grigg, Len Grose, Jack Hannaford, Ken Hannaford, Fred Laing, Ron Martin, Hedley Mundy, Alf Taper, Herbie Taylor, Bill Varcoe, Dick Webber, Ernie Wills and Harry Wooldridge (lengthmen), Mr Bassett, Tom Kent, Percy Martin and Mr Richards (gangers). Nip Grigg and Herbie Taylor later became gangers, as did Ken Hannaford who was also made inspector in 1977, a position he retained until he retired in 1981. An earlier inspector was Art Luke.

Apart from being employed as lengthmen, the following men lived in GWR level crossing gatehouses: Percy Ackrell at Gaverigan, Charlie Billing at Trerice, Hedley Mundy at St Dennis and Alf Taper at St Columb Road. While these men were at work their wives and other members of the family would operate the crossing gates.

The period 1940–43, when the building and development of our north coast military airfields was in progress, every weekday a goods train consisting of up to ten wagons loaded with Blue Circle cement would arrive at the junction in the afternoon. These wagons would be left in a siding while the engine collected and took away the previous day's emptied wagons for eventual return to the cement factories.

Every day at 5.30p.m. the junction's shunter engine would haul the loaded wagons to St Columb Road goods yard for unloading the following day. It would then return to the junction with the wagons emptied that day. The whole process would be repeated daily.

On one occasion during 1942 a train comprising an engine, a coach, a box van, an open wagon, and a flat-bed wagon with an anti-aircraft gun mounted on it, all painted in a green and black camouflage pattern, arrived at the junction. It was manned by soldiers and was positioned on a siding near the waste tip, and remained at the junction for about two weeks without being called into action.

Personal Reminiscences of K.H. Rickard

My experiences of the Great Western Railway started in 1936, when I lived at St Dennis Junction, and continued until 1948 when I moved to St Dennis after which I retained an interest from a distance. In my memories I have referred to the steam locomotives as engines as they were known in those days.

As a boy all my spare time was spent around the junction either playing or watching. The fascination of watching steam-powered engines shunting and moving around the yard from the A30 road bridge sometimes surrounded by steam, is something I will never forget.

To watch the daily working was always interesting. To have a train set was most boys' dream in those days, but to have a real situation on our own doorstep made my friends and I very lucky.

I had a hobby at one time of recording engine numbers. One day in 1999 my wife and I visited the Great Western Society's Didcot Railway Centre and we had the pleasure of riding on a small train hauled by steam engine No. 3738, a number I well remembered from my boyhood. This engine, all clean and shiny in its original colours, was in working order, despite starting its life probably in the 1930s, and working in the demanding Cornish mineral industry for many years. It was a tribute to the British engineering industry of that era.

During the Second World War china-clay production was reduced considerably, resulting in less mineral traffic. This was offset by the increase in goods and equipment traffic required for the building programme at the military airfields, the general goods traffic for other military services, and Blitz rubble for the tip.

The same applied to passenger trains; whereas local services were reduced, special troop trains to and from Newquay carrying men to training schools, and convalescent and rehabilitation centres took their place.

The mineral traffic started to increase as soon as the war ended in 1945 and reached its peak in the 1950s. Its demise started in 1960 and by 1966 the mineral branch to St Dennis was closed. The Retew branch was kept going until 1983 when it closed. The St Dennis Junction signal-box was closed in 1986.

British Rail replaced the GWR name in 1948 when the railways were nationalised. Steam locomotives were withdrawn in 1962 and were replaced with diesel-powered units.

In 2003 the junction is only a shadow of its former self with only a single track serving the Par–Newquay branch line, which passes under two road bridges (the additional bridge was built in 1995 to carry the Indian Queens bypass). All buildings and other facilities have been demolished and removed.

The tip is virtually overgrown with willow and gorse, with the old track and sidings area likely to follow suit in the very near future.

The Railway Waste Tip

This tip was situated on the south-west corner of Goss Moor and was started in 1896 when the Great Western Railway took over the Cornwall Minerals Railway's operations. It was originally used for the dumping of trackside maintenance and repair waste, soiled ballast, and the residue from emptied coal trucks.

The loaded wagons were unloaded manually by a gang of lengthmen at the St Dennis Junction marshalling yard complex. The tip gradually became wider and higher, and encroached onto the moor. This, however, was set to change.

During the Second World War, as a result of the extensive bombing of Plymouth by the German Luftwaffe in 1940–41, the rubble from the blitzed buildings had to be removed. A considerable percentage of this rubble was thus transported by rail to the St Dennis Junction tip for disposal. To cater for this there was an almost-daily flow of various types of full and empty wagons from and to Plymouth, and the tip became one of the largest and busiest of its kind in the GWR south-west region.

As the tip grew the original GWR boundary fences were buried and the unstable track proved too dangerous for the heavy steam locomotives to travel very far onto the siding. Shunting the full and empty wagons was achieved by using a 'rake' of wagons in front of the locomotive. Some wagons were pushed too far and ended up going over the stop blocks and down the tip embankment; their recovery depended on their final position.

The increase in tonnage to be unloaded had brought about a manpower problem which was beyond the capacity of the GWR. However, the utilisation of Italian prisoners of war from the POW camp at Whitecross solved the problem. Up to 20 POWs were transported by bus from Whitecross to St Dennis Junction daily (not Sundays). The lengthmen's hut near the Retew branch line junction was taken over as a canteen where they would cook their midday meal. More often than not these POWs came to work without a guard; when this occurred a senior rank of their own would supervise them while working under the control of a GWR ganger. These men, who were content in their captivity and resigned to a quiet life away from the war, soon settled into the daily routine and efficiently carried out their task.

The final working days of the signal-box in 1987. B. Cole

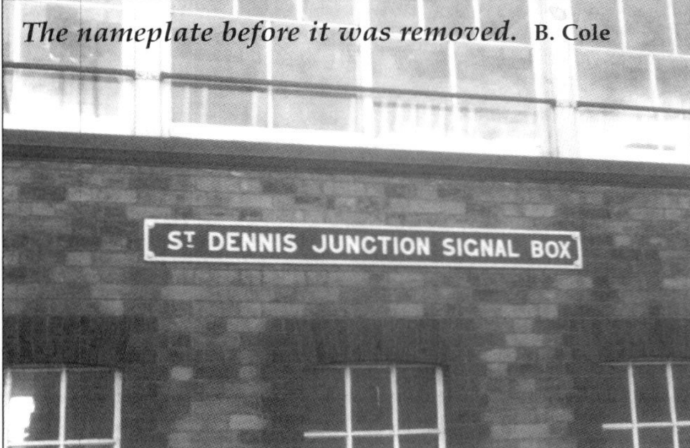

The nameplate before it was removed. B. Cole

The now-redundant signal-box being demolished in 1987. M. Cole

After completing their daily unloading, which would vary according to the number of wagons brought down from Plymouth, the POWs ventured onto the moor to cut small willow branches which they would use to construct baskets of various sizes to sell locally. This sort of article was in short supply during the war so it sold well and brought in cash for extra food and cigarettes. The POWs also utilised any brass and aluminium found during their unloading work to make various models and ashtrays.

During 1945 the tip started to smoulder, probably caused by internal combustion due to the variation of its contents. This, apart from making the surface very warm, also made it dangerous as it had the tendency to collapse unexpectedly under foot. Some men had very nasty experiences falling into little hollows when this occurred and had to be rescued by their workmates. One incident which could have had serious consequences was when a ganger supervising Italian POWs became trapped up to his chest. The POWs thought this was hilarious, not realising the danger he was in until a lengthman who was working nearby saw the ganger's predicament and quickly organised his rescue.

Another more natural problem was that the heat of the tip attracted various forms of wildlife, especially snakes; adders were the most prominent and, as they are venomous, the most dangerous. When the track was moved sideways as the tip grew, they were disturbed. To overcome their presence one of the lengthmen's gang would be appointed as the adder killer armed with a hefty stick. The most adders killed in one day, according to Bill Edyvean, an old railway lengthman, was 76.

In 1946 after the war had ended, the Italian POWs were repatriated to their own country and the Plymouth Blitz rubble disposed of at this site virtually ceased. The tip reverted back to its original use. By this time the site had expanded from its pre-1940s position some 250 yards into the moor and had a second siding on it. The GWR's use of the tip ceased in the 1960s when the Bristol Parkway tip proved more convenient for the region.

Local knowledge of the tip and its contents always attracted interest. In 1983 a small local firm called Shepherds Minerals obtained planning permission, mineral rights and an agreement with British Rail to work the tip and part of the moor for its recovery value.

The extraction of raw sand, etc., from the moor, at a site adjacent to the tip, was made difficult by the fact that it was a very wet area. The south-west corner of the moor is notoriously wet with numerous swamps and bogs. This condition is mainly brought about by the position of the tip and railway embankment which restricts natural drainage to the River Fal. An RB10 excavator with a drag-line was brought in to enable sand recovery from the moor to take place. One man who worked for Shepherds Minerals from day one on this site was Reg Crocker of St Dennis; he operated the drag-line. This activity stopped after a while when the sand proved to be of poor quality and the speed of recovery too slow.

It is worth recording that sand recovered from the moor contained two per cent tin, which was deemed at that time as not viable to pursue. The tip contents were excavated, washed, graded and screened. This produced small quantities of wood and metal, a reasonable quantity of coal, and a large quantity of sand and stone, all of which were sold locally. Whereas most materials recovered came from sources already mentioned, the coal content came from the practice of washing out empty railway coal wagons on the tip for many years. During 1986–87 several hundred tons of fine coal were purchased by the then-named ECCI Ltd, for use at their Central Power Station at Drinnick.

These top five photographs capture the building of the new A30 road bridge for the Indian Queens bypass from foundations to completion in 1994.
M. Cole/KHR

A 1996 photograph of the remaining track and the A30 road bridge. KHR

The junction's old trackbed area in 2002. KHR

A 2002 photograph of the remaining track and the A30 road bridge showing the area gradually being overtaken by nature. KHR

As the demand for aggregates increased, sand and stone was purchased from local china-clay companies and quarries to supplement site production. The production plant included classifiers, conveyors and a crusher. Mobile plants, including loaders, dumpers and a swing-shovel, were hired from a local contractor, Mr R. Brewer.

In 1987, Shepherds Minerals were taken over by a firm called Ken Abrahams who specialised in supplying sand, aggregates and ready-mixed concrete. The Abrahams business previously based in Wadebridge was then transferred to the newly acquired site at St Dennis Junction. It was at this time that Mr Crocker's son, Mark, joined the firm as a driver.

Vehicular access to the site was from the B3279 below Domellick Manor, across the moor to the old railway embankment, then along the embankment to St Dennis Junction. As the number of vehicles using this access track increased, the B3279 regularly became soiled with mud and debris. To counteract this, a mechanical sweeper was acquired to clean the road on a daily basis.

As the ready-mixed concrete business increased, more and more of the sand and aggregates had to be purchased from local companies. One major ready-mixed concrete contract was for the Indian Queens bypass project. Halfway through the contract Ken Abrahams sold the business to the Ready-Mix Concrete Co., who continued with the contract until the project was completed in 1995. A few months later the planning approval for the site was not renewed. The site was closed and cleared by the Ready-Mix Concrete Co., and the business transferred to a newly acquired site at Bodmin. In 2003 Mark Crocker still drives a concrete-mixer lorry for the Ready-Mix Concrete Co.

A discussion with Ken Abrahams revealed that when sand extraction from the moor stopped, the pools which soon developed became home to a family of swans. A site visit in 2001 revealed that the whole tip had returned to nature with gorse and willow being very prominent. The visit included a look at the sand-extraction pools, but no evidence of swans was found. Unfortunately these pools, which extend to and beyond the original course of the River Fal, have left the river unrecognisable as such.

Left: *Probably taken in the 1940s, this picture shows one of the many incidents which occurred on the tip sidings due to the primitive tracks and stop blocks.* KHR/Coll

These pools in the south of the moor near the old railway embankment were created by the tin-recovery exploration and sand extraction carried out in the 1980s. KHR

Chapter 17

Block and Sand Works

Concrete Block Works

Utilising the sand reserves for the manufacture of concrete products such as blocks was the first major sand-extraction industry on the moor when it was started in the 1920s by a Mr H. Wheeler. Apart from concrete blocks he also made other concrete products such as slabs, dog kennels, bird troughs and coal bunkers, examples of which were displayed beside the A30 to attract customers. Mr Wheeler operated the business until 1939 when he sold it to Mark Richards & Son.

The production plant was situated some 300 yards in from the level crossing over the GWR double-tracked Par–Newquay branch line near the Poplars cottage on the A30. The site was accessed by a sand and gravel hardstanding track which also served the shooting lodge and the old mining and sand pits further into the moor. It was chosen because of its proximity to a tributary of the River Fal and previously washed sand and gravel, the remains of old tin-mining and streaming workings. These natural resources provided two of the three main components required for concrete products.

The production site consisted of a long shed in which the concrete was mixed and then placed in wooden moulds. There was a narrow-gauge tramway running the full length of the shed and to the outside stacking area where the products were taken after they had set. There was also a galvanised lock-up shed in which the bagged cement was kept. The sand and gravel was dug from the old tin-streaming sites by men working horses and wagons to transport it to the shed.

Teams of one man with a horse and cart were hired from local farmers. Some of these known teams were: Jack Burnett and his brother Vernon, who worked their father's horses and carts, and Charlie Osborne who worked a horse and cart belonging to Viv Smale.

The demand for concrete blocks increased in 1939 as a result of military construction projects such as camps and airfields. Consequently, the horse and cart proved too slow and was replaced by pairs of men who worked on a narrow-gauge tramway digging the sand and gravel, loading the trams and transferring the material to the production shed.

In 1946 a block-making plant was established near one of the sand-classifier plants, to supplement the production of the original block works and to utilise surplus stocks of processed sand and gravel.

Men known to have worked at the block works were: Bill Edyvean, Cyril Endean, Ken Hannaford, Den Harris, Dick Hicks, Bill Keast, Sid Roberts, Bill Smale, Dick Webber and Denny Westlake.

The demand for concrete blocks remained constant for many years after the Second World War because of a vibrant construction industry. However, with the increasing cost of sand and gravel production, the growing need to comply with quality standards, and the fact that china-clay-work sand was proving cheaper, of a better quality and available in vast reserves, the site on Goss Moor was closed and the operation was transferred to a new site at the Anchor China Clay Works, near Melbur, in 1958.

Mark Richards & Son carried on the block-making business on the new site for many years until ECLP & Co. Ltd purchased the Anchor China Clay Company and the lease for the site was not renewed. The site was taken over by their quarries division.

Sand Extraction

Sand extraction from Goss Moor started in the 1920s in a small way when a Mr H. Wheeler extracted sand and gravel for his concrete-block-making works. As outlined above, he sold the business to Mark Richards & Son in 1939.

The road into the moor from the A30 that accessed the block works, then continued past the shooting lodge to the old tin-dredging pool (known locally as Tin Mine), also led to the site of the first large-scale sand- and gravel-extraction operation. This pit was closed prematurely when extraction too close to the pool caused the pit to flood.

Two larger pits with permanent pumps and classifiers were soon developed further into the moor, the first of which was near an old mining site called Green Banks. The second of these pits was near fresh reserves of sand, etc., near an old mining site known as the Upper Fal Tin Pits. Both pits used the same production process of digging, washing and classifying the sand and gravel.

Top left: *This level crossing from the A30 road was the only access to the moor used by the lorries serving the sand and block works in the 1940s, when it was quite normal for it to be used up to 150 times a day. This photograph taken in 2002 shows a different picture from the 1940s when the railway was a double track and the gates were wooden and much wider.* KHR

Above: *Here we see a fairly level area which is still recognisable in the early-twenty-first century as the site of the old block works which, by the time of closure in 1958, had operated here for nearly 30 years.* KHR

Above: *There are many pools on the moor; this one was the site of tin-dredging operations in the 1920s. Nature and industrial pollution have eroded most of the pool, seen in here in 2002.* KHR

The River Fal flows through this pool, pictured in 2002, created by tin-dredging operations, before flowing southwards to the railway embankment bridge. **KHR**

Men working in pairs at the moor-face end of narrow-gauge tramways would dig and load the raw sand onto trams, which were then pushed to the slurry pool where the material was washed and pumped into a rotating classifier that graded the slurry into sand, gravel and waste. It was not uncommon for up to six teams of men to be working in one pit. As the demand for sand and gravel increased the primitive and time-consuming method of drivers loading their own lorries with a large shovel proved too slow and alternative methods were sought. The first major improvement was the hire of a Mr Ambrose Matthews of Trefullock Moor, Summercourt, to operate a steam-driven excavator which was then used to load the lorries. The excavator belonged to Richard Costain, the contractor who was building the airfields at St Eval and St Mawgan. It ran on standard-gauge tracks and had a crane-like lifting jib with a mechanical grab attached capable of lifting five–six cwts at a time. The power was supplied by a locomotive-type steam engine, which was fired by coal and had an upright boiler. It was manned by a fireman called Reg Davey from Enniscaven, with the driver being Ambrose Matthews. The former had to start work two hours before the driver in order to light the fire to enable the boiler to reach the correct steam pressure by the time the first lorries arrived for loading. The steam-powered excavator was positioned at the Green Bank site on a length of track alongside the classifier bays so that it could load whatever grade of sand was required. It did have a habit of breaking down which usually caused chaos.

The excavator was brought by road to the railway crossing and then unloaded onto a length of track complete with wooden sleepers. There were actually two lengths of track; the excavator used its jib as a crane to place the second length of track in front of the first, then move forward onto it after it had been bolted together. This process was repeated many times before the humpback bridge was reached. To overcome this obstacle the section of the River Fal was filled with stacks of railway sleepers until the level of the road on each side of the river was reached. The track was then placed on top of the sleepers. This crossing caused much concern and was anxiously watched by many people. Happily, it was achieved without incident and the final destination reached after about seven days of effort. When the excavator started work, everyone was delighted – the drivers because it made their lives easier and the management because it brought about increased sales.

When the building of RAF St Eval was virtually completed the steam excavator was recalled by Costains and was removed from the moor after working there for nearly two years.

Another improvement was the purchase of a Ruston-Buycrus RB10 tracked excavator with a shovel that could excavate the raw material from the pit face and load it onto the trams. John Kellow of St Dennis became the permanent driver of this machine.

These are all photographs of the Mark Richards sand-extraction storage and loading silos last used in the 1940s which, as seen here in 2002, are still in remarkable condition and are a credit to their builders. KHR

The ultimate improvement was the building of a concrete-block silo at Upper Fal Tin Pits. The classified sand and gravel was conveyed and stored in various bays of the silo under which lorries would reverse to be loaded by gravity.

For safety reasons the road crossing over the railway track was normally manned by an operator who would control the lorries crossing by opening and shutting the gates. One long-serving crossing-gate operator was a local lady called May Wooldridge. On a normal day there would be up to

150 lorry crossings over the railway tracks and on average up to ten passenger and goods/mineral trains using the track in each direction.

However, there were accidents involving collisions between lorries and trains. Most of these occurred when the crossing was unmanned with the worst one being when a train hit a lorry driven by Ken Tabb of Fraddon. The lorry was written off and Mr Tabb seriously injured, although he made a complete recovery and was eventually able to carry on with his driving livelihood. Another incident involved a lorry driven by Garfield Kent, which resulted in the lorry being badly damaged, but Garfield was unhurt.

The fact that tin streaming and mining had taken place virtually all over the moor meant that large quantities of washed sand and gravel were still in a reasonable state and could be easily recovered. Overburden was never a big problem with only about 18ins of soil, heather or gorse to remove. The removal of overburden was assisted by the use of a manually-steered two-wheeled petrol-driven Trustee tractor known as an iron horse, which was used to plough the overburden prior to removal.

One of the main resources required for sand and gravel extraction is obviously water, of which there was always an abundance available from the River Fal and its tributaries, and the many pools formed at old mining sites. The unwanted residue after classifying was always stored and allowed to settle in an old pit before the water was returned to the Fal.

There was a problem in 1942 which threatened the supply of sand and gravel to the airfield construction contract when certain moorland vegetation roots were not being separated from the gravel by the classifiers. These roots then found their way into the concrete being used for runways, which in turn damaged the surface once they had dried out and thus created holes. The firm's remedy to overcome this problem was to remove the roots by hand at the classifier, which eventually proved successful.

Construction of airfields began in 1939 with RAF St Eval, RAF Trebelzue, RAF Perranporth and RNAS St Merryn. It finished in 1944 with the completion of RAF St Mawgan. The majority of the sand and gravel was carried by Richards' and Osborne's fleet of over 30 American-made Reo Speed Wagons, nicknamed Reos, which carried about five yards worth of materials. These wagons were designed to carry a four-yard load, but when it was discovered that they could easily carry five, they were all fitted with higher sideboards to carry the additional yard. The wagons made four or five journeys a day, six days a week. Other local hauliers were hired as and when required. A rough calculation reveals that in five years over one million yards of sand and gravel were excavated from Goss Moor.

Although there are no records available, memories of local people suggest that very little sand and gravel excavation was made after the end of the war, except for whatever was needed to supply the block works, which remained on this site until 1958.

Today the only evidence of the sand- and gravel-extraction industry is the remains of the concrete-block sand silo and large pools of water at the pit sites. The pools, however, are considerably smaller in size when compared with their working days of the 1940s. This is as a result of the natural process of erosion by the soil material and flora of the moor.

Some remembered names who worked the sand- and gravel-production sites were: Fred Bale, Mr Beard (foreman), Les and Fernley Caddy, Bill Luke, Stan Pearce, Dick Runnalls, Wes Stephens, Maurice Tonkin, Norman 'Panshine' Wills and Lew Yelland, who worked the pumps and engine house at Green Banks.

Some remembered drivers who were employed by Richards and Osborne were: Les Allen, Ron and Reg Chappell, Harold May, Stan May, 'Dicker' Parsons, Garnet Rowe, 'Lightning' Rowe, Ken and George Tabb.

The lorry-loading doors at the bottom of the silos, under which the lorries would reverse to load, seen in 2003. KHR

A veteran from the Second World War, this 'Reo Speed Wagon' lorry is identical to the Richards and Osborne fleet of over 30 which they operated to carry sand and gravel from the Goss Moor to the north coast airfield construction sites in the early 1940s. This vehicle is now owned by Mr Rex Curtis of Roche who has restored it to its former glory. KHR/Coll

Chapter 18

Electricity Installations

Since the early-twentieth century, Goss Moor has been home to many high-voltage power lines and pylons. The Central Electricity Board constructed a National Grid high-voltage electricity supply system of 132 KV in 1934. During its construction across the moor in the early 1930s the author's father, being at that time employed by the Cornwall Electricity Company, worked on this project. Pylons were erected by trained riggers with local men being employed as labourers. Locally owned cart-horses were hired to carry out general haulage work including pulling cables into place and tightening them.

In 1950, as a result of the increased demand for electricity nationally, the construction of a national super-grid of 275 KV was started. The original lines were replaced and new pylons were installed. This grid was upgraded in the mid-1960s to 400 KV. Much larger pylons were erected that were capable of carrying the heavier cables. Local contractors were engaged to supply hardcore for the construction of access roads to the sites, heavy plant for excavation work, and ready-mixed concrete for pylon footings and anchorage. The power lines were hauled into position by mechanically powered winches mounted on heavy vehicles. With the new excavations for footings having to be bigger and deeper than before, tales of finding the well-preserved remains of cattle lost in the bogs over the years are well known locally.

In the early 1970s the National Grid Company decided that a new large sub-station switch yard was required to serve the most westerly point of the National Grid. A site was chosen on Goss Moor, south of the old railway embankment near Domellick Manor Farm on property originally known as Ennis Veor. After much opposition from local people planning permission was eventually granted and the Indian Queens Power Facility was established. A sub-station switch yard was built in 1975 and was the most westerly point of the 400 KV National Grid. The sub-station controls the electricity supply of most of Cornwall on 275 KV and 132 KV power lines.

In 1995 a generating facility was added to the site. An oil-fired gas turbine was built by John Brown Engineering Ltd, of Clydebank, for Destic Energy of Texas, USA, to provide power compensation and peak power service for the National Grid. This plant became operational in 1996. As a matter of interest the nearest generation facility to Indian Queens is Hinkley Point in Somerset, some 100 miles away.

Both the sub-station and the generating plant are located in an environmentally sensitive rural area near the villages of Indian Queens and St Dennis. During respective planning applications there was a considerable amount of local opposition. In each case, when planning approval was granted, it was with conditions that noise and omission levels be set and maintained. At the time of writing there is no record of these levels having been exceeded.

The earliest documentary reference to Ennis Veor seems to be dated 1345, when the smallholding was called Ynysmour. In 1748 Martyn's map referred to the site as Ennis, and the title schedule in 1840 named it as Ennis Veor, which was owned by Joseph and Thomas Hawkey who rented it to a William Hey as a farmstead comprising four buildings. By 1880 the farmstead had shrunk to only one building and had disappeared by 1908.

The situation today is that there are two lines of 400 KV which are part of the National Grid, a sub-station site comprising a switch yard and a generating plant, and two lines of 132 KV supplying power to the St Austell and St Germans areas. Lines going west from the sub-station are hardly on the moor, however, the most important of these is a 275 KV line to Hayle. Others are the 132 KV lines, one to Fraddon and one to St Tudy.

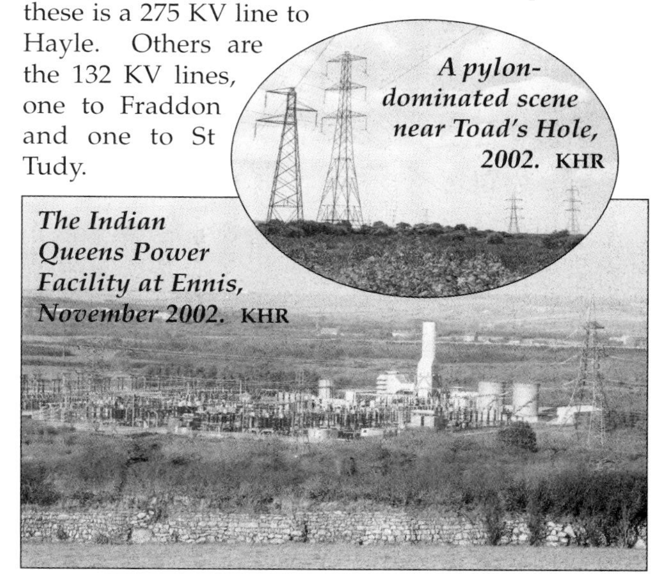

A pylon-dominated scene near Toad's Hole, 2002. KHR

The Indian Queens Power Facility at Ennis, November 2002. KHR

Left: ***The road bridge over the River Fal near Tregoss in July 2002.*** **KHR**

Background: ***Davey's Bridge over the River Fal on the Enniscaven to Dyehouse road in July 2002.*** **KHR**

Below and below left: ***The River Fal near Tregoss with the man-made weirs funded by the Environment Agency in 1996.*** **KHR**

Above: *An access bridge over the River Fal built in 1998 by English Nature.* KHR

Above: *A centre-of-the-moor scene with the River Fal winding its way through typical flora on 1 October 2002.* KHR

Left: *The site of the old weir known many years ago as 'Waterfall' – sadly today no physical evidence of its existence remains.* KHR

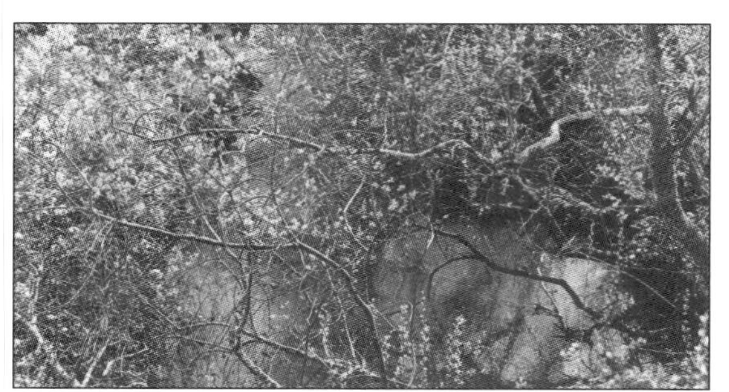

Right: *The River Fal, just off the old A30, which was once the site of an American Army water-filtration plant in 1944.* KHR

Chapter 19

The River Fal

The River Fal rises in the Coldreath area of the Hensbarrow granite mass before entering Goss Moor with its many tributaries. These join the main river before it reaches the bridge under the embankment, which was part of the St Dennis Junction–St Dennis railway branch line. The bridge is near the site of the old ground-frame hut which was part of the railway signalling and control system. In the days of tin streaming, the old 'streamers' utilised water from the Fal as a source of power for driving their waterwheels and for assisting with the production process.

Sand extraction from the moor, which reached its peak in the years 1940–46, used the river to wash the raw sand, which produced slurry. During this period there were some examples of tributaries being re-routed to gain access to deposits of sand. Sand extraction created a large amount of soiled water; this was retained in a disused sandpit where it was allowed to settle before being released back into the river. During the block-making business era, which spanned over two decades, one of the tributaries provided water for the concrete-mixing process.

After the river flowed under the embankment bridge it met a man-made concrete weir which was known locally as 'Waterfall'. At one side of the weir there was a sluice-gate which could be raised or lowered as required to control the flow of water into a man-made channel. This carried water to the Wheal Remfry brickworks, as the Fal at Wheal Remfry was too low for gravity to feed a water-supply to the brickworks. The channel was made with a lesser gradient than the river, which meant the water from the weir was fed by gravity to the brickworks. When the weir and the sluice-gate were built is unknown, although they both appear on the Ordnance Survey map of 1881.

It was not until 1936, when electrically powered pumps were introduced, that the water-supply channel was made redundant. In the 1940s the sluice-gate became damaged through lack of use and the channel started to fill with silt.

Many memories of the Fal revolve around the weir area in the 1940s; there was much playing, fishing (without much success) and bathing. The latter was made possible by walking some 300 yards upstream then building a dam to make a pool. This was only possible in the summer, as during the winter and rainy periods the river would become a raging torrent in which it was far too dangerous to play. Materials for the dam came from the river banks in the form of stones and 'tabs' of earth and grass.

In the 1970s the Fal in the Tregoss area became so silted up that two bridges, one near Tregoss and one called Davey's Bridge nearby, became completely blocked with sand and the like. This was attributed to the poor controls exercised by ECCI (now known as Imerys) in their management of polluted waste water from their Karslake area china-clay works. The blocked river caused flooding to local farm land, which brought about complaints from the farmers who eventually had to seek legal pressure to encourage ECCI to redress the problem. This resulted in ECCI clearing the blockages and cleaning up the river. Unfortunately during this operation the excavator driver was rather overenthusiastic and undermined the foundations of the bridges. This resulted in the need to divert the river around each bridge while the foundations were stabilised with concrete.

It is a well-known fact, especially to those of us who were employed in the china-clay industry, that the main producer was using hundreds of tons of chemicals per week in its production process. It was fairly obvious that any polluted waste from the Karslake area which found its way into the Fal contained some chemicals. This probably contributed to the decline in plant, fish and insect life along the river.

It is important to note that in more modern times china-clay producers go to great lengths to prevent contamination of our streams and rivers.

The River Fal south of the old railway embankment continues over the moor on a similar gradient to and parallel with the old Retew railway branch line down to the old Gaverigan road crossing, after which it flows into the aptly named Fal Valley.

In 1992 English Nature cleared some overgrown parts of the river bank in the Tregoss area, which gives access on foot along the river bank down as far as the old sand silo. In 1996 small stone weirs were made to encourage the return of Odonata and fish.

Above: *The old chapel at Enniscaven which was closed as such in 1908, and later used as an institute.* KHR

Top right: *Leghorn Cottages at Goss Moor.* KHR

Above: *One of the new enterprises which has replaced farming on the Goss Moor.* KHR

Above left: *Mr W.H. Key with his horse and cart at Ennis Farm in 1938.* KHR/Coll

Left: *Fred Couch in his working attire with his version of a mobile shop.* KHR/Coll

Below: *Tregoss Mill, 2003.* KHR

Chapter 19

Hamlets and People

Enniscaven, Gothers and St Dennis Junction

The hamlets of Enniscaven, Gothers, St Dennis Junction (also known as Goss Moor) and Tregoss are on the fringes of the moor. Other moorland residences include a single dwelling near Skilley Davey's Bridge over the River Fal on the Enniscaven–Dyehouse road. In the past this property has used a small wind turbine to generate its own electricity.

Two semi-detached houses known as House on the Common are situated on the Tregoss Moor by the embankment below the girder bridge. They are reached from the A30 over a railway crossing.

The Treranke Cottages are positioned on the edge of the Tregoss Moor by the B3274 near the Roche Cross junctions, and were originally three semi-detached cottages which at one time also included a small shop. The site of these dwellings was also known as Poorhouse. The cottages had no mains water or electricity until the 1960s – up until then drinking-water was obtained from a well by a windlass and bucket, and oil-lamps provided light. At Enniscaven six separate dwellings are situated on Goss Moor, one cottage is known as Salt Box, there is another nearby, with the other four in an area known as Toad's Hole. All are remotely situated and are served by their own tracks. Another residence near Tregoss is called Moor View. Mains water was not available in this area until 1960.

Enniscaven and Gothers are close-knit communities with the same families having lived there for generations. However, towards the end of the twentieth century this trend has not been quite so pronounced; some families have virtually died out or moved on and other people have moved in. Family names which have long been associated with Gothers and Enniscaven are: Davey, Docking, Dymond, Glanville, Hicks, Jay, Liddicoat, Runnalls, Tabb, Truscott and Williams.

In the past Enniscaven had its own band, football and darts teams, as well as a chapel and Sunday school, an Institute, and a War Memorial. The chapel is still going strong today, as is the War Memorial. Many years ago Enniscaven held an annual Band Fête and Garden Show.

During the 1940s the child Bernard Bresslaw, who went on to be a famous actor, stayed in Gothers as an evacuee. He lived with Mr and Mrs Leonard Tabb.

A well-known feature on the moor at Enniscaven was an object nicknamed the Tube – a metal chimney stack (30ft by 5ft) originally intended to be used on a Pochin's mica-drying kiln in the early-twentieth century, although this never happened. The stack was left on the moor for many years and was used by children as a plaything and by their parents as a poultry house. It was finally utilised during the Second World War when it was cut up and sent away to be melted down and used as part of the war effort.

Livelihoods were mainly made in farming and china-clay production, until the demise of these industries as major employers in the late-twentieth century. In the nineteenth century virtually all local people utilised Goss Moor in some way to assist with their income, such as working the tin-streaming sites.

One successful farmer who still farms some land bordering the moor at Newmoor is John Blewett of Carsella (see Chapter 3). He farms nearly 1,000 acres in the St Dennis area. The land at Newmoor is only used for sheep grazing.

Goss Moor

In the 1940s this hamlet included the St Dennis Junction area, along the A30 from the Richards and Osborne garage to the Poplars dwelling south of the Tregoss railway road crossing. Exceptions to this were Brenton's Farm, Ruthers Farm, and Hawkins Farm. During the 1930s and '40s the postal address of this hamlet was Goss Moor, Fraddon.

The amount of traffic in those days (excluding the build up to D-Day in 1943–44) was considerably less than today. Indeed, children (the author included) used to play football on the A30, which at that time was only disturbed by the occasional passing vehicle.

The local chapel and Sunday school were in the nearby hamlet of Ruthers where the community enjoyed anniversaries, tea treats with saffron buns, playing bands and sports days.

The author recalls:

There was no electricity at Goss Moor during my time

there – cooking and heating were done by coal- and wood-burning stoves and grates, lighting was provided by oil-lamps and wirelesses were powered by accumulator batteries which had to be recharged weekly at the local garage. These batteries were not very popular as they were heavy and filled with diluted sulphuric acid.

Everyone had an oil-fuelled Primus stove which was a small water and food heater mainly used when the coal-fired stove was not in use. It was not the safest piece of equipment and accidents did occur; in fact I still have a scar inflicted by boiling water to prove it!

There was no mains water; all our water had to be drawn from various wells by using a windlass to wind a bucket on the end of a rope up and down. Rainwater was collected and stored for certain uses.

Having a bath once a week was a luxury which sometimes took place in front of the grate or fire, but mostly it took place in an outside wash-house which had a built-in copper boiler heated by a wood-burning fire. The bath was made of galvanised tin and was portable. It was filled with hot water from the boiler and cold water from a tank. The luxury of a bath was not so popular in the winter as the wash-house was cold and draughty.

Mains sewerage was unheard of – there were no flushing toilets at Goss Moor. Most lavatories were situated at the bottom of the garden away from the house. I must add that we did grow extremely good rhubarb!

Most of our food, except for vegetables, which we grew, was delivered by the Co-op each week. Butchers and bakers called regularly as did the coalman and provender merchants. Our paraffin and methylated spirits were delivered by the Co-op along with the groceries.

Other memories are of assisting various smallholders, as did all neighbours, to harvest the hay and corn crop, and to carry out the threshing of the corn. No wages were paid, but everyone was invited to attend a farmhouse supper when the work was completed each day.

A smallholding, probably built in the nineteenth century, positioned on the edge of the moor south of the railway junction, inland from the old A30 towards Gaverigan Manor Farm, was owned and worked by a Mr Hawken from about 1930 to 1960. He grazed his three or four cows in a few meadows and on parts of the moor, which did not offer the best grazing as it had been turned over many times by past tin workings, and he also had two pigs and a small herd of goats. The one good thing about this area was that there was an abundance of fresh water. People who worked on this smallholding were: Percy Martin, Ed Hawken and Den Hawken. The Hawken family worked the smallholding up to about 1966. Sadly the property has not been lived in for many years and has become derelict.

The author also recalls:

In the 1930s my father kept two pigs and about three dozen fowls (chickens) on an area of the moor called Ladysmith which he rented from a Mr Reg Roberts.

One concrete and two wooden buildings provided shelter for the livestock. The fowls were locked inside by night to protect them from foxes. While home on leave from the Army in 1940, my father dismantled one of these wooden buildings, brought it home and buried it in the back garden at Leghorn Cottages, to act as an air-raid shelter for my mother and me.

The children of the Goss Moor attended the schools at Indian Queens. However, today they use a newer site than the one I attended many years ago.

Local livelihoods relied on farming, the china-clay industry and the railway. At the start of the twenty-first century, this has changed significantly, following the decline of the railway in the 1970s, and the decline of farming and the china-clay industry as major employers in the 1990s. People have had to diversify, with businesses such as a horse-riding stable, a nationally recognised owl sanctuary, a caravan site, and a 'gnome world' being established on previously farmed land. In the 1940s there were 14 farms and smallholdings, but in 2004 there are no more than four that are worked as such. Some fields have been lost to the ever-growing willow, gorse and rushes, whilst others have become waterlogged.

Remembered names at Goss Moor include: Ackford, Barrett, Cocking, Collins, Common, Crago, Crowle, Hannaford, Harvey, Hawken, Hicks, Honeywell, Julian, Keast, May, Osborne, Pratt, Rickard, Rouse, Rowe, Smale, Solomon, Trethewey, Truscott, Williams, Wooldridge, Udy and Varcoe.

After nearly 70 years of trading, the family-run haulage firm of Richards and Osborne still operates in 2004 from its original depot by the Toldish junction on the old A30, which for many years had the postal and business address of 'Goss Moor, Fraddon, Cornwall'. This firm, which over the years has enjoyed much success with its local and long-distance haulage, has progressed from the early three- and four-ton steam-driven lorries of the 1930s to the large, articulated, diesel-powered lorries of modern times.

Tregoss

This is the smallest of the hamlets and is positioned on the grassland island partially bisecting the Tregoss and Goss Moors. It consists of a handful of dwellings, two farms, a railway crossing gate-house, and, in the old days, had a chapel which was closed in 1920. Farming represented the livelihood for most of the inhabitants, with the two farms of Pendine and Tregoss continuing to be successfully worked even in 2004.

Children living in this hamlet have always attended the schools at Roche. At the start of the twenty-first century, any form of social or religious life has to be enjoyed at Enniscaven or Roche.

Names which have long been associated with the hamlet are: Bennetto, Burnett, Cowling, Dunn, Gill, Hill and Trudgeon.

From the 1990s up to the time of writing Tregoss has become well known for being on the route taken by high-sided vehicles that are unable to pass under the girder bridge on the A30. The lack of desire by successive governments to remedy this problem, which was highlighted during the late 1980s, has resulted in significant damage and cost.

Tregoss Mill

Before the twentieth century Tregoss Mill was known as Pendeen Mill. Situated on a remote part of Tregoss Moor, it consisted of a three-storey building with a grinding mill, a saw bench and a residence. It was originally used as a mill for grinding corn and wheat for local farmers. Up to the 1930s levies had to be paid to the church at Roche for every bag of corn milled. The mill was powered by a water-wheel fed by the mill-race, a man-made channel that brought water from springs and pools in the Dyehouse area. In the summer months when the water-levels were too low to supply the mill-race, the River Fal near the normal water-supply pools was blocked and diverted into them.

The stream flowing away from the mill to the River Fal near Tregoss contained an abundance of fish, such as minnows and trout. This was probably because they were attracted by the residue in the water from the mill.

Some known millers were: Mr Bennetto, Russell Edyvean, Sammy Phillips, Mr Richards and Mr Trevenna. The Common family lived at the mill for many years, as did some of the millers. Russell Edyvean, the last miller to operate the site, ceased milling in the 1940s. He dismantled the water-wheel before emigrating to Australia in 1950.

At some point the millstone was buried in the floor, although in recent times it has been dug up and repositioned as a feature in the garden. At the time of writing the property, minus milling gear, is used as a residence and is owned and inhabited by a Mrs Nash. The old millpond has become overgrown and is virtually unrecognisable.

Memories of Fred Couch

edited by the author

The British Tin Syndicate's streaming site on Tregoss Moor near the Treranke Cottages was well known to me as a boy in the 1930s and 1940s.

My father's mother, his sister and her husband lived at these cottages on the edge of Tregoss Moor for many years. When I visited them as a boy I became familiar with this old mining site.

Because of its shallow depression in the contours of the moor, it actually gave the impression of a washed-out river bed. It was utilised as a fowls' run by my auntie and uncle, Dorothy and Fred Couch, who sold the eggs to supplement their income.

Fred was a well-known figure in the surrounding villages. Not long after he married he lost his right arm in an accident sustained while working as a locomotive fireman on the Bodmin–Padstow branch of the Southern Railway. He was fitted with an artificial arm and he used a crook.

As he could not continue to work for the railway he turned to selling groceries from a bicycle which he rode and pushed several miles a day around Treviscoe, St Dennis, Whitemoor, Gothers, Enniscaven, Tregoss, Trezaise, Bugle, Retire, Grogley, Ruthern, Withiel and Be Lovely. He had regular rounds for each area and never stopped for bad weather or illness. His bicycle carried baskets and pannier boxes all protected from the weather by canvas-type coverings.

If ever a man showed resilience to adversity, and determination to overcome his disability, it was Fred Couch. I must add that his achievements were only possible because of the devotion he received from the hard-working and supportive Dorothy.

He had to retire at the age of 63 because of ill health, and had 12 years of retirement in a new home in St Austell before he died in 1975. Dorothy lived to be 93.

Sammy Smith

A well-known poacher called Sammy Smith lived at Raggedass Corner, St Dennis, and carried out his pastime in the Gasson area of the moor along with his dogs. Sammy always carried a few 'smutties' in his 'spoil' bag in case he was challenged by the gamekeeper as to his presence on the moor. When this occurred he would explain that he was collecting firewood and would present his proof.

Kitchener Bragg

In November 1949 a St Dennis man called Kitchener Bragg went duck shooting around the old tin-dredging pools that were surrounded by willow and rushes. When he did not return home a search was mounted the following day. His clothing and gun were found by the side of a large pool, which suggested that Kitchener had shot a wild duck that landed in the pool so he may have swam out to retrieve it and become tangled in the weeds. Three attempts to recover the body were unsuccessful. Then, after waiting a fortnight, a stick of dynamite was detonated and dropped into the pool. This had the effect of bringing the body to the surface, from where it was finally recovered by PC Tom Willey and local men Stuart and Roy Gregor in a rowing boat.

Tommy Kessell

Tommy Kessell worked the smallholding called Brenton's Farm at St Dennis Junction. He also worked as a foreman in charge of some tin-streaming sites on the moor in the late-nineteenth century.

Will Key

Living with his wife Grace at the Ennis Vean homestead below Domellick Farm, Will Key kept a flock of geese. They were driven onto the moor daily via the Domellick cattle arch and driven back home every evening. It is reported that when the geese saw Will they would come to meet him. He also kept ponies ('gossies') on the moor, which were reared for eventual sale as pit ponies. Will also had a sow which was kept in his yard and had a reputation for eating hens.

Gypsies

Gypsy camps were to be found at three different sites on Goss Moor; one at Pitsmingle, one near Davey's Bridge and one near the bridge over the Fal at Tregoss. All three were virtually permanent from the mid-nineteenth century until the 1950s and were sited near running water, plenty of willow (used as a basic material for making clothes-pegs and baskets), grazing for horses and ponies and good cover that provided privacy and some protection from the elements.

During the 1960s a nomadic gypsy gentleman with his horse and caravan was well known for his regular visits to several locations in the area. He was always friendly, especially to those who brought him hot meals. He made a gypsy caravan for a lady that lived on the moor at Enniscaven. The hazel trees at Tregoss provided an ideal source of wood for caravan building. The local nickname for this wood is 'nuttals'.

One of the most well-known local gypsy figures of the twentieth century was a lady called Selina Crocker, who spent some considerable time in the tented camps at Tregoss, Enniscaven and Dyehouse. Selina was a very persuasive and strong-willed person which made any encounter with her very daunting!

Ray Bullock: Aviation Pioneer

Many inhabitants of Goss Moor have fond memories of Ray Bullock from Fraddon and his aviation experiments. He lived at the top of Fraddon Hill where he also had a garage and workshop. He ran a haulage business and worked for Cornwall County Council, collecting and transporting grass and hedge cuttings.

In 1935 he built his own Mignet 'Flying Flea' aeroplane using a set of plans he bought for three guineas. He purchased all the materials he needed so that he could make the plane in his workshop. When it was completed it had the registration G-AEDM (RBI).

Being a true adventurer, Ray took the Flying Flea up to the A30 on Goss Moor, where the road is fairly straight; there was very little traffic in those pre-war days.

Ray proceeded to taxi up and down the road with the noise of the engine and the occasional back-fire shattering the peace and quiet of the moor. As the morning progressed he became more daring so his actions developed into a series of hops and bumps along the road. This was prematurely brought to a halt when the cockpit floor fell out! After repairs, Ray and the Flying Flea finally took off and in doing so frightened the local milkman and his horse, with the noise and smoke.

Ray used a field on the edge of the moor and a field at Parka near St Columb Road. Sadly he eventually crashed the Flea onto the GWR railway line at Whitecross; although he escaped injury the aeroplane was damaged beyond repair. Undaunted, he went on to build a BAC Drone using parts salvaged from the Flea's wreckage. The Drone was a delight to fly but during a landing it went the way of the Flying Flea.

Ray's next plane was a Pixie II Tom Tit, made of parts salvaged from the previous crafts. It was a high-wing monoplane with a petrol tank fitted over the cockpit. To top up the fuel during longer flights, Ray would grip the control stick between his knees to keep the craft steady, take a can of petrol, which made up his seat and, using a funnel, pour petrol into the tank. Only about half the petrol found its way into the tank, with the remainder cleaning the fuselage.

Unfortunately in April 1939 too much fuel was carried and this resulted in the overloaded Pixie crashing near Coswarth Farm, Colan. It was irrevocably damaged and Ray suffered a broken arm and leg.

After this accident and the outbreak of the Second World War, Ray's flying activities had to stop, although during his rehabilitation he started to build another machine. No doubt he will be remembered as a local aviation pioneer and as one of the first, if not the first, aircraft constructor in Cornwall.

In 1937 the Air Ministry's Civil Aviation Division in London learnt of Ray's flying activities. They wrote to him telling him that, as they had no record of him having a private pilot's licence, they would like him to report to the examiner at Plymouth airport to have the formalities attended to. Ray flew his aircraft to Plymouth and landed unannounced using his own unconventional spiral-landing technique, which caused quite a panic with the staff and emergency services. The examiner gave Ray all the appropriate training manuals with the instruction to take them home and not to return until he had read and learnt all of their contents. To accommodate all the manuals Ray sat on them for the flight home. Needless to say, he soon returned to Plymouth and completed his PPL examination and flying test.

Even today Mr Bullock's garage, workshop and aircraft hangar can still be seen on the original site at the top of Fraddon Hill, between Fraddon and Indian Queens on the old A30. Ray's widow, Mrs Bullock, is a charming lady who lives at Indian Queens at the ripe old age of 95.

Chapter 21

The Second World War

The Home Guard

The Home Guard was formed in 1939 at the outbreak of war, although at this stage members were known as Local Defence Volunteers (LDV). There were no uniforms, only an armband. Members were to report and repel any attempt by the enemy to land any of their forces, and to arrest any suspicious-looking characters who may have been enemy spies, such as parachutists and aircrew. Initially men were armed with their own garden tools which they carried on their nightly vigils. After a few months sections and companies were formed and officers were appointed (often local businessmen). Uniforms were issued in 1940 and the name was changed to the Home Guard.

The nearest post to Goss Moor was a disused farm building near the Richards and Osborne garage. It was a pigs' house that had been whitewashed inside, and fitted with bunk beds, a Primus stove and a tilley lamp. Weekly parades and training sessions were introduced, rifles were issued and nightly patrols carried out. Men reported for duty in the evening and returned home the following morning in time to attend their normal employment. Most of the personnel were elderly men and those exempt from military service.

At one training session an officer from Indian Queens, when demonstrating the use of a pistol, accidentally shot a friend of the author in the leg. The injury remained with him for the rest of his life. With hindsight, one wonders how effective the Home Guard would have been against enemy attack, yet at the time it was somewhat reassuring to have them around.

An original member remembered an amusing but true story. Whilst on duty one night at a local Home Guard post, the patrol was summoned to an incident. Before leaving, the officer in charge reminded the men of his previous instruction which was 'at all cost do not let the enemy pass', to which one chap quickly replied 'don't you worry sir, they won't catch us'.

Rationing

Food was in short supply for many reasons during the war, so rationing was introduced along with ration books to help administer and control it.

Food, clothing, petrol and oil, furniture, coal and animal feed were all rationed. This created a black-market trade which was difficult to suppress. In turn, this led to the emergence of the 'spiv' who could seemingly supply most things at a price.

The population was encouraged to produce home-grown food, especially in rural areas. Gardens were fully utilised by growing vegetables and providing a home for a few poultry and a pig. Mothers, sons and daughters quickly learnt the basics of gardening and soon became efficient. The fowls produced a supply of eggs, which proved invaluable to the family diet. Strictly speaking all eggs produced should have been sold to official egg collectors, with the family diet catered for by a ration of powdered egg. There is surely no need to explain what actually happened.

Householders would keep and rear a pig if they had the facilities. The pig would be fattened up by feeding it the household food scraps and milled corn, and when ready it would be killed to supplement the family meat supply.

German Air Raids

When the Blitz on Plymouth reached its height in 1940–41, on a clear night the glow from the fires could be seen in the sky from St Dennis Junction. The German air raids on RAF St Eval and later RAF St Mawgan could be heard, and by night the explosive flashes could be seen. Local people would gather at night on the road bridge while some men would climb up onto the GWR water tank, the highest point around, and report to the people below on any flashes from exploding bombs and anti-aircraft fire.

During daytime air raids German Heinkel and Donier aircraft were seen flying to and returning from our airfield targets – they often flew directly over St Dennis Junction at ground level, low enough for the pilots to be clearly seen. This made everyone very nervous and scared wondering whether they were going to be bombed.

In 1941 the Goss Moor area was bombed by the German Luftwaffe on two occasions. The moor was directly below the bombers' flight path as they flew to their targets of St Eval, St Mawgan and St Merryn from their bases in France.

Left: *US Army tanks awaiting embarkation before D-Day at a local port.*
Imperial War Museum

Right: *A scene repeated all over Cornwall prior to D-Day.*
Imperial War Museum

Below, inset: *This American-supplied 'Oliver 90' tractor dating from the Second World War was restored in 1980 by Mr Rex Curtis of Roche.*
KHR

US Army tanks loading onto a tank-landing craft at a local port.
Imperial War Museum

The Germans were not always successful in their attempts to attack our airfields; sometimes they were beaten off by our fighter planes and ground defences. When this occurred they would release their bombs indiscriminately in order to lighten their load during the dash for home. It was on two such occasions that Goss Moor was bombed. The first proved harmless when at least four bombs were dropped between the old Tin Mine pool and the Gasson pool. The explosions did little damage except for frightening wildlife, destroying gorse, and leaving craters that could be recognised many years later. However, the second occasion was very different. The author recalls:

It was on a dark winter's evening when I had been to the fish-and-chip shop at Indian Queens to purchase our supper to take home to St Dennis Junction. As I approached the old primary school on my bicycle a German bomber dropped a 'stick' of bombs which fell each side of the old A30 near Georgie Williams' shop, which was positioned halfway between the school and the Richards and Osborne garage. A cottage near the shop was damaged and its occupants, who had taken cover under the kitchen table, suffered cuts and bruises and one broken limb. Some kind of warning had been received – probably the sound of the German aircraft's engine which was distinct from Allied aircraft.

Unfortunately more severe damage was inflicted across the road – a piggery belonging to Viv Smale received a direct hit. The building housed a large number of pigs, and tractor fuel, collapsed and caught fire, which resulted in pigs being killed or injured. Many had to be put down the next day; very few survived. Because of the tractor fuel the building burned for two days.

My memories are of the smell, the noise from the injured pigs and the fire as I pushed my bicycle through the debris on the road, hugging the hedge for false security. No emergency services or help had arrived and my only thoughts were to get home as quickly as I could. For a nine-year-old boy this experience was traumatic to say the least and, as if this wasn't enough, when I finally arrived home at St Dennis Junction, I received a row, before I explained my experience, because the fish and chips were cold!

The recovery of animals and materials continued into the next day. A neighbour of ours, Jack Hannaford, also experienced this bombing. He was walking home from Indian Queens where he had been to collect his charged-up wireless accumulator, and had just passed the Angilleys' cottage when the bombs exploded. This resulted in Jack being severely shaken and shocked.

Blackouts

Blackout regulations were introduced in 1939. During darkness all windows had to be completely blacked out. If any light could be seen from outside the local policeman would remind the occupants of the law.

All vehicles' headlights were covered except for a small slit, street lighting was switched off, and cycle lights were banned. Everyone had a torch and shops selling batteries did very well. Danger lurked on the roads and accidents were frequent.

Indian Queens Primary School

Children were encouraged to buy National Savings Stamps and Certificates. There were occasions when Royal Air Force personnel would bring a bomb to the school, supposedly destined to be dropped on Germany, on which children would be encouraged to stick National Savings Stamps. Whether these bombs were actually ever used is a matter of opinion.

In 1940, when gas attacks were considered a possibility, everyone was issued with a gas mask. These had to be carried at all times in a square cardboard box with a string carrying strap. At school pupils had to carry out gas-mask drills at regular intervals, which involved wearing the gas mask for about ten minutes at a time. Most children hated this drill; with a strong smell of rubber and its claustrophobic feeling the gas mask was not popular. Thankfully, the real need to use them never came about.

With all kinds of clothing and footwear being rationed the issue of new rubber boots to schoolchildren was very popular. The issue was carried out by and at the school and was limited to pupils who lived at least two miles away. It was no surprise when the majority of children claimed qualification for the rubber boot (Wellingtons) issue. On one occasion the Canadian Red Cross supplied various items of winter attire such as gloves, scarves, hats, socks, etc., for distribution to schoolchildren. These items were virtually impossible to obtain by civilians in this country. The author received a khaki-coloured balaclava which he gratefully wore in the winter months and treasured for many years.

Children were allowed time off from school to work on farms for a limited number of days each month in the summer. The usual work was picking up potatoes and sugar beet after it had been dug.

Women's Land Army

With the majority of able-bodied men having been conscripted into the Services, farming, along with other industries, was short of labour. The contribution of schoolchildren was far from filling the gap so a Women's Land Army was formed. Women from cities and non-rural areas were conscripted and allocated to various farming areas. The Land Army Girls, as they were known, were billeted on farms where they worked with local families.

They soon became accustomed to their work which they carried out with much enthusiasm. After the war some of the women stayed in the St Dennis and Goss Moor locality and married local men.

Salvage

Lots of surplus materials were collected from the general public in 1940 as part of a Government initiative to provide for the war effort. In rural areas such as Cornwall there was not much to contribute, probably due to the county's standard of living at the time; you could not give what you did not have. Apart from a few tin cans and the occasional old bicycle frame the contribution from Goss Moor (hamlet) was very small.

The tin cans were collected by the local council and stored in one of the old Royalton mine pits at Castle-an-Dinas. A desperate measure, enforced by the War Department in 1941, was the confiscation of all household and public metal gates and railings. These were removed, cut up and sent away to foundaries up country for use in the production of much-needed war equipment.

Military Sites

The locality played its part in the war effort by providing various military sites, such as the Italian prisoner-of-war camp at Whitecross, which was administered and guarded by the British Army's Pioneer Corps. These prisoners were put to work on local farms, the railway, and other suitable services.

The Irish Enniskillan Regiment was stationed at Carworgie Manor, a rather special and secretive location. It was reputed at the time that these soldiers were as tough and fearless as the Gurkha regiments. These soldiers were a rough bunch, when they were not confined to barracks for various reasons, they were out and about in the evenings usually upsetting the locals and creating problems for the police.

A Royal Ordinance Corps supply depot was established at the site of Gothers Clay Dries for the servicing of other military sites in the area. These soldiers formed a good relationship with the village people, and participated in local concerts and football matches. It is a fact that many of these men returned to the area after the war and married local girls. The clay dries at the Anchor China Clay Works near Fraddon were commandeered and used as a bomb store for the airfields at St Eval and St Mawgan.

Evacuees

To protect the children of our large cities from the German Blitz, they were evacuated to rural areas in 1940–41. Cornwall received its share of evacuees with the majority coming from London and Bristol. It was sad to see these children arriving by train with their gas-mask boxes around their necks and a small bundle of possessions, and being mustered in village halls before being designated to local families.

These were difficult times and the new environment presented a completely different lifestyle to what they were used to – there was no running water, no flushing toilets, and no electricity. They had to adopt to country food and a new lifestyle. Nevertheless, most eventually adapted to the situation and stayed until the end of the war when they were able to return to their parents. However, some had no homes or families to return to, some went home and returned to the locality in later years, and quite a few stayed in Cornwall and eventually married local people.

Lend-Lease Tractors

New farm machinery was in short supply in England during the war because the engineering industry was fully occupied by production for the war effort. Under a 1941 agreement between Britain and America called 'Lend-Lease', our farming industry was boosted by a supply of new equipment from the US. Tractors were the most welcome of the machines supplied and, because of its power and size, the American 'Oliver 90' was the most sought after.

Two of these tractors were supplied to farmers in the locality, one to Viv Smale of Goss Moor and the other to Dick Parkyn of Treliver Farm near Ruthers, both of whom were farming contractors. These new tractors benefited all local farms and smallholdings as they were available for hire in order to assist in the cultivation and threshing work.

Ministry of Agriculture

At the outbreak of the war it became obvious that Britain had to be more self-sufficient; the country could not afford to rely on imports to feed the population. The Ministry of Agriculture or, as it was known in Cornwall, the 'War Ag', was given more powers and responsibilities with the aim of encouraging and assisting farmers to achieve maximum productivity from their land. Advice, machinery and manpower were made available to all farmers who needed them. Land which had never been cultivated before, such as downs and heathland, was broken in and tilled with the cost being met by Government subsidies.

The Ministry's machinery was 'pooled' and held in depots around the county. One of the depots was situated on the airfield at Trebelzue, where tractors, ploughs, seed drills, cornbinders, trailers and threshers were kept. Moving the machinery in or out involved crossing the main runway, which was controlled by traffic lights with a reputation for changing very quickly. This resulted in frequent confrontations between the airfield controllers and the drivers, although no accidents were recorded.

Military Aircraft Crashes

There were several aircraft crashes near Cornwall's airfields. As a young lad, the author visited the scene of two such incidents on his bicycle. The first of these occurred on 21 April 1941 at 3.35a.m. on Providence

Farm, just below Castle-an-Dinas. The aircraft was a Lockhead Hudson 'C' of 206 Squadron, St Eval, and had been flying out for patrol duties over the Channel when it suffered engine failure and crashed on a hill-side killing all four crew members. As it lost height, the aircraft narrowly missed the farmhouse at Providence and ploughed a path through the farmyard trees. When the author arrived the next morning the scene, as seen from the next field, was the still-smouldering wreckage with lots of white foam all around it and a distinctive smell. An RAF fire tender was present, as were two or three other RAF vehicles. The aircraft was still armed and three unexploded bombs were in the field, so armed RAF guards kept sightseers away.

An account of the second crash has been supplied by some of the people involved, including Mr L.R. Holmes, MBE, of the Cornish Aviation Society.

On 19 May 1943 Hudson IIIA FH168 of 38 Wing RAF took off from RAF St Eval bound for the Middle East. The aircraft had previously taken off from its base at RAF Netheravon in Wiltshire and had only landed at RAF St Eval to top up with fuel for its long-haul journey. 38 Wing RAF had been formed at Netheravon to provide a link with the 1st Parachute Brigade at Bulford Camp and this link was to prove fatal for the Hudson's most senior passenger. The Hudson was the military version of the American 11-seat Lockhead 14, known as the 'Electra'. It had two Wright Cyclone engines, twin fins and a rudder. The Hudson normally carried a crew of four (pilot, navigator and two air gunners/wireless operators). It was also fitted with two Browning machine-guns that fired through the nose, plus a twin-dorsal turret and a twin-ventral turret in the floor of the aircraft.

The pilot was Flt/Lt R.H. Jesse, navigator pilot officer Arthur Rotenburg, and the wireless operator/air gunner was Flt/Sgt G. Russell. The four other occupants were passengers and included Wing Commander R.W. Hurst, Squadron Leader E.W. Armstrong and Corporal H.A. Palmer. The highest-ranking officer on board was Air Commodore Sir Nigel St Valery Norman, CBE, baronet and son of the Rt Hon. Sir Hendry Norman PC, JP who was about to join 38 Wing Army Cooperation Unit in connection with airborne troops and to prepare for possible attacks on Sicily. He had just been appointed to Air Chief Marshal Sir A.W. Tedder's staff and was to attend an Airborne Forces Planning Conference in the Middle East. It is believed that Sir Nigel may have been piloting the aircraft. Most of the crew were French-Canadian in the Royal Canadian Air Force.

At the same time that Hudson FH168 took off from St Eval, Chief Observer George Gregory was well into his duty watch at the St Columb ROC post. Meanwhile, local farmers William (Bill) Richards and Eddie Thomas left Crugoes Farm, to the south of St Columb, and proceeded to a large wheat field some 400 yards to the east to spread fertiliser. Almost certainly the St Columb Royal Observer Corps crew were tracking the Hudson by this time, as it came within their vicinity. Bill and Eddie heard a spluttering sound and saw an aircraft in distress. One engine was already on fire. The aircraft dipped to the left and lost height and seemed to head straight for them.

It was clear that shortly after take-off the Hudson had lost power in the port engine, and was attempting a forced landing in a field at Crugoes Farm, Blackcross, about 500m south-west of St Columb Royal Observer Corps post.

Bill and Eddie dived for cover under the fertiliser wagon as the plane just cleared a hedge, hit the ground, bounced and slewed across the field in which they worked. A wing broke off, as did part of the tail, and the aircraft ended up partly on top of a hedge. The time was just after 9.50p.m. Mrs Bula Prowse, who lived next door to George Gregory at Little Quoit, recalls hearing the Hudson crash. She ran out to see the aircraft burning 'with bullets exploding all over the place, it was spectacular.'

Initially there was little fire, although the left-hand wing was broken and beginning to burn. The right-hand wing was almost over a gate, which caused part of the aircraft to be off the ground. Bill and Eddie were quickly on the scene, as was Royal Observer member George Gregory.

Two occupants exited the aircraft through a hole in the underside. Fire was beginning to take hold whilst Bill and Eddie looked after the two injured survivors. George Gregory was personally responsible for rescuing four additional members of the crew. George's promptness in obtaining medical aid no doubt helped save their lives. All the survivors were suffering from broken limbs. After the rescue of the six members of the crew, the aircraft burst into flames.

Bill Richards claimed that he remembered seeing the last occupant, Air Commodore Sir Nigel Norman, fighting to get out of the burning cockpit. Until the day he died, Bill Richards maintained that Sir Norman did not die in the crash itself, and, with courage, it may have been possible to save him. However, as the fire had taken hold, no further rescue attempts were made – Sir Nigel Norman died in the blaze. In contrast to Bill Richards' account of Sir Norman's death there is one report which states that he was thrown clear of the aircraft but died of a broken neck.

Bill recalled tracer bullets going off all over the place and feeling sick with the smell of burning flesh. Within 20 minutes the emergency services had arrived. Many local people, including George Collins, Mr Batten, Don Retallick and the Dales, came to the site. Two fire-engines arrived, including one from St Columb, but in order to enter the field a large stone gatepost had to be taken out using a horse. As the fire brigade dampened down the burning wreck the RAF Regiment Police arrived to stand guard. Within 30 minutes the aircraft had burnt out.

After three days the remaining wreckage was carted away by the RAF and after a week virtually all signs of the crash had disappeared. The navigator pilot officer Arthur Rotenburg died of his injuries a few hours later in the hospital at St Eval airfield. A few days after the crash Sir Nigel Norman's wife, Patricia, came to see Bill Richards to thank him for all his efforts following the crash. At the subsequent RAF enquiry, fuel starvation to the port engine was deemed to be the most probable cause of the crash.

Throughout the remainder of the war George Gregory carried out his duties on the post with marked efficiency. On 28 May 1945 the Western Area Commandant, Observer Captain J.W. Sanders, recommended him for the British Empire Medal for his brave actions in 1943 and for his ROC work. It was the first BEM awarded to a member of the Royal Observer Corps in Cornwall.

Airfield Construction

Building and construction materials supplied from the Goss Moor sand works were used in the construction of the military airfields at St Eval (RAF) and St Merryn (RNAS). The former started in 1939: George Wallace Ltd did the levelling and earth moving, Richard Costain Ltd the construction work, and Dorman Long erected the four main hangars. RAF St Eval played a vital role in the air war, carrying out many different duties, with its most successful and important one being as a front-line coastal command station. This fact was known by the enemy, which accounted for the numerous attacks during 1940–41. St Eval closed in 1959 with the remaining squadrons being transferred to RAF St Mawgan.

The St Merryn aerodrome was developed in 1937 for civil use and had one hangar. In 1939 the Admiralty surveyed and acquired the site for military use. Construction started immediately and the base was commissioned on 10 August 1940. The airfield was named RNAS St Merryn, HMS Vulture and was a front-line training establishment for carrier-borne aircraft and crews. Another unit named HMS Curlew joined the base as a second-line training squadron.

The airfield was bombed by German aircraft in 1940–41. A rebuilding programme was carried out in 1944–45. RNAS St Merryn was closed in January 1956, after playing a vital part in during the war and a valuable peacetime role, with all remaining operations being transferred to RNAS Culdrose.

Local Defences

Sand and blocks produced from the Goss Moor sand works were used on many Second World War projects, two of which were anti-aircraft pillars and barricades for roads. In 1940 anti-aircraft pillars were built on the grass verges of the A30 on Goss Moor between the iron girder railway bridge and the road bridge at St Dennis Junction. Each pillar was made from concrete blocks and a concrete post and probably stood about 15ft high. These pillars were meant to discourage any attempt by Germany to land troop-carrying aircraft on the straight and open road. When the threat of any invasion diminished in 1944 the pillars were demolished. A concrete pillbox was built in 1940 on Goss Moor by the access road to the sand and block works. It is not clear why this site was selected, apart from the fact that it did command good views of the A30 (this area was not overgrown in those days). In any emergency it would have been manned by the Home Guard. This pillbox was destroyed using dynamite after the war.

The road barricades were very large concrete sections probably weighing about four to five tons each and were positioned at strategic positions along the A30, including Fraddon Hill, Indian Queens and St Columb Road, plus all road junctions. They were positioned so that with a slight adjustment they could block the road in the event of an enemy invasion, thus impeding any transport progress. The disadvantage was that these sites were a nuisance to local traffic, especially buses which had difficulty in negotiating the chicane-type road layout. When the threat of an invasion diminished these barricades were also removed.

The Construction of RAF St Mawgan, 1942–44

Trebelzue opened for passenger flights in 1933, which ceased in 1939 when the aerodrome was taken over by the military and used as a satellite airfield for RAF St Eval. Two hardstanding runways were completed in 1940 and military operational flying began in 1942.

The construction of RAF St Mawgan started in 1942 with Trebelzue being integrated with it. The new site engulfed the hamlets of Trenoon, Deerpark

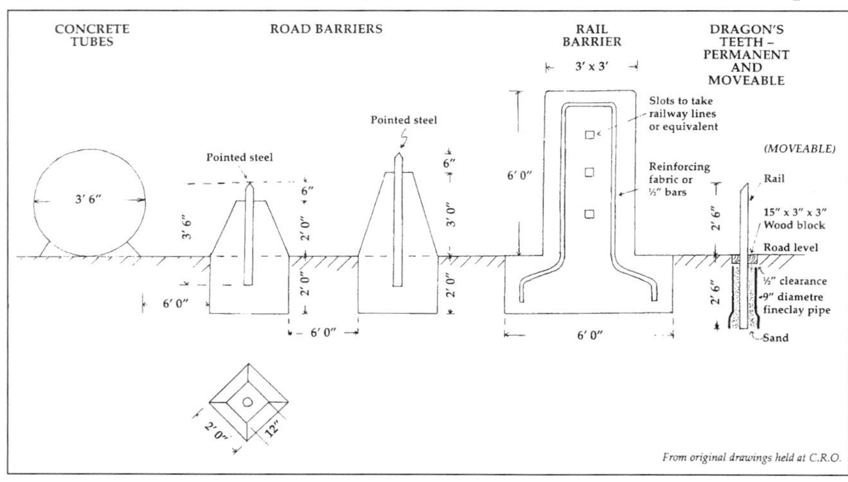

The County Council installed road barriers. KHR/Coll

and Mawgan Cross. The main contractor for RAF St Mawgan was Richard Costain, a firm experienced in airfield construction. The airfield construction spanned the period 1939–40 for Trebelzue and 1942–44 for St Mawgan.

The author's mother was employed as a cook in the workmen's canteen at the St Mawgan site. Transport was provided to convey her to and from work by way of riding in a lorry belonging to Richards and Osborne. The usual driver was a Mr Wes Rowe from Roche. The author remembers riding with Mr Rowe in his lorry delivering sand to the Trebelzue end of the site and being told on arrival that the site had just been attacked by a German aeroplane which had probably been carrying out reconnaissance work. They were warned that if it returned they were to take cover under the lorry. There were no casualties but the large cement mixer was damaged by machine-gun fire, with the bullet holes clearly visible. Dust was still in the air from damaged bags of cement and the heaps of sand which had obviously been hit. There was an anti-aircraft gun emplacement surrounded by a wall of protective sandbags near the cement mixer so it was likely that this was the German aircraft's target.

After this incident and on many other occasions Canadian-piloted P51 American Mustang fighter planes would taxi close by, sometimes struggling in the muddy conditions, on the way to or from their task as escorts for Allied bombers. The pilots were always cheerful and always gave a wave as they passed by. Canvas repair hangars were nearby with mechanics working on damaged aircraft, re-arming and maintenance. The danger of war was all around yet it was accepted as part of everyday life at that time.

The first concrete runway at St Mawgan was completed in July 1943 and the first military aircraft to land was an American B24 Liberator. Two more concrete runways were completed in August 1943 and the main runway was extended in 1944, making it one of the longest in the country, as it still is today. Major construction work ceased in 1944.

This project had given the local economy a much-needed boost as it utilised local labour and materials. Around 500,000 tons of sand, aggregates and concrete blocks had been used with 90 per cent of that coming from the Richards and Osborne sand works.

The Build-Up to D-Day

One day in 1944 the inhabitants of St Dennis Junction and other neighbouring villages and hamlets were woken by the noise of a continuous road convoy of American troop-moving trucks and other military equipment. This movement continued for many weeks. Although there were a few British Army convoys, they were nowhere near the scale of the American presence. Tank convoys were the noisiest and took two or three hours to pass. To the locals it was an awesome display of military resources, the likes of which they had never seen before.

When convoys halted for troop-comfort stops and meals the half-blocked roads would be chaotic with civil and military vehicles, aircraft-carrying articulated units and trailers all struggling to progress to their respective destinations. These stops brought friendly exchanges between locals and troops. Fresh water, milk and eggs were always favourites with the troops, while the locals received cigarettes, fruit, sweets and chocolate in return. 'K' ration boxes and sometimes their contents, cigarette packets and chewing-gum wrappers littered the grass verges. The small waterproof cartons of 'K' rations contained emergency packs of powdered food and drink, chocolate, cigarettes and other comforts and were issued to all American troops in combat and standby situations.

All these conveys were heading west to holding parks and camps situated near harbours, river inlets and recently constructed slipways, to await embarkation on D-Day. Then, one day, the convoys stopped passing by and proceeded to turn onto local byroads, which quickly became filled with vehicles and troops (all suitable space around the A30 west of Goss Moor was filled). This was the build-up for the invasion of Europe – right on the doorstep of this small Cornish community.

All vehicles and equipment were camouflaged with nets and foliage, tents were erected, field kitchens were set up, latrines were dug and anti-aircraft guns were positioned. Some fields were turned into tented camps for the combat troops, with engineers and guards living by their equipment and guns and sleeping in two-man bivouacs.

The nearest of these encampments to St Dennis Junction was an engineering construction company which virtually filled the road to Blackacre Farm with cranes, graders, bulldozers and trucks. Local children spent many hours with these troops eagerly awaiting the gifts of chocolate, sweets and fruit which were usually on offer. This particular company consisted of black Americans with white officers.

There was a field kitchen on the byroad to Blackacre Farm, plus one near Ennisworgey and one near Providence Farm. They all produced an excellent standard of food which was far superior to and more plentiful than the locals' meagre rations. On the edge of Goss Moor, on a tributary of the Fal, a water-filtration plant was set up to produce drinking-water for the American troops. A moorland plantation on the brow of the hill by the A30 near Shalimar, Roche, became a large field kitchen in one half and a large fuel dump (in jerry cans) in the other.

On the A30 just west of the Tregoss crossing gatehouse there was a bad left-hand bend with a deep ditch alongside, which many overenthusiastic American drivers managed to find. A large six-wheeled recovery truck was permanently stationed

A recently vacated US Army camp prior to D-Day.
Imperial War Museum

at this site. It is a pity that the concern for keeping the traffic moving was more of a priority in those days than it is today! Every crossroad and junction had military police encamped by it to control traffic and keep the A30 clear. Many locals remember cigar-smoking jeep drivers were always tearing around seemingly intent on destroying the jeeps and themselves, with little regard for other vehicles, people and animals, and all hell-bent on getting somewhere before they started.

The areas around Roche, Be Lovely, Whitemoor, St Dennis, Castle-an-Dinas, Ruthvoes, St Columb, Indian Queens, Penhale, Gothers and Enniscaven were full of troops, vehicles and equipment. Local people were issued with passes to enable them to carry on with their everyday lives and safely move around the locality. Children were not issued with passes as they were not considered a security threat.

The American troops had a service similar to our NAAFI called Post Exchange, usually referred to as the PX, where they could purchase toiletries, cigarettes and luxuries, etc. It was run by the military and was stationed 'in the field' for the convenience of the troops in the surrounding area; they were allowed one visit per week. The Americans were permitted certain recreational times; these were spent in local villages, public houses and village dance halls. There were regular disturbances at Indian Queens between white and black American troops, which often developed into serious fights, reflecting the racial tensions that existed in America at that time.

Some minor road improvements were made by American engineers. An American officer had been given the job of planning and building a road around the low girder bridge on the A30 which caused the Americans problems with high loads. However, D-Day meant that this work was never completed.

The author remembers a situation in 1944, which he describes as 'terrifying':

One day I was taking my one-year-old brother in a pram from our home at St Dennis Junction to Treranke Cottages, near Roche, along the A30 to visit our Gran. Walking on the right-hand side of the road, facing the oncoming traffic, as I was always taught to do, some 800 yards into the journey we met a US Army tank convoy travelling west. These tanks were not the easiest of vehicles to drive on hard roads at the best of times, but to unexpectedly be faced with a young lad pushing a pram which could only be seen at the last minute was not easy to cope with, as the evasive manoeuvres of some drivers proved. I had to keep on the road, as the grass verges were too soft and overgrown for me to successfully push a pram.

I'll never forget the sight and noise of the tank tracks and the smell of heated engines being so close – to say I was frightened was an understatement.

We did eventually reach Treranke Cottages unscathed and very thankful. Needless to say I never repeated that kind of journey again.

To put the situation into perspective, at the time of this incident the A30 was not as wide as it is today. It was not until after the war that the County Council widened the road across the moor.

With D-Day imminent and the American troops moved out, within a couple of days everything was gone – they had all moved west to their designated embarkation points along the south coast. Here, special concrete loading ramps nicknamed 'hards' had been constructed along river banks and inlets to enable organised embarkation onto various types of landing-craft to take place, irrespective of tides, etc. For example, the dock facilities at Falmouth were used for the loading of the large and heavy equipment.

The debris and gear left behind, such as empty jerry cans, cases and boxes, tables, seats and anything else that could not be practically carried into an invasion-landing situation soon disappeared as locals recovered anything that could be of use. Certain items and material was hard to come by in those days so it was an opportunity not to be missed!

The tented camps were soon dismantled and removed by a US Army unit not designated for the initial landings. Gates and hedges were repaired and fields returned to their normal use and humans and animals returned to normal life. The military build-up and preparation for D-Day was spectacular, very well organised and unforgettable.

It is hard not to wonder how many of these brave men, who were all from the 15th Combat Troop of the American 29th Division, which landed with the second wave of landings at Omaha Beach in Normandy on D-Day, survived the landings or indeed the whole war. Americans suffered huge losses in the initial landings in France, as did our own troops. To commemorate the American Forces' embarkation from Turnaware Beach on D-Day, a granite memorial stone has been erected at Tolverne on the bank of the Fal next to the Smugglers Cottage near Philleigh on the Roseland Peninsula.

APPENDIX 1:

Flora and Fauna

Flora

The Goss and Tregoss Moors contain a pattern of different habitats including dry and wet heath-land, grassland, bog, swamp, fern and inundation communities, open water and dense willow. Natural drainage has been stifled by what some have called mismanagement during the tin-streaming days, which has resulted in the southern region becoming a wetland vegetation area. Large areas of the moor remain partly or wholly submerged for most of the year, only drying out in the summer months. During heavy rain a large area of the moor becomes totally inaccessible, even on foot. During these times the moor can be a dangerous place, especially to people who are unfamiliar with it. The wet areas occasionally contain open water but are usually characterised by a marsh vegetation. The Tregoss Moor has areas of dry heath, wet heath and bog moss while northern Goss Moor has damp and variable purple moor grass pasture.

Colour patterns on the moor are made up of heathers, gorse and grassland, dominated by purple moor grass, wavy hairgrass and orchids. Gorse is always in abundance with its yellows and greens, adding a colourful dimension to the landscape. Wet hollows and areas with poor drainage support vegetation such as purple moor grass, cross-leaved heath, early marsh orchid and the lesser butterfly orchid (see 142).

There are 15 ponds or pools on the moors; on the more open ponds a variety of vegetation is found (see table). There are even some lily ponds either side of the A30 road near the Poplars residence. One has yellow lilies, despite the fact that the area has long been used as an unofficial dumping ground. The other pool, on the opposite side of the A30 and some distance into the moor, has the white lilies. This pond is reputed to have been the site of a drowning many years ago with the lilies being planted as mark of remembrance.

The information that follows has been compiled from a field survey carried out in 1994 and from the author's experiences. It represents a true but not necessarily complete account of wildlife on the Goss and Tregoss Moors.

The Utilisation of Vegetation

Willow grows all over the moor and was utilised in many ways. Local household gardeners would use the long straight branches to support and assist the growing of peas and beans ('pea sticks' and 'bean sticks'). Gardeners would go onto the moor to select and then cut these sticks, tie them into bundles, and carry them home on their backs or on their bicycles.

Willow is not a large tree as such, with only the main trunk of the older trees of any significant size. Only the younger straight branches would be used as pea and bean sticks. The larger, older willow tree trunks were cut down and sawn into logs as fire-wood. This practice was prominent during the Second World War when coal was in short supply, but is not carried out today. The practice of cutting pea and bean sticks virtually ceased in the 1970s, as did the making of clothes-pegs and baskets from willow.

Whereas the willow grows more densely on the western side of the moor, hazelnut trees were found mainly in the Tregoss area. These produced nuts which were edible by both humans and animals and a wood which was strong and flexible. This wood was popular with the gypsies up until the 1960s, for the making and repair of their horse-drawn caravans.

Rushes were cut and collected by smallholders for use as thatching for their hay- and straw-ricks. Ferns were also cut and dried for use as animal bedding. Peat was cut and dug from bogs. It was stored and dried before eventual use as fuel for fires. It is uncertain when the practice of using rushes, ferns and peat stopped, and it is very doubtful if it continues today.

Fruits and nuts included blueberries ('erts'), blackberries, wild strawberries, wild apples and hazelnuts. Blackberries and blueberries have always been picked and eaten by local people.

In the days of steam railway locomotives the moor was regularly a victim of fire caused by sparks from the smokestacks. Gorse and dried grass, etc. was the main fuel for these fires in the dry season. Gorse would never completely burn and the charred remains were nick-named 'smutties'. These were collected by local people for use as fuel to heat their water boilers, etc. In the dry summer season fires on the moor were almost a daily occurrence. These

Just some of the flora and fauna found on the Goss and Tregoss Moors

Dry heath

Purple Moor Grass	Cross-leaved Heath	Marsh Violet	Devil's Bit Scabious
Southern Marsh Orchid	Bog Myrtle	Lesser Butterfly Orchid	Bog Asphodel
Black Bog Rush	Bog Pimpernel	Greater Bird's-Foot Trefoil	Jointed Rush

Wet heath

Common Heather	Bell Heather	Western Gorse	Common Gorse
Tormentil	Bristle Bent	Wood Sage	Purple Moor Grass
Foxglove	Bilberry (herts)	Heath Spotted Orchid	Ivy-leaved Bellflower
Betony Lousewort	Bracken		

Marshy grasslands

Yellow Loosestrife	Marsh Violet	Tussock Sedge	Greater Bird's-Foot Trefoil
Yellow Iris	Common Valerian Reedmace	Hemlock Water Dropwort	Marsh Thistle
Marsh St John's Wort	Southern Marsh Orchid	Heath Spotted Orchid	Lesser Butterfly Orchid
Devil's Bit Scabious	Water Mint		

Bogs

Bog Moss	Common Cotton Grass	Round-leaved Sundew	Marsh Cinquefoil
Bog Bean	Sedges	Southern Marsh Orchid	Wavy-leaved St John's Wort
Water Horsetail	Marsh Lousewort	Bog Pimpernel	

Pond/pool margins and marshland

Broad-leaved Pondweeds	Spiked Water-millfoil	Greater Bladderwort	Water Horsetail
Bog Beam	Yellow Loosestrife	Marsh Cinquefoil	Marsh St John's Wort
Sharp Flowered Rush			

Many ponds are surrounded by tall fern vegetation such as:

Reedmace	Bottle Sedge	Rushes	Water Mint
Grey Willow			

Mature Willow Woodland and Willow Scrub

Extensive Willow Carr Lichen	Broad Buckler Fern	Lady Fern	Royal Fern (uncommon)
Yellow Iris	Reedmace	Hemlock	Water Dropwort
Enchanter's Nightshade	Water Horsetail	Tussock Sedge	

Trackways

Yellow Centavoy	Three-lobed Crowfoot	Greater Bird's-Foot Trefoil	Allseed

Former trampling by cattle and ponies, as well as compaction by gravel lorries, has enabled an unusual and rare community of minute plants to colonise the rutted and disturbed ground.

moorland fires did no significant damage and, more often than not, helped with the regeneration of the plant and vegetation life. After a fire was out new shoots of plant and vegetation would appear within days and all the wildlife dependant on that particular stretch of land would vacate the area, returning when the threat from fire had been extinguished. The Odonata's ability to survive moorland fires and adapt to a new habitat means that it has become less of a concern for those organisations today that are in favour of a further urbanisation of the moor.

When the railways changed from steam-powered to diesel-powered locomotives in 1962, the moorland fires virtually ceased. The few exceptions which did occur were by acts of vandalism which unfortunately still happens today, albeit very rarely. Perhaps the lack of fires, gypsies and old traditional practices are responsible for the overgrown state which exists on many parts of the moor today.

Fauna

Odonata (Dragonflies and Damselflies)

The diverse wetland habitats on Goss and Tregoss Moors support an outstanding assemblage of 16 breeding species of Odonata; keeled skimmer and black darter breed in the more acidic pools, whereas beautiful demoiselle and golden-ringed dragonfly breed along the streams open ditches. The neutral ponds support the azure damselfly, common darter and the regionally uncommon red-eyed damselfly. Of particular note is the presence of large populations of small red damselfly and variable damselfly, both nationally scarce species.

Lepidoptera (Butterflies and Moths)

Over 100 species of Lepidoptera have been recorded, including 30 species of butterfly. Of note are the silver-studded blue and the marsh fritillary. Of the moth community, silky wave and narrow-bordered bee hawkmoth are both nationally scarce, but present here. Other rare invertebrates include beetles, and the bog bush cricket.

Amphibians

The common frog and the common toad have always been found in the wetland areas of the moor.

Mammals

A wide range of animals have always enjoyed the freedom of the moor, such as badger, fox, hedgehog, rabbit, hare, vole, woodmouse, roe deer and red deer.

The hare was more prominent in the early 1900s than it is today, when it was the prey for organised hunts. Roe and red deer are relatively new to the moor with evidence of their presence only having been found since the 1990s.

Reptiles

The moor provides an ideal habitat for the venomous adder, the grass snake and lizard. As with most reptiles, these like the warmth of the sun and are most likely to be seen in the summer months. All three hibernate in the cold winter months.

Birds

A recent survey found the following species nesting on the moor: woodpigeon, cuckoo, swallow, wren, dunnock, robin, blackbird, song thrush, garden warbler, goldcrest, long-tailed tit, blue tit, coal tit, jay, magpie, chaffinch, linnet, bullfinch, sparrowhawk, stonechat, tree popit, little owl and raven. Buzzards and herring gull have also been seen, but they do not appear to nest in the area as there is no suitable habitat for them.

In the 1940s snipes, moorhens, wild ducks and swans were common sights on the moor but sadly none of these can be found there today. Having said that, a local survey carried out in the 1990s actually reported 58 species of birds on the moors.

Chordata (Fish)

From the early-twentieth century up to the 1960s there were fish in the streams, clear-water pools and the River Fal. Brown trout, eels, minnows and the rare brook lampney were reasonably prominent. However, the contamination of the Fal in the 1960s virtually put paid to any survival of fish life. It is believed that in the 1970s and '80s two northern pools were stocked with brown trout, trench, bream, carp, roach and rudd, by local angling clubs. Although fish numbers are unknown today, an indication of the low numbers is reflected in the fact that there is no active angling club at the time of writing.

Recent moves to clean and clear the River Fal are hoped to result in the return of fish and also increased Odonata presence.

Livestock

With the abundance of water and various grasses the Goss Moor offered local householders, farmers and smallholders cheap grazing for their animals, although this virtually ceased in the 1960s. In 1930 there were over 200 head of cattle on the moor.

Traditionally many local families living on the Enniscaven and Penrose side of the moor owned a single cow to provide milk, cream and butter for their own consumption, with any surplus being sold to neighbours. Smallholders would have three or four cows, with some farmers having larger numbers.

Anyone grazing animals on the moor was obliged to pay a small annual fee to Viscount Falmouth. This was collected by his gamekeeper when he could prove who owned each cow.

Smallholders and farmers had various ways of identifying their own cattle, some were known to have included a white cow in their herd to make it easier. There is a local story about a smallholder called Runnalls who used his dog to bring home his cattle. He would take his dog onto the moor, identify his cattle, lift the dog up onto his shoulder and point to his herd. Runnalls would then return to his smallholding and leave the dog to bring home the cattle, which it always did.

With the moor being made up of streams, pools, bogs and swamps it was not uncommon for cattle to become trapped and stranded. When this occurred it was a case of all available locals assisting with the recovery. The majority were successfully recovered, but some were not.

Today there are at least two farmers who exercise their commoners' rights to graze cattle on the moor. Moorland cattle do not usually have any contact with cattle grazed on normal grassland because of the possibility of contamination of moorland-related diseases. Most of the moorland cattle are Charalais crosses which adapt to the conditions better than other breeds.

Although sheep grazing was rare, several people kept geese on the moor. Some were kept in little flocks of two or three geese and a gander. The owners would select a position for the nest, preferably in a bank or burrow made by old tin-mining workings where the geese could lay their eggs and hatch their young. Normally the geese would forage for their own food but during the breeding season their owners would feed them grain. After the goslings were hatched and reared to three to four months old they would either be sold to dealers or at the St Dennis Fair held in November in Trelavour Square. However, some geese would be kept and fattened up for sale at Christmas

There were some people, such as a Mr Will Key from Ennis Vean, who kept flocks of geese on the moor. He reared his own goslings and had up to 30 in his flock. These would be taken out onto the Goss Moor via the cattle arch at Domellick every morning and brought back to the security of the smallholding by night. The practice of breeding geese on the moor was started by the early tin streamers to supplement their income, and reached prominence in the 1800s. By 1940 the practice had virtually died out.

In the late-nineteenth century trains ran at night over the Goss Moor carrying iron ore. This was not popular with the geese owners as some geese had the habit of roosting on or near the railway tracks. The worst accident to occur was one night when a train brought a premature end to 18 geese.

Goats

Nearly all moorland people kept goats on the moor at some time, with herds varying in numbers. They were primarily reared for their milk, some of which was used in the family homes, but the bulk of the milk was used as food for pigs which invariably everyone kept.

Incidentally pigs were very rarely seen on the moor, as most were kept on smallholdings or in gardens.

Poultry

Most people who lived on the edge of the moor kept poultry. By day they were in a wire run and by night they roosted in a chicken house to protect them from foxes. Poultry were kept for eggs and eventually for the family table. For the privilege of running stock on the moor owners had to pay an annual rent to Tregothnan estate. A few people who had access to a stream or pond kept ducks.

Ponies and Donkeys

Moorland people kept ponies for use as a form of transport, and to assist with work on smallholdings. Ponies would pull traps, carts and other equipment for these duties. When not being worked the animals were turned out onto the moor to graze.

From very early times up to the mid-twentieth century a pony and trap was a familiar sight around the hamlets and country lanes. (A trap is a pony-drawn two-wheeled carriage with side seats accessed from the rear capable of carrying up to four people or their equivalent weight.)

There were only a couple of people who kept donkeys on the moor. A donkey provided transport by either carrying a person on its back or being harnessed into a shay (a pair of shafts attached to a frame with a pair of lightweight wheels and a single seat).

Wild Ponies

Wild ponies, known locally as 'gossies', were introduced to the moor in the nineteenth century. The gossies were so well known that people living on or near the moor were often referred to by the nickname Goss Moor gossies. In the early-twentieth century Mr Will Key of Ennis Vean and Mr Richard Pethick of Domellick Manor Farm kept ponies on the moor to breed for eventual sale as pit ponies to the coal mines of South Wales. The latter, who called everyone 'old dear' was eventually nicknamed Old Dear Pethick.

The normal breeding process ensured that numbers were maintained. The gossies had the freedom of the moor to seek out good sources of grazing and water. Although water was plentiful, good grazing was at times more difficult to find. This resulted in the gossies encroaching onto local farms,

Top picture: *The marsh fritillary butterfly.*
Peter Belton

Above left: *Swans – majestic inhabitants of the moorland pools .* KHR

Above: *The golden-ringed dragonfly.* R.J. Evenden

Left: *A snipe. This bird is a regular on the moor.*
Cornwall Wildlife Trust

Western gorse flowering on Tregoss Moor, 2002. **KHR**

Right: *The moor near Tregoss, 2002.* KHR

Below: *The River Fal with Himalayan balsam in the foreground.* KHR

Below: *Marsh thistle.* KHR

Bottom left: *Honeysuckle.* KHR

Left: *Common valerian.* KHR

Below: *Wet willow woodland with royal fern.* KHR

Below left: *Tufted veach and soft rush.* KHR

Bottom: *Willow on the southern part of the moor.* KHR

Above: Crocosmia monbretia, *a garden escapee.* KHR

Left: *Invasive weeds – rosebay willow herb (pink) and Japanese knotweed.* KHR

Left: *Western gorse and bell heather.* KHR

Right: *Western dry heath growing on the tin-streamed landscape – Western and European gorse and heathers growing on the drier hummocks.* KHR

Bell heather. KHR

The Goss Moor looking south to St Dennis Church showing the medieval field system on slopes around the church. **KHR**

Right: *Devil's bit scabious – the larval food plant of the marsh fritillary butterfly.* KHR

Below: *Blackberry or bramble.* KHR

Top picture: *Bell heather.* KHR
Centre: *A moor view near Pitsmingle.* KHR
Bottom: *A Tregoss view.* KHR

Right: *Common ragwort.* KHR

Centre: *Water mint.* KHR

Bottom: *A colourful view of the railway cutting on the northern part of the moor.* KHR

usually in the Pendine area, seeking good grass. When this occurred, the farmers would impound the ponies and seek a levy from the owners for their release. If the levies were not paid, the farmers would sell off the ponies to dealers as pit ponies.

In around 1950 Old Dear Pethick claimed ownership of the remaining gossies and sold them to a Mr James of Redruth. When Mr James moved the ponies off the moor it brought to an end a long-standing tradition of the Goss Moor which had spanned 100 years.

Horses

In very early times, when the moor was drier and safer than it is today, hunting probably involved the the use of horses. However, as the moor became more waterlogged in the twentieth century it also became unsuitable for horses. There were and still are some dangerous swamps and bogs in the southern wetlands of the moor. One unfortunate incident occurred in 1930 when a horse, belonging to Mr Bert Hawken, a St Dennis Junction man, got stuck in a swamp in an area between the old A30 and the railway line. Attempts involving many helpers were made to rescue the animal, all to no avail.

Horses were used at the block works prior to 1940, where they travelled on hardcore roads and were not subjected to the dangers of the moor.

Right: *The moor near Tregoss, 2002.* KHR

Below: *Willow on the southern part of the moor.* KHR

Left: *The Standardised China Clay Company's old ruins on Belowda Beacon, built in 1912 and seen here in 2001.* KHR

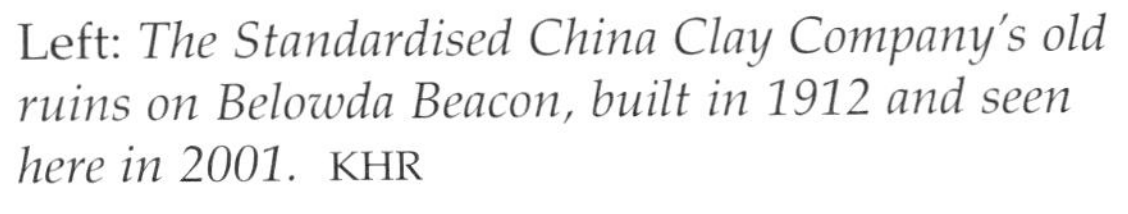

The disused china-clay pit on Belowda Beacon in 2001. **KHR**

The ruins of Parka Tin Mine near Toldish in 2001 – this mine last worked in 1913. **KHR**

Above: ***Belowda Beacon south shaft engine house and stack built in the later part of the nineteenth century and still in good condition in 2001, being utilised as a farm building.*** **KHR**

Right: ***The Ruthers Iron Mine stack still in remarkable condition today.*** **KHR**

Left: ***The old Halloon Mine stack, near St Columb Road in 2001; this mine was started in 1848.*** **KHR**

Background picture: ***The ruins of Ruthers Iron Mine in 2001. Records show that this mine first worked in 1754.*** **KHR**

Appendix 2:

Old Mining Sites

Mining Sites Around the Goss Moor

Tregonetha

An old iron mine, probably represented by old open works and shafts on the western side of Tregonetha Downs, one-and-a-half miles south-west of St Wenn. The open works are in lines trending about 15° east and appear to be all in alluvial or head deposits. Between 1873 and 1876 1,543 tons of iron ore were produced.

Belowda

Two miles north-west of Roche. Also known as Belowda Beacon, Beacon Hill and Be Lovely, it was on the highest part of the granite mass of Belowda Beacon. Although the mine was in operation for 30 years (closing in 1902), it never showed large returns. Only 45 tons of black tin are recorded for the years 1872–75, 1880 and 1894–96, while under the name Be Lovely 4 tons were produced in 1899–1902. The remains of a shaft can be seen on the summit of the hill, and the remains of the shaft workings on Wheal Dora lode near Belowda village are in remarkable condition. The buildings around the engine house are used as cattle sheds by a local farmer.

Beacon Clay Works

In 1912 the Standardised China Clay Co. was formed and developed the site as a china-clay production pit and plant, which included refining and drying. The company had German managers with a local workforce. The ruins of the refining and process buildings and the opencast pits and waste tips can still be seen on the site beside the A3274 to Tregonetha. The manager and assistant manager were, at the outbreak of the First World War in 1914, interned to the Isle of Man for the duration of the war. It was claimed that they had spied on Allied shipping passing along the north coast and passed information to a contact in Newquay who was later imprisoned for spying.

Royalton Tin Mine

Also known as Old Castle-an-Dinas, this mine was half a mile south of the summit of Castle-an-Dinas hill. Work was in progress here during 1836–37, at which time the purser was a Mr Merrifield – probably a descendant of the Elizabethan John Merryfelde. Trials in 1853 apparently showed traces of gold. This was discredited by George Henwood who reported that he had found no gold, just evidence of tin-bearing lodes. He advised the directors to abandon the search for gold and to concentrate on the stanniferous elvan. However, the company ceased operations shortly afterwards. The elvan was later worked in a series of opencast pits or quarries, two of which were still to be seen in 1963, adjoining Royalton Farm. Records show that 24 tons of ore were produced in 1870–73. In the 1940s two of the pits were full of water and the third was being used as a refuse tip and collecting point for used tin cans to be recycled as part of the war effort. The pits are now overgrown.

Treliver Iron Mine

Treliver was an opencast mine positioned about 400 yards west-north-west of Ruthvoes (also known as Ruthers). There are no records of any underground working. Records show that the mine was worked in 1856–61 when 1,380 tons of iron ore were mined. Treliver, along with the mines at Ruthvoes and Toldish, were all part of the Indian Queens Iron Mines. They all worked the same lode, said to be 18ft wide. In the 1940s, the site was a shallow depression used by farmers for the disposal of dead animals. Today, however, the site is completely overgrown.

Toldish Iron Mine

This mine was situated south-east of the Ruthvoes mine, and consisted of a shaft and an opencast pit virtually in Toldish village, plus an opencast work on the opposite side of the old A30 and a shaft in the lane which connected the A30 to the B3279 at Gaverigan. This lane was known for many years as Iron Mine Lane. From 1899 to 1903 this mine was owned by the Indian Queens Mining and Colour Co. Ltd. Underground work took place in 1899–1900 and surface work during 1901–02. The mine later produced colour pigment and was taken over by the Golden Valley Ochre Company in 1946. In 1944 the opencast pit by the old A30 was used as a waste tip by the American troops during the build-up to D-Day. It has been filled in since then as the area was developed as a site for the Richards and Osborne transport company.

Ruthvoes Iron Mine

Also known as Ruthers, and Indian Queens Iron Mine, this mine was a mile north of Indian Queens and 500 yards south of Ruthvoes, in red-stained killas country. The lode consisted of quartz with some haematite and limonite and some manganese oxide. It was cut through by the Toldish railway tunnel (now disused) that passes east–west through the Ruthvoes sett, and was said to consist of clear iron ore. The lode exposed in 1942 was of dark brown limonite, with some quartz in places. Ruthvoes was worked for iron ore in 1754, although later the mine was exploited for ochre and umber. Ruthvoes later produced pigment and was taken over by the Golden Valley Ochre Company in 1946. It is unlikely that the mine was worked beyond the early 1950s. The remains of surface buildings can still be seen, as can the engine house smokestack, which is in a remarkably good condition.

Toldish Tin Mine

Also known as Parka Consols, Toldish Tin Mine lies west of the iron mine of the same name. There were reputed to be three east–west lodes crossed by the Great Lode, stated to be of quartz and chlorite, with patches of cassiterite. This mine was worked in 1909–12 as the Toldish Tin Mine, and in 1913 by the Fraddon Mining Syndicate. The best year as far as employment goes was in 1910 when eight men were employed, four above ground and four below. Only two men were employed in 1912. The mine produced 28 tons of black tin in 1881–83 and was last worked in 1913. It eventually became flooded and was initially utilised by the Newquay Water Company as a water source. The Ordnance Survey maps show that one old shaft could have had a private residence built on it. The old mine workings continue to be used as a mains water-supply by South West Water. The engine-house stack, in a reduced form, can still be seen, although the top half has been demolished.

Halloon Pits

Situated near the Halloon Barton Farm on the opposite side of the A39, Halloon Pits consisted of three opencast pits, all worked around 1800. Clay from these pits was used by the nearby brickworks at St Columb Road, which in those days was also called Halloon. After operations ceased the pits became flooded and overgrown. It is documented that in 1809 a prehistoric find of a bronze low-flanged palstave was recovered from a pool between Blue Anchor and St Columb Major.

Halloon Mine

Also known as Parka Mine, Halloon Mine was near the B3275 south of the railway station at St Columb Road. This small mine was started or restarted around 1848. A shaft was put down to a depth of 30 fathoms and an engine erected, but through lack of funds no further work was done. It is said that the mine yielded nickel, silver and even gold. In 1854 the Mining Journal *reported that George Henwood had had 'a massive ring made from its produce'. The gold was said to be of a deep-red hue but on being refined assumed its usual bright-yellow colour. In 1875 Foster described the unusual type of rock that contained cassiterite and quartz, with the chief ore being lenses of tinstone. The recorded outputs were 557 tons of black tin between 1873 and 1879 and 24 tons in 1882–83 when the mine was worked by the Trevarren United Mines Company.*

Fatwork and Virtue Mine

This mine was situated on the edge of Goss Moor. According to Jenkins it was a site likely to have been exploited by 'streamers' in earlier times. The property was re-worked as Wheal Cornwall when it was equipped with a 12ft diameter water-wheel and six head of stamps. Advertised for sale in 1835 as Fatwork, it was claimed to have raised 4,000 sacks of tin. In 1852 an engine was erected which did duty for pumping and stamping. However, the company consisted of poor adventurers and within two years the workings were abandoned. Operations were resumed in November 1880 under the name of Indian Queens Consols. A year later, the company sold the property to Trevarren United Mines which had acquired the Parka mines together with the Gover Mine in St Mewan. After the closure of the mine the old opencast excavation was used as a place of worship by local Methodists, with services held there during the summer. The site is now known as Queens Pit and is kept in good condition by local people.

Gaverigan Tin Mine

This mine was 250 yards north of Gaverigan Manor Farm. An advertisement in the West Briton *of 6 March 1835 mentions five alluvial tin setts in this neighbourhood as available for granting by the High Lord's estate. In the course of streaming, four tin lodes were discovered adjacent to the River Fal. These were later found in the Gaverigan Mine. Records show that 13 tons of black tin were mined in 1837, 1838 and 1866. The mine was re-worked in 1849 by a Manchester company under the name of Wheal Vivian. A 24ins pumping engine, two water-wheels and six head of stamps were offered for sale by auction in 1855.*

Chypraze Tin Mine

Also known as Trefullock, Chypraze was no more than a tin prospect. In 1842 a cost-book company was formed to work part of the St Enoder sett under the name of Chypraze Tin Mine. Most of the adventurers hailed from Truro although towards the end of the company's life a number of shares were sold to London speculators. Operations started in 1842 but were suspended in 1846. At the eventual sale the engine was purchased by the Medlyn Mine in Wendron. After the mine was closed it was revealed in the mining press that the manager and the purser were under suspicion for selling their shares at high prices to London investors when they were aware that the mine was about to close. Working resumed in 1850 under the name of Chypraze Consols but this ceased in 1853. The only record of output is two and a half tons of black tin in 1852.

Background: ***Chypraze Mine stack a little worse for wear in 2001.*** **KHR**

Bibliography

Barton, D.B., *The Historical Survey of Mines and Mineral Railways in East Cornwall and West Devon*, Truro, 1964

Collins, Joseph Henry, *West of England Mining Regions*, William Brendan, Plymouth, 1912

Dines, H.G., *The Metalliferous Mining Region of S.W. England*, HMSO, 1956

Great Britain Geological Survey, *Geology of Bodmin and St Austell*, HMSO, 1909

Hamilton-Jenkin, A.K., *Mines and Miners of Cornwall Part 9*, Truro Bookshop, 1964

Payne, H.M. Creswell, *The Story of Roche*, Newquay, c.1950

Penhallurick, R.D., *Tin in Antiquity*, London, 1986

Spargo, Thomas, *Mines of Devon and Cornwall*, Bradford Barton, Truro, 1960

Trunson, J.H., *The Cornish Mineral Industry 1937–51*, Mining Publications Ltd, London, 1942

Trunson, J.H., *Mining in Cornwall Vol. 2*, Tempus, 1999

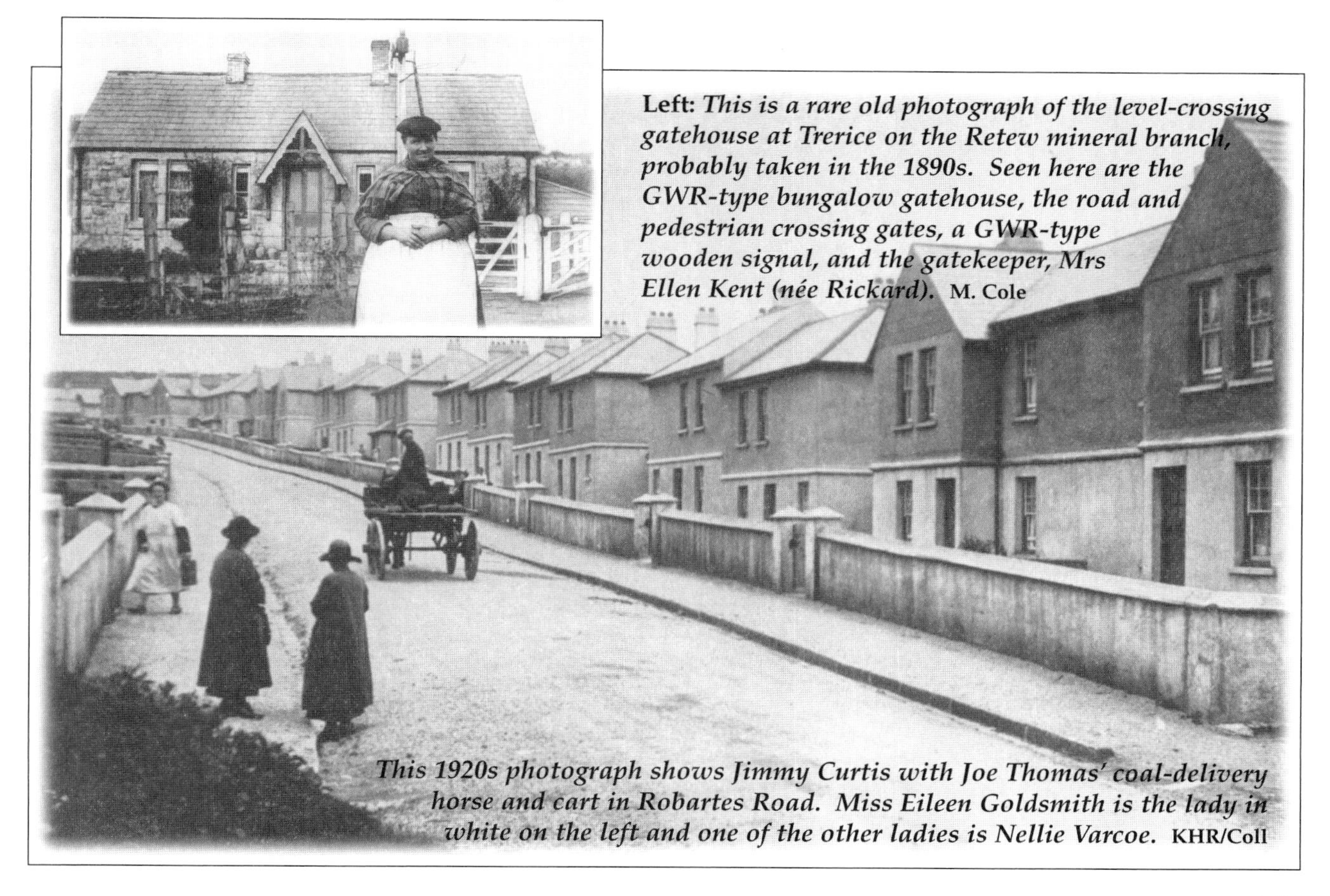

Left: *This is a rare old photograph of the level-crossing gatehouse at Trerice on the Retew mineral branch, probably taken in the 1890s. Seen here are the GWR-type bungalow gatehouse, the road and pedestrian crossing gates, a GWR-type wooden signal, and the gatekeeper, Mrs Ellen Kent (née Rickard).* **M. Cole**

This 1920s photograph shows Jimmy Curtis with Joe Thomas' coal-delivery horse and cart in Robartes Road. Miss Eileen Goldsmith is the lady in white on the left and one of the other ladies is Nellie Varcoe. **KHR/Coll**

Subscribers

Mr and Mrs Joan and Denzil Ackrell, Menawartha, St Dennis
Alistair J. Allen, Newquay, Cornwall
Glenda and Graham Allen, St Dennis
John E. Allen, St Dennis, Cornwall
David Applegate D.C.A., Foxhole, Cornwall
Geoff Ashley, St Dennis, Cornwall
Alan A. Astle, St Dennis
Chris and Kay Bailey, Westmancote, Gloucestershire
Arthur John Baker, Gothers, St Dennis
John Barbery, Bethal, St Austell, Cornwall
Tim Barbery, St Dennis, Cornwall
Lee, Carole and Liam Barkwill, St Columb Road, Cornwall
Robert John Barkwill, St Columb Road, Cornwall
Carole Barlow (née Hick), Whitemoor, Cornwall
Maureen Barnard, South Australia
Harry and Muriel Barrett, Wellington Road, St Dennis
John Barrett, Hendra Road, St Dennis
Mr and Mrs Philip L. Barrett, Goss Moor, St Columb
Mr Stephen J. Barrett, St Columb
Sarah Barrett, St Dennis
Jennifer Ann Bennetto (née Grigg), St Dennis
Andrew N. Best, Culcheth, Cheshire
Colin K. Best, Culcheth, Warrington, Cheshire
Mr R. Best, Lakeview, Hebburn, Newcastle-Upon-Tyne
Mr R. Best, Robartes Road, St Dennis
Russell Best, Saltash, Cornwall
Mr and Mrs A. Bilkey
M.W. Blake, Tywardreath, Cornwall
Mr and Mrs J.T. Blewett, Carsella Farm
Mr Fernleigh Blight, St Dennis, Cornwall
Ivor Bowditch, Tregony, Truro, Cornwall
Dave and Chris Braddon (née Bragg), Fiddlers Green
Sharon Bragg (née Bicknell), Newquay
H. Bray, St Dennis, Cornwall
Derek Brewer, St Austell, Cornwall
Julie Brewer
Richard M. Brown, St Dennis, Cornwall
Richard L. Budge, Robartes Road, St Dennis
Mrs Dorothy F. Bullen (née Trudgeon), St Austell, Cornwall
Claude and Eveline Bunt and Philip Bunt, Cheshire
Graham E. Bunt, Trewoon
Graham Burnett, St Stephen, Cornwall
John Daniel Burnett
Malcolm Burnett, St Dennis, Cornwall
Nigel J. Burnett, Grampound Road, Cornwall
Tony Burnett-Biscombe, Dominica, West Indies
K.J. Burrow, Bucks Cross, Devon
Anne Burton, Trispen, Truro
Mrs Dorothy Olive Caddy, Kestle Mill, Newquay
Peter F. Card, Mawnan Smith, Cornwall
Derek Chapman, Gothers, St Dennis, Cornwall
Harold Chapman, Enniscaven, St Dennis
Julia Clarke, St Dennis, Cornwall
Peter Clarke, St Dennis, Cornwall
B. Coad, St Dennis, Cornwall
Mrs Essie Coffin, Hall Road, St Dennis
Mr and Mrs R. Coffin, Whitemoor
Mr and Mrs Barry Cole, St Dennis, Cornwall
Mr and Mrs Michael Cole, St Dennis Junction
Mr and Mrs R. Cole, Fraddon Hill, Fraddon
Rowena and Cynthia Coon, St Dennis, Cornwall
Terence W. Cory, St Dennis, Cornwall
Ken and Vera Couch, Trelavour Road, St Dennis
Gwen Courts, Perranporth
Martin Courts and Tim Russ, St Dennis
Mrs S. Cox, Lansalson Farm, Ruddlemoor, St Austell
Mr and Mrs G. Craddock, St Dennis, Cornwall
Kenneth Craddock, St Dennis
Mr and Mrs Norman Crews
Tony Cross, St Austell, Cornwall
Muriel Darby (formerly Trudgian), Trevarren, Cornwall
Dianne Darch (née Richards), Summercourt, Cornwall
Maurice Dart, St Austell, Cornwall
Howard Davey
R.J. Alan Davey, Enniscaven, St Dennis
S. and D. Davey, St Dennis, Cornwall
Mrs Brenda Davies, St Austell, Cornwall
Pam and Peter Dickin, St Austell
Cyril Dingle, St Dennis
Graham Docking, Australia
Hazel E. Dowrick, Coombe, St Austell
Paul Dunstan, Hall Farm, St Dennis
Bob and Sylvia Ede, formerly tenants of Penrose Veor Farm, St Dennis, for 40 years
Barrie and Ginny Edwards, St Dennis
C.R. Edyvean, Trethurgy, St Austell, Cornwall
Denis Ellery, Fowey
Patricia J. Fisher, St Dennis, Cornwall
Mrs Betty Flack (née Davey), St Dennis
Jennifer Fouracres, St Dennis
Mrs Kathleen D. Fox, St Dennis, Cornwall
Mr Albert Gilbert, Hall Road, St Dennis
Andrew Gilbert, St Dennis
Mr Bevan Gilbert
Mr Colin Gilbert, St Austell, Cornwall
Mr Marshall Eric Gilbert, St Dennis
Raymond G. Gilbert
Richard Gilbert, Overstone Lodge, Northants
T. Gilbert, St Dennis
Margaret Giles, Menna Wartha, St Dennis
Arthur R. Giles, St Dennis, Cornwall
Mr T.R. Gill, Gothers, St Dennis
Miss Tamsyn Godfrey, St Columb Road, Cornwall
Hazel and Stan Goodman, St Dennis
Christopher Goodwyn, Plymouth
Connie Goudge, St Dennis, Cornwall
Charmian Gregor, St Dennis
Roy Gregor, St Dennis
Stuart Gregor, Polgooth
Ken Grigg, St Stephen, Cornwall
Donald and Lidia Grigg, Melrose, St Dennis
Barry Grime, St Austell
Marie Gurnett, Gillingham, Dorset
Stan and Eunice Hadland, Mosman Park, Western Australia
Kenneth G. Hambly, Hendra Downs 1943
Brian J. Hancock, Foxhole, St Austell, Cornwall
Mr and Mrs R. Hancock, Cornwall
Mr and Mrs E. Happs, Bolton-on-Dearne, South Yorkshire
Mrs Yvonne Harper, Bodmin, Cornwall
Mr Cleon and Mrs Barbara Harvey
Miss Julie Harvey, Foxhole, St Austell, Cornwall
Mrs Pamela Harvey, Whitemoor, Cornwall
Miss Rachael Harvey, Foxhole, St Austell, Cornwall
Stephen V. Harvey, St Dennis, Cornwall
Mr and Mrs Denis Hawke, Rossdorf, Germany
Beatrice Hayward
Marie Heard (née Veall), Newquay
Sharlene E. Heathcote, St Dennis, Cornwall
Dr Anthony Hellen, Rowlands Gill, Tyne and Wear
David T. Helyar, Fraddon, Cornwall
Mrs Margaret Higgins (née Caddy), formerly of Gilley Mill, Roche, now St Columb
Raymond Hill, The Meadows, St Dennis
Gillian Hockaday, granddaughter of William Percival Martyn (deceased)
Ken and Penny Holden, St Dennis, Cornwall
Mr Andrew J. Hones, St Dennis, Cornwall
John (Jack) Hooper, Indian Queens, Cornwall
Hilary Hooper (née Barkwill), St Columb Road, Cornwall
Brian and Carletta Hugh
Mr Shaun Hugh, St Dennis, Cornwall
Rex Hugh, St Dennis, Cornwall
Hil's and Ken Hutton, Gothers, St Dennis, Cornwall
Mr and Mrs Colin James, Orchard House, Hatt, Saltash
Eddie James, Indian Queens, Cornwall
Alan and Candice Jay, St Dennis, Cornwall
Mrs May Jewels, St Dennis, Cornwall
Miss Annette Johns, St Dennis, Cornwall
Ivor Johns, Church Road, St Dennis
Joyce Johns, Quintrell Downs, Cornwall
Raymond and Jeannette Johnson, St Dennis, Cornwall
Roger Jones, St Austell, Cornwall
Pauline Juleff (née Pelleymounter), Exeter
M.J. and B.J. Keast

R.G. Keast, Treliver Farm, Ruthvoes, Cornwall
R. Norman Keast, Indian Queens, Cornwall
Mr and Mrs T.J. Keast, St Dennis, Cornwall
Colin and Diana Keen, The Shop, St Dennis
Roy Kellaway, Cobbity, Australia
Trevor Kellow, St Dennis
Graham Kent, Thirsk, N. Yorkshire
Jonathan Kent
Ronald Kent
Ruby M. Kent, St Dennis, Cornwall
Trevor Kent, Cubert, Cornwall
Enid Kessell, Toldish Farm, Toldish
Trevor Kessell, Whitegate Garage, St Dennis, Cornwall
Mr and Mrs Leslie Merlin Key
Mr and Mrs Merlin Key,
Darran R.C. Key, Greendale View, St Dennis
Robin G. Key
Mrs J. King (née Coombe), Trewoon, Cornwall
Colin Kneller, Gothers House (1946–56)
Colin Lagor, born St Dennis
Kenneth John Liddicoat, Newquay, Cornwall
Mr and Mrs Stewart Lindman, Minneapolis, Minnesota, USA
Joyce Luke, St Dennis, Cornwall
Phyllis M. Luke, St Dennis, Cornwall
G.R. Mannell, Truro, Cornwall
Roma Mannell (née Gilbert)
Alan J. Martin, St Dennis, Cornwall
Barry Martyn, Ennis Vean, St Dennis
James Edward Martin, St Dennis, Cornwall
Kenneth S. Martin, Saltash, Cornwall
R. Barry Martin, Swindon, Wiltshire
Mr Percy Martyn, Ennis, St Dennis, Cornwall
Colin May, Boscawen Road, St Dennis
David May, Boscawen Road, St Dennis
Vivian May, St Dennis, Cornwall
Malcolm McCarthy, Padstow
Shirley E. McGirl, St Dennis, Cornwall
Mr Samuel John Mennear, St Stephen
Mrs Peggy Metherell, Trelavour Road, St Dennis
Hilda and Sandy Metherell
Ivor and Marlene Minear, Trewoon, Cornwall
Mr Leslie Donnithorne Mitchell, Cornwall
Mr Mervyn Moon, Portslade, East Sussex (grandson of Emma Doris Kent)
Colin and Margo Morcom, Bodmin, Cornwall
Owen Morcom, Witney, Oxon
Gordon Nancarrow, Indian Queens, Cornwall
Barry Richard Nance, St Dennis, Cornwall
Jason E. Nance, St Dennis, Cornwall
Marlene Netting (née Cross), Lostwithiel, Cornwall
M. and R. Newman
Merle Oliver, St Dennis, Cornwall
Mr William Oliver, St Dennis, Cornwall
Len and Joan Osborne, St Dennis, Cornwall
Melville Lonnie Osborne
Gary Oxenham, St Dennis, Cornwall
Mrs Doreen Ann Page (née Hill), Belowda, Roche, Cornwall
Anne Parry (née Lagor), born St Dennis
Jeff Parsons, St Dennis Junction, Indian Queens
Barbara Pascoe, St Dennis, Cornwall
Marlene Penhaligon, St Dennis
Pam and Derek Penhaligon, Fore Street, St Dennis
Donald W. Pethick
Lloyd Pethick, St Dennis, Cornwall
June and Geoff Pittard, St Dennis Junction, Goss Moor
Margaret Pomphrey (née Greenslade), St Dennis
Adrian Pope, Barnstaple
John C.C. Probert, Redruth
Edna Quelcuti (née Varcoe), St Dennis, Cornwall
Martin Rabey, Whitemoor, Cornwall
Mary Rabey, St Dennis, Cornwall
Michael Rabey, Redruth, Cornwall
Shaun Rabey, Treviscoe, Cornwall
Sylvia Rabey, St Austell, Cornwall
Trevor and Susan Rabey, St Dennis, Cornwall
Harold F. Rapson, Enniscaven, Nr St Dennis
Betty Rawlings, Weston-super-Mare, Somerset
Claire Richards, St Dennis, Cornwall
Susan M. Richards, St Dennis, Cornwall
Mark Richards, R. and O. Ltd, Goss Moor
Mr Rodney Richards, St Austell, Cornwall
Gary and Beverley Rickard, Elviria, 29600 Marbella, Spain
Mr Arthur Christopher Rickard, St Dennis
Mr Mark Roberts, Indian Queens, Cornwall
Peggy D. Robson, St Dennis, Cornwall
Charlie and Blanche Rogers, Penryn, Cornwall
Joyce Rowe, Three Milestone, Truro, formerly of St Dennis
Royce Runnalls, Gothers, St Dennis, Cornwall
Mrs K. Russ
Ryan and Rhys, Brecon Lodge, Hendra Prazey, St Dennis
Austin and Eleanor Vera Sampson, Mount Elgon, Hendra Down, St Dennis
Alan Sanders, Falmouth, Cornwall
Mr and Mrs Richard Sargent, Fore Street, St Dennis
Val Sawyer, Higham Ferrers, Northants
Graham Nigel Sears, Gunvena, St Francis Road, Indian Queens
Michael Sheaff, Plymouth, Devon
Rodney Sheaff, Lady Barn, Manchester
Will Sheaff, Saltash, Cornwall
Mrs Gillian Side (née Docking), Par, Cornwall
Bernard N. Simmonds, Indian Queens, Cornwall
Coleen M. Sleeman, St Dennis, Cornwall
Mrs Florence Neva Sleeman, St Dennis, Cornwall
Courtenay V. Smale, Newquay, Cornwall
Tony Smale, formerly of St Dennis
Denis J. Smith, St Dennis, Cornwall
Yvonne Smith (née Hawkey), Wanganui, New Zealand
Timothy Soloman, St Austell, Cornwall
E. Solomon, St Dennis
The Sowell Family, Peterborough
Donald J. Sparrow, St Dennis, Cornwall
St Dennis Community Primary School
Barrie Stark, New Jersey, USA
Trevor Stephens, Whitemoor, Nanpean
Joe, Berrie and Terry Stocks, St Dennis
Mr Rex Stone, Treviscoe
Dorothy L. Stoneman, St Dennis, Cornwall
Douglas Stoneman, St Dennis
Trevor James Bunt Stoneman, Nanpean
W. and T. Stoneman, St Dennis
Maurice Leonard Stribley
David Malcolm Stribley, Gothers, St Dennis
Peter Hooper Strongman, St Dennis
Brian M. Sweet, St Stephen
Stuart Tabb, Gothers, St Dennis, Cornwall
Charles Dennis Tabb, Enniscaven, St Dennis
Edith and Peter Taylor, Nanpean, Cornwall
Mervyn, Suzanne and Dani Thomas, Enniscaven, St Dennis
Graham Thorne, Maldon, Essex
W. John Tonkin, formerly of Bugle
Mrs S. Trebell (née Taylor), St Dennis
Maurneen Trebilcock, Tywardreath
Mr and Mrs D. Trendall, St Dennis, Cornwall
Arthur Trenerry, Fraddon (formerly Trerice)
Mr and Mrs Alan Trethewey, Carne Cottage, Carne Hill, St Dennis
Mrs R. Mona Trethewey, St Dennis, Cornwall
Mrs Olga F. Trethewey, St Dennis, Cornwall
Tim Trevenna, St Dennis
Arthur Truscott, St Dennis
E.H. Truscott, St Columb Road, Cornwall
Mrs Janet A. Truscott (née Ruse), St Dennis, Cornwall
M.G. Truscott, St Austell, Cornwall
W. Peter Truscott, St Dennis, Cornwall
Richard Turner, St Austell, Cornwall
F. Joy Turner (née Best), Lostwithiel
Mrs Maud Varcoe, Newquay, Cornwall
Les Varcoe, Indian Queens
Edna Vercoe (née Angilley), St Dennis, Cornwall
Dilys Vincent (née Hawken), St Dennis Junction, Goss Moor
John F.W. Walling, Newton Abbot, Devon
Cunteller An Brewyon. M.F. Waters, St Austell, Kernow
Dick Watters, St Dennis
Malcolm Watters, Guisborough, Cleveland
W.A. and A.K. Watters, St Dennis, Cornwall
M.J. Weaver, Hendra, St Dennis
Madeline M. Webber, St Dennis, Cornwall
Stephen P. West, Trelavour Road, St Dennis
Tom and Clarice Westlake, St Dennis
Graham Wherry, St Stephen, St Austell, Cornwall
Lyn White (née Osborne), St Dennis, Cornwall
C.N. Wiblin, Shrewton, Wiltshire
Vivian Willcock, St Dennis Band 1955–1963
Mr Albert Henry Williams, ex Gothers Road, Enniscaven
Derek and Frances Williams (née Truscott), St Dennis, Cornwall
G.V.R. Williams, Liskeard, Cornwall
Wendy Williams, Indian Queens, St Dennis Junction
R.A. and C.A. Wisdom, Harvenna House, St Dennis
James Wright, Newquay, Cornwall
Frank Yelland

Community Histories

The Book of Addiscombe • Canning and Clyde Road Residents Association and Friends
The Book of Addiscombe, Vol. II • Canning and Clyde Road Residents Association and Friends
The Book of Axminster with Kilmington • Les Berry and Gerald Gosling
The Book of Bampton • Caroline Seward
The Book of Barnstaple • Avril Stone
The Book of Barnstaple, Vol. II • Avril Stone
The Book of The Bedwyns • Bedwyn History Society
The Book of Bickington • Stuart Hands
Blandford Forum: A Millennium Portrait • Blandford Forum Town Council
The Book of Bramford • Bramford Local History Group
The Book of Breage & Germoe • Stephen Polglase
The Book of Bridestowe • D. Richard Cann
The Book of Bridport • Rodney Legg
The Book of Brixham • Frank Pearce
The Book of Buckfastleigh • Sandra Coleman
The Book of Buckland Monachorum & Yelverton • Pauline Hamilton-Leggett
The Book of Carharrack • Carharrack Old Cornwall Society
The Book of Carshalton • Stella Wilks and Gordon Rookledge
The Parish Book of Cerne Abbas • Vivian and Patricia Vale
The Book of Chagford • Iain Rice
The Book of Chapel-en-le-Frith • Mike Smith
The Book of Chittlehamholt with Warkleigh & Satterleigh • Richard Lethbridge
The Book of Chittlehampton • Various
The Book of Colney Heath • Bryan Lilley
The Book of Constantine • Moore and Trethowan
The Book of Cornwood and Lutton • Compiled by the People of the Parish
The Book of Creech St Michael • June Small
The Book of Cullompton • Compiled by the People of the Parish
The Book of Dawlish • Frank Pearce
The Book of Dulverton, Brushford, Bury & Exebridge • Dulverton and District Civic Society
The Book of Dunster • Hilary Binding
The Book of Edale • Gordon Miller
The Ellacombe Book • Sydney R. Langmead
The Book of Exmouth • W.H. Pascoe
The Book of Grampound with Creed • Bane and Oliver
The Book of Hayling Island & Langstone • Peter Rogers
The Book of Helston • Jenkin with Carter
The Book of Hemyock • Clist and Dracott
The Book of Herne Hill • Patricia Jenkyns
The Book of Hethersett • Hethersett Society Research Group
The Book of High Bickington • Avril Stone
The Book of Ilsington • Dick Wills
The Book of Kingskerswell • Carsewella Local History Group
The Book of Lamerton • Ann Cole and Friends
Lanner, A Cornish Mining Parish • Sharron Schwartz and Roger Parker
The Book of Leigh & Bransford • Malcolm Scott
The Book of Litcham with Lexham & Mileham • Litcham Historical and Amenity Society
The Book of Loddiswell • Loddiswell Parish History Group
The New Book of Lostwithiel • Barbara Fraser
The Book of Lulworth • Rodney Legg
The Book of Lustleigh • Joe Crowdy
The Book of Lyme Regis • Rodney Legg
The Book of Manaton • Compiled by the People of the Parish
The Book of Markyate • Markyate Local History Society
The Book of Mawnan • Mawnan Local History Group
The Book of Meavy • Pauline Hemery
The Book of Minehead with Alcombe • Binding and Stevens
The Book of Morchard Bishop • Jeff Kingaby
The Book of Newdigate • John Callcut
The Book of Nidderdale • Nidderdale Museum Society
The Book of Northlew with Ashbury • Northlew History Group
The Book of North Newton • J.C. and K.C. Robins
The Book of North Tawton • Baker, Hoare and Shields
The Book of Nynehead • Nynehead & District History Society
The Book of Okehampton • Roy and Ursula Radford
The Book of Paignton • Frank Pearce
The Book of Penge, Anerley & Crystal Palace • Peter Abbott
The Book of Peter Tavy with Cudlipptown • Peter Tavy Heritage Group
The Book of Pimperne • Jean Coull
The Book of Plymtree • Tony Eames
The Book of Porlock • Dennis Corner
Postbridge – The Heart of Dartmoor • Reg Bellamy
The Book of Priddy • Albert Thompson
The Book of Princetown • Dr Gardner-Thorpe
The Book of Rattery • By the People of the Parish
The Book of St Day • Joseph Mills and Paul Annear
The Book of Sampford Courtenay with Honeychurch • Stephanie Pouya
The Book of Sculthorpe • Gary Windeler
The Book of Seaton • Ted Gosling
The Book of Sidmouth • Ted Gosling and Sheila Luxton
The Book of Silverton • Silverton Local History Society
The Book of South Molton • Jonathan Edmunds
The Book of South Stoke with Midford • Edited by Robert Parfitt
South Tawton & South Zeal with Sticklepath • Roy and Ursula Radford
The Book of Sparkwell with Hemerdon & Lee Mill • Pam James
The Book of Staverton • Pete Lavis
The Book of Stithians • Stithians Parish History Group
The Book of Stogumber, Monksilver, Nettlecombe & Elworthy • Maurice and Joyce Chidgey
The Book of Studland • Rodney Legg
The Book of Swanage • Rodney Legg
The Book of Tavistock • Gerry Woodcock
The Book of Thorley • Various
The Book of Torbay • Frank Pearce
The Book of Watchet • Compiled by David Banks
The Book of West Huntspill • By the People of the Parish
Widecombe-in-the-Moor • Stephen Woods
Widecombe – Uncle Tom Cobley & All • Stephen Woods
The Book of Williton • Michael Williams
The Book of Witheridge • Peter and Freda Tout and John Usmar
The Book of Withycombe • Chris Boyles
Woodbury: The Twentieth Century Revisited • Roger Stokes
The Book of Woolmer Green • Compiled by the People of the Parish

For details of any of the above titles or if you are interested in writing your own history, please contact: Commissioning Editor, Community Histories, Halsgrove House, Lower Moor Way, Tiverton Business Park, Tiverton, Devon EX16 6SS, England; email: katyc@halsgrove.com